THE
RIDDLES
OF THE
SPHINX

THE
RIDDLES
OF THE
SPHINX

Inheriting the Feminist History
of the Crossword Puzzle

ANNA SHECHTMAN

HARPERONE
An Imprint of HarperCollinsPublishers

Portions of Chapter 1 of this book previously appeared in the *New Yorker* ("Black-and-White Thinking" published December 20, 2023).

HarperCollins books may be purchased for educational, business, or sales promotional use. For information, please email the Special Markets Department at SPsales @harpercollins.com.

FIRST EDITION

Designed by Janet Evans-Scanlon

Library of Congress Cataloging-in-Publication Data has been applied for.

ISBN 978-0-06-327547-8
ISBN 978-0-06-339400-1 (ANZ)

23 24 25 26 27 LBC 5 4 3 2 1

To Bonnie and Emily

CONTENTS

I PRONOUNS THEE

Across

1 Kind of eatery where Meg Ryan's Sally Albright faked an orgasm
9 "Mountain of God," in Exodus
14 Fanatical
15 Bit of finger food
16 Runway model?
17 Line on a weather map
18 Playwright Simon
19 Multitasker's browserful
21 "Nevertheless" . . . informally
22 "Gross!"
25 L.G.B.T. History Mo.
27 U.N. agcy. created by the Treaty of Versailles
28 Observed
31 Half of none?
33 More humid
35 Expert
36 One way to get around a city
38 Dante Alighieri e Francesco Petrarca
39 Some airport postings: Abbr.
41 Challenges for cryptologists
43 College app exams
44 Challenges for cryptologists
46 Rockefeller Center statue
48 ___ Speedwagon
49 It's "usually just a case of mistaken nonentity," per Barbara Stanwyck
51 Fib
52 Attraction at Seattle's Museum of Flight, for short
53 Half-___ (coffee order)
54 You can bank on it?
55 Pop
57 "La Marseillaise" and "O Canada"
58 Tabula ___
61 *Abolition Geography* author ___ Wilson Gilmore
65 Backdrop for the final scene of Antonioni's *L'Avventura*
68 Inherited wealth
71 Even-tempered
72 Displaced
73 Turkey's neighbor
74 Big deposit?

Down

1 Riddle in Zen Buddhism
2 Award created by the *Village Voice*
3 Prozac or Paxil, for short
4 Mindless followers, per right-wing propaganda
5 Broadband inits.
6 That: Sp.
7 March fast?
8 It's a thought
9 Owns
10 Artist given a writer's credit on the 1971 song "Imagine" in 2017
11 V on an old TV?
12 Certain embellishments, from the French word for "little shoulders"
13 Impressionist painter and frequent subject of Édouard Manet, her brother-in-law
15 "Welcome to the human network" sloganeer
20 Epithet for a Hollywood blonde . . . or the 1933 Jean Harlow movie that coined it
23 Entanglement
24 "The Brian Lehrer Show" producer
26 Inside info
28 Summer programs for future astronauts
29 Without humility
30 "Gaslighting" in 2022 and "Vaccine" in 2021, per Merriam-Webster
32 *Portrait of a Lady on Fire* director Céline
34 Help line?
37 Fitting
40 Collector's goal
42 Stated
45 Pop star and co-writer of the 2012 Rihanna hit "Diamonds"
47 Mediterranean, e.g.
50 Valuable violin, for short
56 Salivate
59 Romantic poet whose "The Story of the Three Bears" became the basis for the Goldilocks tale
60 Iams competitor
62 "___ Me? I do not know you": Emily Dickinson
63 Ticked (off)
64 Literary alter ego
66 Onetime cable giant acquired by AT&T
67 Actress Long
69 ___ & the Women (2000 Altman film)
70 Crystal Bridges Museum architect ___ Safdie

THE
RIDDLES
OF THE
SPHINX

Black-and-White Thinking

Twenty letters for "In myth, the question 'Which creature has one voice and yet becomes four-footed and two-footed and three-footed?'"

Twenty letters for "What Freud called the question 'Where do babies come from?'"

Twenty letters for "In Greek mythology, its solution is 'Man,' but in Freudian theory, its solution is 'Woman'"

Answer: THE RIDDLE OF THE SPHINX

THE SPHINX POSES A RIDDLE, AND SHE PRESENTS AN ENIGMA. IN THE myth of Oedipus, written by Sophocles and revived by Freud, the Sphinx is a hybrid figure. Part human, part lion, and part bird, she's as inscrutable as her words. She guards the entrance to Thebes, a threshold that Oedipus must pass if he is to return home and fulfill his prophesized fate (the patricide and incest for which his story is more often remembered). If Oedipus fails to solve the Sphinx's riddle, she will descend from her perch and devour him, as she has so many men before. But Oedipus solves it: the creature with "one voice [who] becomes four-footed and two-footed and three-footed" is "man, who crawls on all fours as a baby, then walks on two feet as an adult, and then uses a walking stick in old age." Oedipus prevails, and the Sphinx falls to her death. Or, in some tellings, she devours herself.

The Riddle of the Sphinx, in other words, is a zero-sum game. It's a contest for which there is only one victor, one victim, and one solution, which amounts to the death of the creature who is both a woman and not properly human at all. Language is the Sphinx's doing and her undoing. Her riddle is meant to create logical order (baby, adult, old man) from the wavy incidence of human life. But she is disorderly: at once bestial and cerebral, she is a symbol of man's fear and his fantasy, of woman's appetite and her mystery.

Like the Sphinx, the crossword puzzle constructor creates problems with language. To write a good crossword clue—a hard clue, one that frequent solvers will recognize because it's appended with a question mark, signaling its deception—the puzzle-maker has to loosen a word or phrase from its common set of associations. She has to unsettle its forms—attending to the chance encounters between synonyms and homonyms, idioms and clichés—before she can set them down again. She reverse engineers the solver's process, a task that involves scrutinizing a clue's language for its ulterior meanings, latent puns, and allusions:

Seven letters for "Complex character?"
    Answer: OEDIPUS

A complex character, a trope of literary fiction, is typically a protagonist with conflicting motives and, therefore, one imagines, psychological depth. Because of the clue's question mark, however, the solver knows that she's being misdirected. She must take each word on its own, rummaging through its various meanings with the dexterity of a human thesaurus or a literary New Critic. *Character* could mean personality trait ("She had an unpleasant character"), alphabetic letter ("謎 is a Chinese character"), or eccentric ("She's such a character!"); or, as in this case, it could mean a literary personage ("Oedipus is the titular character of a play by Sophocles"). *Complex*, meanwhile, could mean structure ("She lived in an apartment complex"); it could be an adjective ("I'll never understand. It's too complex"); or, as in this case, it could mean neurosis ("She has some sort of complex"). Through this process—unearthing the mundane magic of language's overdetermination—the solver arrives at a solution: OEDIPUS is the character of a Freudian complex. The process repeats itself, clue by clue:

Seven letters for "Sphinx-like?"
    Answer: RIDDLES

In other words, the crossword constructor makes chaos out of language and then restores its order in the form of a neat solution. This relentless activity—tearing language apart and piecing it back together—was what I enjoyed most when I started making crosswords at age fifteen. Before discovering the grammar—to say nothing of the art—of writing clues, I simply wanted to get words to intersect, their letters to interlock in the squares of my graph paper notebook. I'd squint at words until they lost their meaning—until they were only a string of letters to be arranged and rearranged into units that were recognizably words again.

I didn't imagine a solver for my puzzles because, initially, I wrote them for myself. An aspiring Sphinx without an Oedipus, I wasn't working to exhaust anyone else's mental effort, so much as to test my own. Without a solver in mind, I wasn't creating any real solutions, but false problems (*What's a three-letter word that ends in Z? What's a synonym for X?*) to distract from real ones and to tire my restless mind. I was consuming time, energy, and eventually my sense of self with word games. I wanted to retreat into the recesses of language—unsettling and resetting its forms—and I wanted to devour myself. To tear myself up and start anew.

———

I WANTED TO SEE MYSELF AS A COMPLEX CHARACTER—SOMEONE worthy of inquiry, which is to say attention—but I had no proof of my psychological depth. I wanted to be read as unreadable, legible as illegible, understood to be a woman, or really a girl, of mystery. Like most teenagers, I wanted to be something more than what I was. I had to invent my complexity, and so, to put it plainly, I began writing crossword puzzles and I began to starve myself. The connection between puzzle-making and anorexia will strike most people as tenuous or arbitrary, but to me, it felt intuitive: both were efforts to make my mental strength, the willed intensity of my interiority, obvious. Both were also extensions of adolescent megalomania, allowing me to feel that I was mastering forms that should be unmasterable—that the body of language and my body could be brought to heel with the brute power of cognition. But neither words nor bodies are zero-sum games. Neither can be defeated, however hard I tried.

In the five years that I wrote crossword puzzles for no one, I clung to anorexia, as a set of restrictive food behaviors and as an anchor for my wayward identity. I was acting willfully and then compulsively. I was reaching for sublimity—to become a boundless mind, to defeat matter—only to find myself in a bureaucratized world of doctors, therapists, scales, and blood samples. I had notebooks and planners filled with calorie counts and puns, meal plans and puzzle themes. My relationship to words and to food was highly formalized—as if both were basically immaterial, existing more powerfully in my mind than on the page or the plate. Their material forms (the notebooks and meals) were, at best, incidental and, at worst, a painful burden. I had achieved complexity, and I was miserable.

I first learned about the people who create crossword puzzles when, at age fifteen, I watched the documentary *Wordplay*. The indie film featured celebrity crossword fans, as well as a handful of puzzle constructors, and reached its narrative denouement at the American Crossword Puzzle Tournament, a weekend-long speed-solving contest, and by all measures, the apex of American nerdery. It was through *Wordplay* that I learned that crossword-makers are called "constructors"—not "writers," nor "setters," as they're called in the UK—and only sometimes, albeit rarely with a straight face, "cruciverbalists."

It wasn't so much *Wordplay*'s star cameos, its speed-solving prodigies, or their collective ethos of jittery intelligence that captivated me. Instead, I was drawn to the movie's C plot, the actual creation of a crossword, performed onscreen by Merl Reagle, a prolific, syndicated constructor based in Tampa Bay, Florida. Reagle's star turn in *Wordplay* is distinctly unglamorous: he's featured in a midsize sedan, driving along strip malls, riffing on roadside signage: "Dunkin' Donuts: put the *D* at the end, you get *Unkind Donuts*, which I've had a few of in my day." Like many puzzle fanatics, Reagle lived in a house full of crossword paraphernalia: black-and-white ties, mugs, and, as was prominently featured in *Wordplay*, a crossword mural in his living room. "Noah's Ark right there?" he says on his drive, referencing a local pet store. "You switch the *S* and the *H* around, and that's *No, a Shark*!"

The hard-core kitsch aesthetics of Reagle's life weren't exactly what drew me in. With these simple puns, the lowest form of humor, he seemed to be accessing something foundational about language—a quasi-mathematical code that could be rearranged and manipulated through brain power alone. When the filmmakers took us into Reagle's dining room, where he plots out a crossword with grid paper and pencil, I internalized the puzzle's protocols: perfect 180-degree symmetry, elegantly interlocking words, a minimum of black squares, no jargon or linguistic waste, only "good words."

What makes for a good word, in the eyes of a crossword puzzle constructor? The language of aesthetic judgment is gustatory—one has "good taste" or feels something in "one's gut"—but crosswords are meant to transcend physical sensations. Solvers of the *Times* puzzle may have heard of the "Sunday morning breakfast test," the paper's requirement that its crosswords not turn the stomach of a morning solver. ("URINE would bail me out of a corner a million times a year," Reagle says in *Wordplay*. "Same with ENEMA," he adds. "Talk about great letters. But you gotta keep those words out of puzzles.") This was one of many rules instituted by the architect of the contemporary puzzle, Margaret Farrar, the *Times*'s first crossword editor. She believed that a crossword should activate your mind, not your body.

Perhaps, then, it is of little surprise that crossword constructors have imported the language of math into their process. A "good word" might be a term with a high vowel-to-consonant ratio (AREA, ERIE, OREO) or extreme anagramability (LIVE, EVIL, VEIL, VILE). The latter tend to have a near equal number of vowels and consonants, making them useful for filling in the grid between less balanced—or predictable—words.

But like the assessment of a mathematical proof's "elegance," the standards for a good crossword word might be more capricious. Why was it so rewarding to watch solvers in *Wordplay* fill in the squares for 1-Across ("Stark and richly detailed, as writing") with ZOLAESQUE? Was it the unlikely combination of *Z* and *Q*? The word's improbable specificity? Its rolling sound off the tongue? When I started writing puzzles, ascribing arbitrary but absolute value to words and letters came to me naturally. Anorexics, like crossword constructors, are predisposed to black-and-white thinking.

———

I DON'T REMEMBER WHERE I FIRST HEARD ABOUT ANOREXIA. THE word floated around my world, lower Manhattan in the 1990s and early aughts, as omnipresent yet meaningless to me as the back-of-the-magazine crossword puzzles that traveled, untouched, in and out of my home. That is, until anorexia—and crosswords—assumed unreasonable meaning in my imagination. At the start of tenth grade, I read in a health-class textbook that high-achieving, affluent young white women were the population most likely to succumb to anorexia. I found in this portrait, and in the common identifiers of the disease—extreme thinness, eagerness to please, a penchant for self-punishment—a near-description of me. Or, more precisely, an aspirational description of "me." A "me" I could love, if I worked at it.

Anorexia became a rigid template on which to trace my pubescent identity, as the gap between *it* and *I* became a gap that I could close, if only I starved. It was a distorted fantasy of success that, despite the textbook's illustration, ignored the actual demographic reach of eating disorders and betrayed the stony limits of my teenaged imagination.

Diagnoses for mental illness are notoriously reductive, and I wanted to be reduced.

After two weeks of fasting—eating nothing at school, picking at my dinner at home—I visited my older sister at college. I wasn't yet ready to disclose my new identity to her, and so I ate what she ate. I did so without fear, something I wouldn't be able to replicate for five years. And yet, I couldn't really do it then: when I woke up in her dorm room the next morning, tallying up what I'd eaten the night before, panic ran its course through my body. I had erred; I had lost myself. But I settled my nerves, feeling relief and even gratitude, that with this fresh day I could return to order, return to anorexia, which was already a return to "me."

There was a single word of the textbook's description of anorexia that fueled my new attachment to it. Anorexic girls, the book said, tended to be "perfectionistic." Whether willfully misreading or simply falling prey to a malapropism, I know that I split the word in half in my mind, hearing not "perfectionistic," but "perfect" instead. Anorexic girls were perfect, and I could be too. By the winter of tenth grade, the error of my thinking had become obvious: I wasn't perfect but stuck; I wasn't perfect but cause for concern.

I had locked myself into a strict pattern of behavior, and I couldn't simply go back to another way of thinking or eating. I wasn't experimenting with a new weight regimen; I had conceded my autonomy to an autocratic weight regime. Eventually, doctors and parents—and my own fear instincts—intervened. I would have to gain weight to stay in school and avoid hospitalization. I decided that I would gain the weight but retain control: I would do so by eating arbitrarily but truculently defined "good" foods, not "bad" ones. I would eat four large meals a day, and between each one I would write a crossword puzzle. My war with my body at a temporary cease-fire, I escaped into an abstract matrix of letters and words. The simple fifteen-by-fifteen-square grid gave order to my racing thoughts and offered a replacement high for that of starvation. If, by the dumb logic of my eating disorder, I was losing something special about myself by gaining weight, I was bolstering my fragile self-esteem by creating puzzles.

In fact, "crossword puzzle constructor," I found, was a compatible identity container with "anorexic." *She has a discipline*, I imagined people thinking, *so she must be disciplined*. A little neurotic, maybe—but the cultural residue of female hysteria, made trite by its distance from Freud's couch, might have them convinced that this simply meant "adorable." And, without a doubt, she must be smart. I was using these highly impersonal labels to develop a personality. I was misrecognizing myself in their image.

The French psychoanalyst Jacques Lacan describes such scenes of misrecognition—scenes in which we feel the gap between who we are and who we want to be—as foundational to the development of the ego. But his English translators always retain the French spelling of misrecognition (*méconaissance*) in his writings, because Lacan was playing with French to unmask this psychic truth. He understood "self-knowledge" (or, a pun on the French reflexive pronoun *me* and the French word for knowledge, *conaissance*) as the flip side of "misrecognition."

Méconaissance (misrecognition) = *me-conaissance* (self-knowledge). By this logic, there is no way to know the self outside of a tragicomic interplay between who we are and who we aren't, who we could be and how we feel. The anorexic, then, is just another person trying to be a better version of herself. That she risks death in so trying is the most disastrous paradox of the disease.

A PREVAILING CULTURAL LOGIC ASSUMES THAT THE ANOREXIC'S desire to fast is triggered by the overly literal intake of commercial images— in magazines, on Instagram—of stick-thin supermodels and celebrities. As the feminist critic Abigail Bray writes, many people believe that anorexia is both an eating disorder and a "reading disorder." Accordingly, anorexics are twice victims of improper consumption. Bray, however, rejects this etiology of the disease, which implies that the anorexic suffers simply from an inability to distinguish fact from fiction. The anorexic does flirt with literalism—*The culture tells me to be thin; here you go, I've done it!*—but she is just as likely to practice a highly creative misreading of cultural cues, as I did when I took my textbook's cautionary tale as aspirational.

The puzzle of anorexic reading habits was made most apparent to me when, at age nineteen, I left college and checked in to an inpatient treatment center for women with eating disorders, in the infelicitously named town of Paradise, Utah. I didn't write crosswords in Paradise. I have never liked to work with other people watching: the supervisory gaze interrupts the escapist conceit that I might exist only in a virtual space of moving letters on a page. And everything in Paradise—eating, sleeping, shitting, reading—was highly supervised. As a budding English major, I brought more books than clothes, hoping a self-guided course in American literature would suit my convalescence. My favorites were the works of Saul Bellow and Philip Roth, whose matter-of-fact bawdiness was a welcome antidote to the facility's earnest mix of Mormonism and group therapy.

I learned that my books were being monitored in treatment when my therapist prevented me from reading Roth's *Anatomy Lesson*. The title suggested to him some perverted relation to the medicalized body, and to be fair, he wasn't entirely wrong. When I asked what books, in particular, were banned from Paradise, I was told that this was ultimately left to the therapist's discretion, but that they tended to belong to one of two genres: books promoting dieting, and those detailing the conditions of Holocaust internment. Each, I was told, might be perilously read as instructional.

The anorexic's attraction to the stories of Holocaust victims could be seen as yet another symptom of her "reading disorder"—consuming descriptive texts as prescriptive. But as I understand it, this perverse attraction reveals a more structural condition of the starving mind: one that is rooted in obsessive fixation and the logic of substitution, allowing a single feature of the human body to stand in for the totality of one's self-worth—or allowing the signs of starvation, in Auschwitz or Utah, to stand in for each other as abstract equivalents.

Linguists call this way of thinking "paradigmatic." It's a method of focusing on language's interchangeable patterns (*I, you,* and *we* are all the same parts of speech, for example), as opposed to how language operates in context, connecting various parts of speech to each other in meaningful syntax. Both the anorexic and the crossword constructor tend to think paradigmatically. Crossword clues and answers must be perfect substitutions for one another. A crossword puzzle has no syntax, just sets of words that interlock and interchange. Likewise, the anorexic stops seeing herself in syntactical relations: she doesn't think of herself as existing in time, in space, harmoniously or disharmoniously with others. Or at least, these relations are subordinated to her thinking in patterns of substitution. Of course, *weight loss = good; weight gain = bad* is the governing pattern that determines many of the smaller ones—what to eat, and when, and how—that freight her day and her self-image.

IN 2010, A FEW MONTHS BEFORE I LEFT FOR TREATMENT, MY BOY-friend persuaded me to start submitting my crosswords to the *New York Times*. My first was a puzzle with a "Grade Inflation" theme. The college I was then attending was famous for resisting grade inflation (our unofficial motto was "Anywhere else it would have been an A"), and with that maxim in mind, I created a puzzle that did the inflating my professors wouldn't. All of the *B*s in the grid were turned into *A*s, making new (and frankly goofy) phrases as a result: *nine letters for* "Monk's karate blows?" (answer: LAMA CHOPS).

Will Shortz, the newspaper's longtime puzzle editor, encouraged me: if I was quick with my revisions, he said, I could be the young-est woman to publish a crossword in the paper's history. (I wasn't that quick; I became the second youngest.) At the time, I didn't know that the process for constructing puzzles had been digitized and therefore expedited. Most constructors now use software with imported word databases to help them write their puzzles. An algorithm slots words from their curated databases into their grid designs. In the age of software-based construction, the puzzle-maker's obsessive energy, once focused on interlocking words, has been displaced onto building and refining a word database. The constructor places her black squares in the program's interface, adds "seed entries" (either the entries that make up a puzzle's theme, if it has one, or words that she generally wants to see in her grids), and presses a button labeled "autofill." Based on how the constructor has ranked the words in her database (0: don't include it in the grid; 100: include it whenever possible), the program will fill the grid with words around the black squares and seed entries. The process is not, ultimately, automatic. Like a singer using Auto-Tune or a photographer using a digital camera's automatic focus, the constructor using software is still responsible for several variables that inform its computerized output. Most significantly, she still writes the clues. But now that clue databases exist, listing every clue that's ever run for every word in every major outlet, it is fair to say that, at every step of contemporary puzzle-making, little boxes cede to Big Data.

Before I left for Paradise—and for many years after—I was still using graph paper and pencil to make crosswords, just as Merl Reagle had done in *Wordplay*. I wasn't looking to make the best puzzles or to publish the most grids the most efficiently. My process wasn't competitive; instead, it was some form of catharsis. The puzzles I wrote were reflections of my daily preoccupations, featuring words, allusions, and little jokes that I enjoyed, not particularly aware of any future solver or even why the word game gratified me when so little else could. My second puzzle appeared in the *Times* when I was in treatment. Its theme was "It's All Greek to Me," and its answers included words with Greek letters nested inside them. I had written it before Paradise, while on a break from school, when my doctors and parents had given me another ultimatum. I needed to gain weight to return.

I had just read Virginia Woolf's "On Not Knowing Greek," an essay that seems to imply a feminist complaint—the study of Greek in Edwardian England was a privilege reserved for upper-class boys and men—but transforms into a treatise on the unknowability of Ancient Greek because no one, no prep school boy or classics professor, knows how it sounds. Learning to read Greek, then, can only teach you how little it can be known. The essay incited in me a shallow form of hunger: I wanted all the erudition that Oxford or Cambridge afforded its schoolboys. More,

I wanted the knowledge that Woolf had earned to wield it against them, allying herself instead with Thomas Hardy, George Eliot, and Siegfried Sassoon, who would know better than to think they could *know* Greek. But because I wrote the puzzle on a school break, I wasn't spending my time learning. My principal task was eating. And so I turned to my own dead language—words and phrases I had engineered to only make sense on the page—and wrote a crossword puzzle between my meals. Freud's "oral phase," I discovered, contained the Greek letter *alpha* in its middle: ORAL PHASE. That answer, with the Greek letter (α) buried in one square, was the puzzle's answer to 1-Down: "First part of psychosexual development" (answer: ORαSE.) The resulting crossword—filled with unspeakable words and displays of my own striving learnedness—was a testament to my fixations, oral and otherwise.

After spending the better half of a year in Paradise, I returned home to New York City, my recovery precarious but hard-won. I was learning to trust my body's hunger cues and to reimagine my days in terms of opportunities and responsibilities—relations with a syntax—not willfully overdetermined by food rules and restrictions. Nothing about life in recovery felt natural to me. My older sister and I even went to couples therapy to rediscover the cadences of our connection, which, like so much else, had been disarticulated by my eating disorder. I had to figure out who I was without anorexia—how I related to myself as a woman, as a student, as a body in space, to other women and to men, and even to crossword puzzles. I had to figure out that these relationships couldn't be "solved" but only developed and hewn through perpetual, ever-humbling misrecognitions.

That fall, I returned to college, and during intractable periods of body dysmorphia—when all I could think was a cloud of undifferentiated malice (*I hate my body; I hate myself*)—I returned to the grid. These boxed-up words were harmless—they were nothing more than letters— and so constructing crosswords remained a primary source of solace, but something had changed. I was beginning to be recognized by the audience I had ambivalently courted in the pages of the *Times*. I was invited to Facebook groups and email listservs for puzzle-makers, where I began to sense that I was an outlier in what has come to be known as the Cross-World, a highly devoted set of mostly male, mostly STEM-educated speed solvers and constructors. Other outlets, looking to diversify their bylines, solicited my puzzles. I was known not just as a constructor but as a woman constructor.

When I graduated college in 2013, Will Shortz offered to hire me as his assistant. I was reluctant to accept the post. Resolutely committed to my recovery, I worried that giving my time over so fully to crosswords would somehow prove symptomatic of relapse. But instead of succumbing to this classically paradigmatic train of thought (in which puzzles = disembodiment = anorexia = relapse), I took the job. Four days a week, I rode the Metro-North train from Grand Central to Pleasantville, New York, to join Shortz at his home office, a room, like Reagle's, flooded with crossword ephemera and walled with reference books, holdovers from his pre-Google editing days.

I imagined that I was benefiting from a kind of affirmative action. During Shortz's thirty-year tenure at the *Times*, roughly 80 percent of the paper's puzzles had been created by men, a gender disparity that had steadily worsened over time. Some have accused the male editors at prestige papers of implicit bias; others have suggested that the digitization of crossword-constructing labor has reshaped the demographics of the CrossWorld in Silicon Valley's image. There were, I knew, many young men creating crosswords who were more prolific than I, a handful of whom even expressly wanted to be "the next Will Shortz." Still, if my appointment at the *Times* was political, so too was my output.

Shortz was known for editing up to 95 percent of the clues in a crossword submission, tailoring its references to suit a desired level of difficulty and an imagined audience—one that could be as broad or as narrow as Shortz wanted it to be. We tangled, mostly amicably, over this question of audience. We had markedly different frames of reference—he was a sixty-one-year-old who had grown up on a horse farm in Indiana, and I was a twenty-three-year-old who grew up in Tribeca—and the collision of our backgrounds made for good conversation and better crosswords. I remember getting him to rewrite the clue for BRO (traditionally, "Sister's sib" or "Sibling for sis") as "Preppy, party-loving, egotistical male, in modern lingo." But when I constructed a puzzle that prominently featured the term MALE GAZE in the grid, he insisted that the phrase wouldn't be in the average *Times* solver's lexicon; it wasn't "puzzle-worthy."

During my time with Shortz, I received both credit and flak for modulating the voice behind the puzzle's clues: for including words and idioms from my generation and perspective. In 2014, as a constructor for the American Crossword Puzzle Tournament, I was not on a mission to draw attention to my difference. My puzzle, however, did that work for me. In the grid's southeast corner, JESSA (48-Across: "One of the girls on *Girls*") intersected with JANSPORT (48-Down: "Backpack brand"). I thought both were "gettable" answers. (*Girls*-talk was, after all, abundant in 2014.) But apparently the JESSA / JANSPORT crossing had damaged some contestants' scores and sunk their tournament rankings. I had created what in crossword jargon is called a "Natick," an unjustified intersection of two obscure answers, leaving the solver with no hope but to guess at the solution: TESSA / TANSPORT? NESSA / NANSPORT?

The term *Natick*, coined by the puzzle blogger Rex Parker, stems from a 2008 *Times* puzzle in which NC WYETH (1-Down: "'Treasure Island' illustrator, 1911") intersected with NATICK (1-Across: "Town at the eighth mile of the Boston Marathon")—crossword esoterica, to be sure. But to think of my puzzle crossing as a Natick was to confess to never having watched the hit HBO show (no sin there) or to never having bought school supplies or gone to childcare drop-off (more damning, perhaps). You might even say it was to confess to being a man.

BETWEEN PARADISE AND PLEASANTVILLE, MY RELATIONSHIP TO the puzzle shifted—from a private to a public activity, from a coping mechanism to a practice with a politics, and I began to see myself filling one box in the public imagination and then another. Part of the appeal of a young woman crossword constructor is that she is focusing her intelligence on a frivolity; she is making her smarts unthreatening and benign. Of course, nothing about my relationship to crosswords— neither its reflection of cultural misogyny nor its origins in my willful self-destruction—was benign. Surely this is not what the mothers who approached me at the American Crossword Puzzle Tournament had in mind when they tried to set me up with their doctor or lawyer sons.

Since 2014, my constructing process has been digitized. I now use software, which expedites and improves the quality of my puzzles. And the CrossWorld—spurred by online puzzle outlets that work explicitly to mentor and publish women and nonbinary constructors—has become slightly more diversified. I still don't conform to the image or demographics of the contemporary constructor, but the conditions under which I am a token are far more complicated than byline bias or the dearth of women in STEM. The daily crossword is a site of paradoxes: it's a form of popular ephemera with weighty cultural capital; it's a marginal part of the newspaper with an outsize impact on the bottom line; it's a custodian of common usage and an outlet for language's subversion through wordplay. How these paradoxes intersect with the evolution of labor and gender norms in the United States is at once complex and revelatory—like any good puzzle.

The history of the crossword is intimately entwined with the history of first- and second-wave feminism—the history of first- and second-wave white feminism, in particular. Despite the data trends from the last thirty years, dutifully scrutinized and debated by crossword blogs and crossword Twitter, the puzzle has been indelibly shaped by women as constructors, editors, solvers, and polemicists. It was, we must concede, invented by a man. In December 1913, Arthur Wynne, editor of the *New York World*'s Sunday "FUN" page, published the first "word-cross," as it was then called. The diamond-shaped grid sat next to the paper's usual riddles, math problems, anagrams, and word squares. Those squares— sets of words that can be read the same vertically and horizontally—were predecessors to the modern crossword that derive from the Sator Square, a relic of ancient Rome.

Wynne's word-cross liberated the word square from its tight conventions, offering puzzle-makers like himself a much more flexible framework for wordplay. As he put it, "All I did was take an idea as old as language and modernize it by the introduction of black squares." Years later, Margaret Farrar, who took over for Wynne at the *World,* echoed

S	A	T	O	R		S	P	O	R	T
A	R	E	P	O		P	A	P	E	R
T	E	N	E	T		O	P	E	R	A
O	P	E	R	A		R	E	R	U	N
R	O	T	A	S		T	R	A	N	S

Sator Square	Modern Word Square

his sentiment: "The [crossword] is as old as the Sphinx—and as fatal in its fascination."

Wynne published his own puzzles anonymously, but in early 1914, he began accepting outside submissions, and the first puzzle he published under a byline was created by Mrs. M. B. Wood, a member of the Woman's Christian Temperance Union. In 1924, the Amateur Cross Word Puzzle League of America, led by Ruth Hale, stalwart of the Algonquin Round Table, established the rules governing crossword construction. That same year, Mrs. Helen Haven, the founding puzzle editor of the *New York Herald Tribune*, pioneered the crossword puzzle solving contest. Hale was a judge, and Ruth von Phul won it. In 1934, Elizabeth S. Kingsley invented the double-crostic (or acrostic puzzle, as they're now called), in which the solutions to crossword-like clues provide the letters that, once anagrammed, reveal a quote that can only be discovered upon the puzzle's completion. Kingsley's first double-crostic left the solver with three lines from Alfred, Lord Tennyson's "Ulysses," a traditionalist response to her despair that "students embraced twentieth-century scribblers like James Joyce." (That she was scribbling and scrambling letters in a Joycean fashion to achieve this puzzle peon to Tennyson was a paradox that apparently eluded her.) Between 1921 and 1969, Margaret Farrar standardized the grammar of the American puzzle,

FUN'S *Word-Cross Puzzle.*

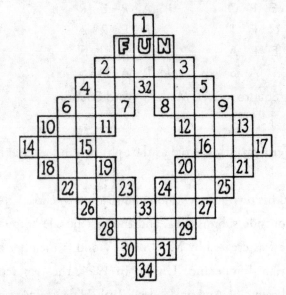

First "word-cross" puzzle, 1913.

CREDIT: Science Photo Library. Used with permission.

Fill in the small squares with words which agree with the following definitions:

2-3. What bargain hunters enjoy.
4-5. A written acknowledgement.
6-7. Such and nothing more.
10-11. A bird.
14-15. Opposed to less.
18-19. What this puzzle is.
22-23. An animal of prey.
26-27. The close of a day.
28-29. To elude.
30-31. The plural of is.
8-9. To cultivate.
12-13. A bar of wood or iron.
16-17. What artists learn to do.
20-21. Fastened.
24-25. Found on the seashore.

10-18. The fibre of the gomuti palm.
6-22. What we all should be.
4-26. A day dream.
2-11. A talon.
19-28. A pigeon.
F-7. Part of your head.
23-30. A river in Russia.
1-32. To govern.
33-34. An aromatic plant.
N-8. A fist.
24-31. To agree with.
3-12. Part of a ship.
20-29. One.
5-27. Exchanging.
9-25. Sunk in mud.
13-21. A boy.

editing the Simon & Schuster crossword puzzle books and then the *Times* crossword. For these white housewives—some self-identified suffragists, some self-identified conservatives—writing puzzles offered three unique satisfactions: a job in journalism, a profession that might otherwise exclude them; a political tool with which to shape the canon of "common knowledge"; and, perhaps above all, a coping mechanism for a life under patriarchy.

These demographics didn't survive the 1970s. The number of women producing puzzles declined as more entered the formal workforce, even though some independent feminist presses began publishing women-made crosswords as consciousness-raising devices alongside feminist dictionaries and encyclopedias. The result has been a pipeline problem—editors receive far fewer puzzles from women than from men—which is to say, it's a structural problem.

I can't make a living on crosswords. With the exception of a handful of daily puzzle editors at the *New York Times*, the *New Yorker*, and *USA Today*, constructors are freelancers. They're not in it for the money ($500 for a puzzle in the *Times*, $750 at the *New Yorker*, $150 at *USA Today*) but for the gratification of a byline and seeing their words in the world. Passion projects are a social privilege, and as most women are still expected to do the majority of childcare and housekeeping as well as work full-time, few find time for this rarified, underpaid work. Meanwhile, the puzzle has only gained prestige in the public imagination—attached to institutions like the *Times* and new media technologies—which has encouraged those with training in computer science to try their hand. Now the creation of a crossword puzzle is a job largely performed by men. But like botany, film editing, library science, and computing before it, it was once a form of feminized labor.

One purpose of this book is to rediscover the women who developed the American crossword—and to trace the puzzle's history through its intersections with forms of women's work and women's writing in the past one hundred years. White women flappers were icons of the initial "crossword craze" in the 1920s and '30s, when the country was reportedly in the throes of "crossword puzzleitis." White housewives were the puzzle's stewards from the 1940s through the '60s. But to be clear, the history of the American crossword is white all the way down. Will Shortz believes that the first Black man to publish a crossword in the Times was Wesley Johnson in 1996. The first Black woman to publish a *Times* crossword was Soleil Saint-Cyr in 2021. These data points are, I think, shocking. The overwhelming whiteness of the CrossWorld is also the result of a structural problem, but an analysis that focuses on labor alone—on who has the leisure time to write a puzzle—doesn't fully account for its endurance. Crosswords have always been understood, however subliminally, as a product of "white culture" in the US—a product of white culture that nonetheless passes itself off as the guardian of common knowledge and a test of racially unmarked intelligence.

In the earliest days of the crossword puzzle, newspapers and humor magazines were filled with images and comics of white Americans newly gripped by the crossword craze: images of mothers neglecting their household duties, redirecting their attention from their children to the grid, and married couples spatting, having their first "cross words" over the right and wrong entries of a puzzle. One cartoon from a 1924 issue of *Judge* magazine brings to the surface an otherwise latent symptom of the crossword craze: the puzzle's function as a way of testing and restricting knowledge along racial lines. The cartoon features two minstrel figures, a man and woman in blackface. She says to him: "Man, you don't mean nothin' to me, youse just de black parts of a crossword puzzle, you is!"

The cartoon plots the coordinates of racial difference along the crossword's black-and-white design: white squares are filled with all that is "meaningful" or worth knowing; black squares mean nothing. It's a

"Man, you don't mean nothin' to me, youse just de black parts of a crossword puzzle, you is!"

Judge *magazine* comic, April 4, 1925.

rather neat metaphor for white supremacy. The white squares are where cultural relevance lies, but there could be no white squares (or shape to that relevance) if not for the buttressing black squares. That the cartoon is written in Black dialect—with words that, at the time, would never have been deemed "puzzle-worthy"—only emphasizes, again by way of metaphor, the crossword's historical project of legislating language's proper use by coding "good words" as "white" ones. Or more precisely, "good words" as "not Black" ones.

Words, per se, don't have identity politics. But when launched into circulation—*By whom? In what context? With what intent?*—they become load-bearing devices. They carry political implications, erecting borders that are inevitably fraught with the psychic and material baggage of identity. Some words carry this baggage in almost every context. We call these words "coded": *grammarian* (woman-coded); *slang* (Black-coded, queer-coded). Because creating and solving crossword clues requires attention to language's unwieldiness—the many ways that words signify in different contexts—the life experience of the constructor will invariably inform her puzzles. However much she might want to imagine that the words in her puzzle are a product of her mind only, the material lives of words (where and how she experienced them—and how she felt) will always inform her process. Having said that, there's no reason to believe that a white constructor will use "white words" (if such a thing exists) in her puzzles; nor that a woman constructor will use "women's language" (although some of the women in this book have tried to create such a separatist idiom, using wordplay, in general, and the crossword puzzle, in particular, to do so). But words, and the images they conjure, fuel our attachments and aversions—our many misrecognitions. I doubt, for example, that I would have started creating crosswords as a teenager if, instead of "disciplined, perfectionistic, and obsessive," I had associated puzzles with housewives, flappers, and suffragists.

There is, however, a startling similarity between the language used about crosswords in the earliest days of the "craze" and the way I now understand their relationship to my eating disorder. *Judge* magazine's racist crossword cartoon, for example, is surrounded by images and articles that present the 1920s fad for puzzles as a "vice." The crossword was a distraction from the home and from more serious forms of knowledge production and consumption. Americans—white Americans—were becoming crossword "addicts," unable to go about their day without dipping into the puzzle or rummaging through reference books. They could go without food but not without the crossword. This puzzle "dependency"—as it was hysterically construed—wasn't a simple proxy for alcoholism in the days of Temperance. There's an air of self-congratulation circulating in these images: *We're addicted to knowledge. We can't help but test our intelligence every hour of the day.* Put otherwise, the crossword was an ironic vice—both a vice and a sign of white virtue. Both a guilty pleasure and a symbol of supremacy.

A vice that is also a sign of white virtue: this is how anorexia circulates in the popular imagination, even though eating disorders affect men and women from all races and ethnicities at a similar rate. When, at fourteen, I misrecognized myself in the image of "the anorexic" and that of "the crossword constructor," I wasn't thinking about whiteness. I was trying to imagine a virtuous version of myself, and perhaps unsurprisingly, I internalized an ugly logic buried deep within both "vices": to be virtuous is to be self-controlled; to be self-controlled is to be white.

In her 2019 book *Fearing the Black Body: The Racial Origins of Fat Phobia*, Sabrina Strings describes the origins of this logic in the rise of the transatlantic slave trade and the spread of Protestantism. By the nineteenth century, she writes, these twinned phenomena produced a "coherent ideology" in the United States—"a synchronized repression of 'savage' blackness and the generation of disciplined whiteness." However noxious this ideology—and however much it informed my attraction to both anorexia and the crossword puzzle—neither the body nor language can ever truly be disciplined. Lacking nutrients, the anorexic brain suffers cognitive distortions, wresting from the anorexic the control she so desperately sought. The crossword puzzle unleashes the chaos of language, maximizing its polymorphic perversity through wordplay, just as it promises to rein language in—to make it neat, orderly, and gridded.

Various efforts to draw attention to the crossword puzzle's

exclusions—the lack of diversity among constructors and its failure to incorporate Black slang and women- and queer-coded language into its lexicon—have been met with some resistance by longtime puzzle fans. Why turn a source of daily pleasure into a source of political anxiety? Why politicize a trivial pastime? These responses rest on a fairly narrow definition of the political; they also imply that those working to change the crossword to accommodate a larger, more inclusive public are humorless. We're taking ourselves—and the puzzle—way too seriously. Feminists will find these arguments familiar.

It's a truism of second-wave feminism that the "personal is political" and that the domestic sphere, the spaces and activities that produce comfort for the worker in his off-hours, are no less worthy of political scrutiny and organization than the picket line or the ballot box. Another truism of the second wave, although perhaps one that gained more traction in academic circles than in the public sphere, is that the modes of representation available to us are inevitably informed by patriarchal ideology. The way we speak and the way we write, how we are represented in images and in prose, reproduce the tropes and social mechanisms that subordinate women to men.

In her 1975 essay that coined the term the *male gaze*—the very term about which Shortz and I disagreed—film theorist Laura Mulvey identified the techniques that Hollywood films use to represent women as passive recipients of an active male "gazer." Whether femme fatale or future bride, women in Hollywood films, she wrote, are always the "bearer[s] of meaning, not maker[s] of meaning." In 1977, Mulvey and her then husband, Peter Wollen, made an experimental film that was meant to disrupt these objectifying techniques and to imagine a cinematic language that represents women otherwise. That film was called *Riddles of the*

Sphinx. In a direct address to the viewer at the start of the film, Mulvey says, "To the patriarchy, the Sphinx as woman is a threat and a riddle, but women within patriarchy are faced with a never-ending series of threats and riddles—dilemmas which are hard for women to solve, because the culture within which they must think is not theirs." How can feminists create a language for women—through words or images—without falling into familiar misogynistic norms? Can women's writing exist that doesn't collapse "all women" into a monolith or that doesn't essentialize "women's language" as "poetic," "anti-serious," or "illogical"? These are the Riddles of the Sphinx, as Mulvey described them.

In their film, Mulvey and Wollen marshaled a diverse set of visual strategies to create a kind of women's writing with film. Most startlingly to the viewer, in the film's middle section, they placed the camera in the center of their scenes (a kitchen, a daycare center, a telephone operator's workstation—sites of women's work), rotating it on a slow, 360-degree pan. As a result, women in the film are only ever seen in motion, passing in and out of the camera's view, their movements shaping the film they are in.

Like so many of the women featured in this book, Mulvey was playing with the norms of representation—in her case, the language of cinema; in mine, the materiality of words—to access a new way of looking at gender and the world. Also like the women in this book, Mulvey approached the riddles of patriarchy with a heady "solution." As if the terms by which women are subordinated to men could be reasoned away. As if they were remotely reasonable.

Ruth Hale, Margaret Farrar, Julia Penelope, and Ruth von Phul—the women who feature in each chapter of this book—are more interesting than they need to be for its purposes. Some of them actively shaped the puzzle that I love, but I was attracted to all of them because their lives have helped me understand why I was drawn to the crossword—and to anorexia—in the first place. They have helped me understand the relentless convolutions of my relationship to being "good," being ambitious, being clever, and being political. Their attraction to the crossword as a way to negotiate being women—being good, ambitious, clever, and political women—has helped me understand my own history with anorexia and crossword puzzles as not exactly intuitive or inevitable, but not arbitrary or incidental either.

The conditions of these women's mostly well-to-do lives conditioned them to find an outlet for their intelligence in wordplay. Their circumstances—and often their stubborn-minded paradigmatic thinking—also led them to positions of political reaction (strike-breaking, elitism, transphobia), and sometimes acts of self-harm. I have tried to be generous to the women who populate this feminist history of the crossword puzzle—not to redeem their bad behavior, but to understand them and to know the cultures in which they lived and learned, the forms of knowledge and language that they adopted, which at times occluded their own self-knowledge, humility, or compassion.

This *Riddles of the Sphinx* provides a panorama of the American crossword puzzle from the 1910s to the digital revolutions of the 2010s. It is also a group portrait of women, myself included, who have attached themselves to language rules—and language games—to resist the realities of their lives as women subordinate to men. At the intersection of these two projects is not a Natick, but a nexus for a larger story about the roles women have been allowed to play in American culture, the boxes they've been allowed to fill, and the ways they've used the crossword puzzle to observe and transgress its gendered matrix.

II

Ruth Hale and the Crossword Craze

I WAS SIXTEEN YEARS OLD WHEN A FAMILY FRIEND GAVE ME A COPY of *Dora*, the case study of a teenage hysteric as diagnosed and described by her analyst, Sigmund Freud. Freud saw Dora in 1900 in his office in Vienna; my family friend, a Freudian analyst, saw me in 2006 in a bakery in the West Village. At the time, I had been fasting for more than a year, and my eating disorder was something we spoke about freely, even as it went unspoken that I wouldn't be having milk or sugar in my tea. As I understood it, he was giving me *Dora* as both a gift and a gateway to self-understanding, if not necessarily self-help. He was offering me a Key to All Self-Mythologies, letting me in on the open secret of the unconscious—its enigma and its clues. Was my eating disorder just latter-day hysteria? Was I meant to identify with Dora, whose chronic cough (tussis nervosa), lethargy (taedium vitae), and loss of speech (aphonia) were, as Freud analyzed them, evidence of her displaced sexual desire?

Dora's symptoms presented a puzzle for her analyst. They were clues to her illness that could be solved by parsing her words, dreams, and the encrypted language of her body. With Freud's case study as my guide,

I believed that I could solve the riddle of my own illness—that I could discover its root causes and think my way to a cure. There were many problems with this plan. In identifying with both Freud and Dora—both analyst and patient—I was exercising the same grandiose thinking that led me to anorexia in the first place. I could control everything: my body and my mind, my illness and my convalescence. I thought I had a relevant skill set, which I was cross-training by solving and writing crossword puzzles every day.

Freudian psychoanalysis runs on word association and linguistic sub-stitutions. Freud's case study of Dora is a case in point: his analysis of his patient's second dream, for example, in which, in her telling, she com-pared a darkened forest to a Secessionist painting of woodland nymphs, allowed him to draw out the double meaning on *nymphae*, signifying both mythological sprites and also, evidently, the labia minora. From Dora's dream Freud correctly deduced that she had been covertly reading an encyclopedia—even, and maybe especially, its entries on sex and the body—and that she therefore knew the term's taboo second meaning, however buried it was in her unconscious. He could then make his final deduction: Dora wished to be vaginally penetrated, just as she had en-tered the forest in her dream.

Such symbolic displacement (forest = vagina) is the bread and butter of Freudian psychoanalysis; it should also be familiar to the average solver of a crossword puzzle. Freud was inventing a new language—the language of the unconscious—but it operated according to the logic of the "old" one, as it was being elaborated in the field of modern linguistics during the same period. This new science of language established a general truth of usage: words don't serve as proxies for "real" objects in the world; they serve as proxies for other words, gaining meaning only through these substitutions. The meaning of the word *forest*, for example, is determined as much by its antonyms, its negatively defined substitutions (not *desert*, not *ocean*), as it is by its synonyms (*woods, thicket, jungle*), all of which conjure figurative associations that inhere in the word's meaning. Freud saw the unconscious as the realm of the unspeakable, and so the sexual fantasies it guarded could only be articulated by way of figurative proxies. In other words, a pipe is not just a pipe; a forest is not just a forest.

Crossword clues also play on such substitutions. A clue can be straight-forward: *three letters for* "consume" (answer: EAT); or it can play on linguistic misdirection: *three letters for* "not fast" (answer: EAT). Although crossword clues might provide insight into the mechanisms of the unconscious, they are not, ultimately, written in its language. The average solver wouldn't know what to make of *six letters for* "forest" (answer: VAGINA), but the potential for words to mean so much with so little context remains the puzzler's—and the Freudian's—great pleasure.

I read as many of Freud's case studies as I could find after discovering Dora's. I was attracted to their abject titles (*The Rat Man, The Wolf Man*), just, as I imagine, prurient Dora was drawn to the illicit entries in her family's encyclopedia. I tried to understand my eating disorder as a physical manifestation of latent desire, but I couldn't find its source through willpower and wordplay alone. (That my name shared proximity with my disorder—Anna Rexia—caused me some macabre pleasure, but it didn't get me very far with my unconscious.) My body had become a symbol that was at once glaringly obvious to others and totally inscrutable to me. I was a walking sign of misery and righteousness, slow death and supremacy, self-erasure and self-display. I felt a melancholic disappointment in my inability to produce the key (some repressed trauma, some psychosexual dilemma) that I could use to solve, and presumably cure, myself. But this melancholy was offset by my suspicion—floating some-where between consciousness and unconsciousness—that I didn't want to be cured at all.

My parents described my descent into the disorder as "falling into a well." According to them, I didn't know what I was getting myself into; I couldn't see into its depths; I didn't know how treacherous the climb to recovery would be. Their account was mostly accurate. Like most teenagers, my thinking was myopic: I could hardly see beyond the next meal. But one doesn't usually "fall into a well" with imperious determi-nation, and that's exactly how I approached anorexia. I felt a thrill of triumph over my appetite and my shape, but I didn't know what kind of Pyrrhic victory it would be. Within six weeks of fasting, I had lost weight *and* control of a disorder that was meant to be a display of self-control. I understood the irony of my situation, and frankly, I found it fascinating. In fact, I was able to feel my fascination with my illness more readily than I could feel my shame, fear, or insecurity. If anyone pushed me to access those bad feelings, I felt condescended to, as if they thought I was just some sad teenager (I was) or a demographic cliché (I was), and not the mastermind of my own confounding fate.

Some clinicians have observed that their anorexic and bulimic patients suffer, like Freud's Dora, from a form of aphonia, impeded speech. In *Lost for Words: The Psychoanalysis of Anorexia and Bulimia*, Em Farrell writes that "the pre-verbal, concrete way these women often think and relate makes words both a dangerous and unwanted commodity." Although my thinking could easily be characterized as concrete, I was far from pre-verbal. My fluency—when talking about my own symptoms as much as anything else—was a strong source of pride. I would talk to anyone about my eating disorder, its motives (and my failure to understand them), and its punishing contradictions. I compelled my parents, their friends, teachers, and doctors into an audience for my self-analysis. When I stopped getting my period, I approached my biology teacher to ask her why. She explained to me, with soft sympathy in her eyes, that sex hormones were lipids (fats) and that by depriving my body of fat through food, I was inhibiting the normative function of my endocrine and reproductive systems. I explained to my doctor that food had become terrifying to me—that eating dinner was like being served a plate of spiders—and that I wished some daily pill existed that could provide my basic nutritional needs, expunge my terror, and get these doctors off my back. I was mostly honest and always prolix, but all this talk could hardly be considered talk therapy. It was a narcissistic self-display—perhaps impressive or interesting—but I imagine it was of no comfort to my family, who saw how little effect it had on my daily food intake.

Around the time that I read *Dora*, I also began seeing a therapist: a new audience. She wasn't trained in psychoanalysis—her methods could be traced to a handful of professional acronyms (CBT, FBT)—but she asked questions about my parents, mostly my father, that aligned with my expectations of "the couch" (which was, of course, a chair). I hardly remember our conversations, although I saw her for almost two years. Instead, I remember the peculiar fact that she often began our sessions by finishing a Light + Fit low-calorie yogurt and almost always had an open can of Diet Coke on her desk, aspartame running through her system as we spoke. Although I wasn't there to diagnose her—surely that wasn't what my parents were paying for—I couldn't help myself. I assumed that her clinical practice, treating adolescent anorexics and bulimics, was a symptom of her own eating disorder. I was spending countless hours thinking about food, when and how to eat it if at all, and I suspected that she was too. Unlike me, she could mark those hours as billable.

I also remember having to pee. To be clear, this was not a displaced symptom of oedipal anxiety. I was always clinching my bladder because I drank a gallon of water before therapy, hoping to disguise my weight loss when my therapist weighed me before our sessions. Sometimes I supplemented the water with Diet Coke or Vitaminwater Zero, assuming that the electrolytes would contribute to bloat and a higher number on the scale—they didn't—but if my mind could defy the biological imperative to eat, surely I could distort the physics of body mass too. I wanted the weight of water to offset that week's loss or to demonstrate that I had actually gained when I hadn't. My therapist wanted me to gain weight, and I wanted to please her. I didn't want to disappoint her or the dictates of my disorder, but of course I couldn't appease both. So I lied.

This was one paradox of my illness that I didn't articulate to my various audiences: although I was fixated on a particular image of perfection—of Good Girl-ness—my desire to protect my eating disorder against those who wanted me to recover had led me to become quite bad. In fact, the lies I contrived to sustain my anorexia became increasingly baroque and, when discovered (if they were discovered), increasingly painful to tolerate. When water-loading wasn't enough to sabotage my therapist's scale, I began taping ankle weights to my legs, a relic of my mother's 1990s exercise routine. My therapist didn't notice; she was temporarily satisfied by my progress, unaware that I was contorting my body in her chair, trying to avoid a conspicuous clank of metal weight against its metal frame. It wasn't until after a family therapy session, when my parents took me home in a taxi, that my scam was discovered. In a show of devotion, my mother put her hand on my leg, but her hand didn't touch my leg; it touched my prosthetic pounds.

Getting caught was inevitable. If not in a taxi—or on the scale—then in the obvious disconnect between my words and my behavior. I made no sense. How long did I think I could keep up the ruse of outpatient recovery without recovering at all? I had no endgame, just an increasingly fervid sense that I needed to remain underweight, that gaining weight would constitute a failure, and most of all, that I needed to be anorexic to be myself. Those who wanted me to recover became my antagonists: they were infringing upon my right to exist—or, as it were, my right to die. My thinking became narrower and more conspiratorial as my parents became more surveillant. At the suggestion of my therapist, they consented to the Maudsley model of eating disorder treatment, in which parents assume responsibility for "refeeding" their anorexic child, monitoring her meals, in an effort to avoid her hospitalization. Yet another puzzle: anorexia had allowed me to flaunt my complete independence from bodily need or want, but I found myself locked into a regressive relationship with my parents, as dependent on them to satisfy my needs as I had been in infancy. Instead of submitting to their care, though, I waged war on the domestic front.

At first, my mother planned my meals, sitting with me at breakfast and packing my lunch (and the supplement drink Ensure) for school, where I was to eat in front of a school nurse or a gym teacher. I panicked and devised a scheme, using savings from my bat mitzvah to purchase low-calorie alternatives to my mother's meal plan. I poured out her orange juice and replaced its contents with "50% less sugar Tropicana"; I threw away her loaf of bread and substituted a "thin-sliced" brand in its packaging; I emptied my Ensure and filled the bottle with water, sealing its lid with glue so it would appear untampered. These wasteful tricks took tremendous effort, but at the time, the handful of calories that I was able to shave off my meals seemed well worth it. These were not just symbolic gestures, though they were also that—token victories over my would-be wardens. They were also evidence of my illness's cognitive distortions. The difference between a slice of bread with 100 calories and one with 90 was, at the time, the difference between peril and security. Those 10 calories spared allowed me to feel securely, resolutely still anorexic. Sometimes I think about the waste: not only of food but of thinking. What if I had spent all that self-destructive brainpower on learning an instrument or a new language or how to be a good friend?

Although I only told my parents about my fridge-based insurrection years later, I doubt it surprised them. It wasn't my most outlandish or damaging plot. Around that time, my mother opened the mail to find a package addressed to me from Canada. I had purchased birth control online—or *maybe* it was birth control—hoping that the pills would induce my lost period. (Even if it was birth control, I doubt I would have bled. My body was in a state of starvation; I wasn't getting enough nutrition to sustain myself, let alone an ovum.) I was planning to use this ersatz period to convince my therapist that mine was actually a "healthy" weight. This wasn't the behavior of a Good Girl or a Smart Girl. This was undeniably stupid. This was bad.

In the spring of my sophomore year, my parents took me out of school, although I continued to keep up with my studies, only returning to the classroom to take exams. Like everything at the time, this decision was a battle of wills and a compromise. I wanted to stay in school; I loved learning as much as I loved excelling there, but I was only allowed to stay enrolled if I gained weight. I agreed, but on my terms. Against the advice of my therapist and the tenets of the Maudsley method, I took charge of my meal plans. I would gain the weight but retain control: I would do it by eating "good" foods, not "bad" ones.

Although some of my ideas about food at the time were widely accepted in a fat-phobic culture—high-caloric snacks are "bad"; weight loss is "good"—many of the behaviors and food rituals I adopted over the next year, though sacrosanct in my imagination, would have been unintelligible to an outsider. I could have a full stack of pancakes with as many chocolate chips as the diner's cook would load into the batter—but not a drop of syrup. I wouldn't allow myself a teaspoon of ice cream, but I could eat a pint of frozen yogurt. My mother accompanied me on frantic tours around our neighborhood, treading through freezer aisles in multiple supermarkets to find the only brand and flavor I would tolerate.

However arbitrary, these puzzling food rules had some logic: the pint of frozen yogurt took longer to eat than a calorically equivalent serving of ice cream, and I wanted to prolong my "indulgence" for as many minutes as I could, having fantasized about it all day. Syrup seemed "extra"—an addition to my contrived meal plan—but the chocolate chips scooped into the pancake batter made the meal seem contained into a singular unit. This way, when I imagined my day in terms of the meals I had eaten (the only way I knew how to imagine a day), I could say to myself that I had only eaten "pancakes" (one thing), not "pancakes and syrup" (two things). There are interesting ways to think about food, but these were not those. My thoughts about food were persistent, repetitive, and mind-numbing. As a result, I never brought them into therapy with me. *Did you want to talk about my dad again?* It would have been my pleasure.

Meanwhile, each scene of eating gained new ritualized ceremony: my mother sat with me, and I made her eat what I ate. If she didn't—or didn't finish her meal—I would accuse her of thwarting my recovery. If my father tried to sit with us, I would wave him away from the table or leave it myself. His presence inhibited our ritual, which included food but also two forms of distraction: over breakfast and lunch, my mother and I solved crossword puzzles; over dinner and dessert, we watched television. Both activities diverted my attention from any sensation of fullness; both offered me the conceit of shared intimacy with my mother, even as I was crushing her spirit, gaining malevolent control over her body by punishing mine.

WHY? WHY DID I BECOME THIS TERROR? I DIDN'T BLAME MY PARENTS when they occasionally resorted to moralizing; I also wondered: *Perhaps I'm just not a good person.* But this answer satisfied no one, least of all me, as I tried desperately to compensate for my bad behavior. I did extra chores around the house; I never missed a doctor's appointment (and there were many); and I was always polite to teachers and my parents' friends. I was eager to please, so long as it didn't inconvenience my mental illness. Even so, I was very unpleasant. I stood for no criticism, never crouching into a defensive posture but erupting into self-pitying hysterics if I was ever scolded or told no. I wish I had written down my feelings at the time, but I disdained journaling, associating the therapeutic exercise with maudlin sentimentality and a femininity for which I had no use. Instead, I wrote down little theories, gleaned from Penguin Freud and my own mental gymnastics. Instead, I wrote crossword puzzles.

However cathartic and curious I've found it, the psychoanalytic literature on anorexia continues to offer me little insight into those years. Was my condition oedipal? Was I effectively an "invert," identifying with my father and competing with him for the possession and sexual control of my mother? Was my eating disorder a function of distorted object relations? Did I fail to separate from my mother because she used me as a fetish object, thwarting my individuation? In other words, was my eating disorder an elaborate revenge plot? Or, as one analyst has ventured, was it a classic example of penis envy taken to its literal extreme: Did I want to turn my body *into* a penis, mimicking its taut, muscular shape?

Histories of eating disorders often begin not with anorexia nervosa but with anorexia mirabilis (the miraculous loss of appetite), a medieval "epidemic" of fasting nuns who subsisted on little more than the Eucharist and the Word of God. The most famous of these sainted women was Catherine of Siena (1347–1380), who is said to have eaten only a handful of herbs each day and would reportedly use twigs to induce vomiting if she was forced to eat anything else. Secular fasting, as it were, was first reported in medical literature in 1689 and was named anorexia nervosa (starvation by the mind, not the miracle) by British physician William Gull in 1873. It was, however, a misnomer. Anorexia means "loss of appetite," and despite what they report, anorexics are always hungry.

It wasn't until the early twentieth century, inspired by Freud's discovery of the unconscious, that anorexia began to be studied as a psychological mystery, not a religious miracle or somatic deficit. In case histories of anorexics from the first half of the twentieth century, the patient, who is nearly always a woman, becomes a puzzle for her psychiatrist, who is nearly always a man. The "key" to solving the starving woman's puzzle usually lay in the equation of food and sexuality. Two common solutions were the fear of pregnancy and the repressed desire for fellatio. In 1919, Ellen West, an anorexic and bulimic patient of the psychiatrist Ludwig Binswanger, wrote out her thought pattern as an equation: "Eating = being fertilized = pregnant = getting fat." Hers was paradigmatic thinking at its finest. These logically false but psychically powerful substitutions shaped her unconscious desires and repulsions. In 1942, the psychiatrist Ruth Moulton suggested that the anorexic rejects slimy foods because they remind her of semen or because she wants to be force-fed to satisfy a fantasy for oral sex. Binswanger's patient was sexually timid; Moulton's demonstrated sexual aggression. At once too frigid and too promiscuous within the terms of early psychoanalysis, the anorexic woman's appetites (or lack thereof) were a threat to the cultural order.

Fittingly, for my own history, during the same period that anorexic women became a source of medical suspicion, the crossword puzzle became an object of cultural hysteria. Newspapers and magazines from the 1920s and '30s warned of a "crossword craze" afflicting the country's minds. Hotels considered placing a dictionary next to the Bible in every room; telephone companies tracked increased usage, as solvers phoned friends when stuck on a particularly cryptic clue; baseball teams feared that America's pastime would be usurped, the grid to replace the diamond. The passion for crosswords was described as an "epidemic," a "virulent plague," and a "national menace."

Much of the outcry focused on the puzzle's trivializing waste of brain-power. In 1925, syndicated columnist Arthur Brisbane wrote, "Young people who want to increase their vocabulary should not deceive them-selves with crosswords. Let them read Shakespeare." What if, instead of puzzles, they learned an instrument, or a new language, or how to be a good friend? Or, more relevant to the fears of the time, a good spouse, as many worried that the puzzle was a threat to the family unit. A host of divorces in Ohio were said to have been caused by the daily crossword, with the man-ager of one legal-aid association claiming to have received an average of "ten letters a day" from spouses whose partners were "suffering from 'crossword puzzleitis.'" The caption on a cartoon from the time asks, "What is home without a mother—now?" The illustration, by Donald McGill, features a woman huddled over a puzzle, having abdicated the maternal function, while her apparently emasculated husband is stuck caring for their crying infant. Like an emotional affair, the crossword seemed to be siphoning off energy and intimacy from married life.

This "square vice," as it was once called it, became a locus for displaced anxiety about a movement that was explicitly changing American gender relations: first-wave feminism. In books, comics, and postcards from the time, the New Woman and the crossword puzzler became linked as flouters of Victorian gender conventions. Flora Annie Steel's novel *The Curse of Eve*,

"CROSSWORDS."

"What is home without a mother - now?"

Postcard illustration by Donald McGill, 1925.

published in 1929, featured two antiheroines who are "making a living out of the craze for crossword puzzles." One is a fashionable beer heiress, with more bite and better business instincts than her brothers; the other is a cash-strapped dancer who sees marriage as another form of prostitution. Both are depicted as simultaneously desexed ("in the fullness of her bodily and mental powers she sits free of sex") and oversexed (with an "unconscious desire to attract, unconscious desire to appropriate"). Both are too great a puzzle for the modern man to grasp.

The dangerous fantasy of the crossword-obsessed New Woman also provided the hook for three novelty songs in 1924 and 1925, including "Cross-Word Puzzle Blues" (performed by the Duncan Sisters), in which the duo curse the "demented nut [who] invented this way to sadistic contentment," and "Cross-Words (Between Sweetie and Me)" by Billy Jones, who laments that his sweetie has "been puzzling, [and] don't seem to care / Whether I'm near her or taking the air." The last and most famous of these songs was "Cross-Word Mamma You

"CROSSWORDS."

"You naughty boy - it couldn't be that word!"

Postcard illustration by Donald McGill, 1925.
CREDIT: Shutterstock.

Puzzle Me" by Frank Crumit, about a "puzzling woman" who devotes herself to the crossword as a stand-in for other fashions of the time. Like the flapper, she is liberated from the corsets and customs of the Victorian age. A double-crosser, she is not to be trusted: "You call me 'honey'—that means 'bee'! / Looks like I'll be stung no doubt." The conceit extends across nine verses: "I heard you mention 'butcher'—that means 'meat'! / Who you gonna 'meet' tonight?" But like the Sphinx before her, the Cross-Word Mamma solicits a solution: "Cross-Word Mamma, you puzzle me," the chorus concludes. "But Papa's gonna figure you out."

There are hundreds of other Jazz Age relics that conflate the flapper and the crossword as fixtures of the zeitgeist. In these images, the puzzle represents the enigma of female desire and fuels intimacy between men and women in an otherwise chaste culture of heterosexual courtship. The crossword allows verbal and physical taboos to be breached, as members of the opposite sex say four-letter words to each other, cuddling around the newspaper page. "You naughty boy—it couldn't be that word!" reads the caption of a cartoon featuring two young solvers, a blushing man and a woman clutching her breast. In the 1925 film *The Freshman*, Harold Lloyd's character looks inquisitively over the shoulder of a young woman crossword solver, while sitting next to her on a train; their heads almost touch as they crowd over the grid. "I think I know the word for number 19 vertical," the intertitles read, "Name for the one you love." And the couple starts free-associating together: "sweetheart," "darling," "dearest," "precious," "honeybunch." An older woman behind them, not seeing the grid at their table, cuts in, assuming that they had been exchanging these sweet nothings without the assistance of crossword clues: "Isn't it wonderful to be in love?" she asks. The couple is scandalized and embarrassed, and Lloyd runs out of the car, knocking over a waiter and stumbling into one of his classic pratfalls. By the dual logic of the crossword craze, the woman is the puzzle, and the puzzle brings solvers closer to their desire. The puzzle was, in other words, a sex object.

*Judge magazine covers
from November 1924,
May 1925,
January 1925,
and March 1925.*

ANOTHER CROSSWORD NUMBER!

JUDGE

THE SIX BEST SELLERS

SPECIAL NUMBER FOR DUMB-BELLS!

JUDGE

1 HORIZONTAL—PEACH

The Freshman and "Cross-Word Mamma You Puzzle Me" both premiered in 1925, the high point of the crossword craze. Between November 1924 and May 1925, *Judge* magazine, a humor weekly, ran four covers illustrated with "Crossword Mamas": stylish women puzzling over puzzles or seated in a coquettish pose with a grid overlaying her image. "The Greatest Puzzle of Them All," reads the caption on the earliest of these illustrations. In the pages of these issues and many others that year, *Judge* magazine's contents—short comic sketches and political cartoons—were consistently crossword-themed. The puzzle was a source of an apparently endless stream of magazine content: mock love letters to Crossword Mamas, crossword etiquette manuals, and the fictional testimony of a man who had "shot [his] wife after she asked [him] for the one hundredth time for a word meaning cold oatmeal in Patagonia." He was "quite cheerful," he confessed, "for wherever they would send [him], [he] would never have to give synonyms to a woman with an insatiable appetite for solving crosswords." In 1925, *Judge* readers evidently tired of these tropes as little as they tired of crosswords themselves.

Occupying American minds and the pages of American periodicals, the crossword made its way to Broadway in *Puzzles of 1925*, an Elsie Janis production at the Fulton Theatre on 46th Street. The show featured a scene in a "crossword sanitorium," where patients came to recover from their life-absorbing puzzle addictions. The set design featured black-and-white squares in the pattern of Turkish bath tiles or weaving patterns—both well-suited to a scene of "recovery." On stage, a social worker confesses that she was the originator of the crossword puzzle, and the patients revolt, killing her on the spot. Upon her removal, Jimmy Hussey, the revue's emcee, jokes to the audience: "She came in vertical; she's going out horizontal."

Janis, the show's writer and lead actor, was a vaudeville child star who

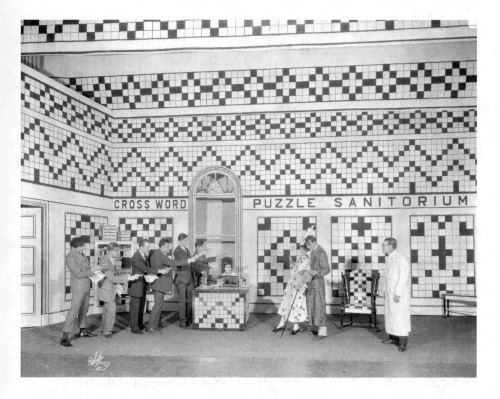

Puzzles of 1925 *at the Fulton Theatre on Broadway.*
CREDIT: New York Public Library Digital Collections. Used with permission.

gained renown as the "playgirl of the Western Front" and the "sweetheart of the AEF" during her time as a USO performer in World War I. While on an American tour in 1924, she began solving crossword puzzles on her train trips between cities. As she described her new fixation in a newspaper column that she wrote that year, "After two hectic months of writhing among words and struggling with synonyms I have decided that I must either give up my career or can the crosswords—I am physically unfit to do both." This was both hyperbole and false modesty: not only was Janis solving crosswords and performing multiple shows a day, she was also writing and planning her next revue, penning columns, and keeping a full social calendar, including many parties at regional veterans' associations that were thrown in her honor. But hyperbole was the spirit of the "craze"—it's what made it into a "craze" at all—and Janis's writing about her puzzle addiction was no exception. She explained:

In the midst of a puzzle, I suddenly thought of my performance and dashed to the theatre to do my stuff. In the midst of my performance, I suddenly thought of a word and wanted to dash back to the hotel to do my puzzle. One night I nearly announced to the audience that I would give them an imitation of a well-known actress whose name suggests an undertaker in nine letters. Of course you have guessed it—Barrymore. Now you know why I must stop.

When *Puzzles of 1925* premiered, Janis's columns were collected in a book titled *If I Know What I Mean*. She borrowed the phrase from her good friend Dorothy Parker, who, Janis wrote in the book's introduction, gave the line to "one of her characters who was prone to talk about things she knew nothing of . . . [and] I thought it was an ideal caption for my efforts." (More false modesty.) In the years after the war, Janis was a sporadic attendee of lunches with the Algonquin Round Table, where Parker was a staple. But as a performer, not a critic, she was just as likely to sit at square tables with the hotel's other luminary diners (John Barrymore among them) as she was to sit with Parker in the round.

In the 1920s, no group did more to fuel the crossword craze and its underlying sensibility—a self-satisfying amalgam of pedantry and wit—than the writers and editors of the Algonquin Round Table. If the group didn't exactly have a leader, it did have an elder statesman in Franklin Pierce Adams, who signed his popular "Conning Tower" column F.P.A. The column, which had a cultlike following, featured limericks, puns, and satirical prose and offered early publishing platforms for Edna Ferber, Edna St. Vincent Millay, and Parker herself. Although Adams started "The Conning Tower" at the *New York Tribune*, he, like so many of his Round Table peers, moved to the *New York World* in the 1920s, where his office was next door to the inventor of the crossword, Arthur Wynne, and the puzzle's first full-time editor, Margaret Farrar, then Margaret Petherbridge, who assumed the role in 1921. Adams was known to use his column as a kind of errata sheet for the previous day's puzzles, criticizing Petherbridge's failures while celebrating this new medium for language's play and display.

The Round Table was a medium for the same. The founding members of the group—Jews, Protestants, Catholics, and atheists; Republicans, Democrats, Socialists, and the avowedly apolitical—shared trades (jobs in publishing and the theater) and traits (a free-floating logophilia). Although Parker is perhaps the best remembered of the coterie, its initial members were many and moved fluidly between publications and genres and from stage to screen.

The group's parlor games were word games. However much they have since been romanticized for their off-the-cuff wit, the Round Table's diversions were often highly structured, with rounds of trivia, anagrams, charades, and something called "I-Can-Give-You-a-Sentence," in which one diner would say to another, for example, "I can give you a sentence with the word 'burlesque,'" adding, "I had two soft-burlesque for breakfast." It's said that the terribly corny game began when Adams walked around the hotel one December wishing everyone "a meretricious and a happy New Year."

Unsurprisingly, the group christened itself with puns and double entendres: most famously, the Vicious Circle, the Luigi Board (named for the server who tended to their table at the Algonquin and the spiritualist novelty of the time), and Wit's End (Parker's name for Alexander Woollcott's apartment, which became an unofficial lodging house for wayward Round Tablers).

Even their first meeting was baptized with a play on words. Woollcott, the *New York Times* theater critic, imposed a number of hostile tics on his peers. Having, like many of the group, worked on the military newspaper *Stars and Stripes* during World War I, he insisted on beginning his many "stories from the front" with the line "From my seat in the theater of war . . ." ("Seat 13, Row Q, no doubt," writer and publicist William B. Murray once replied; "Must have been the last row nearest the exit," editor Art Samuels said.) In 1919, exasperated by Woollcott's bloviation, many of his friends held a luncheon at the Algonquin to officially welcome Woollcott home from war, a year late, hoping it would end his theatrics. A banner in the hotel's dining room read:

AWOL
cot

He was A. Woolcott, to his readers. He was AWOL on the Western front, having missed out on military action while working on a newspaper. And to the guests' further delight, he famously rankled when his name was misspelled. They returned every day for the next decade.

The Round Table didn't just have a shared sensibility with the crossword craze; they were also its victims and proselytizers. Harold Ross, who founded the *New Yorker* in 1925 with his wife, Jane Grant, was the editor of *Judge* when it ran its four crossword puzzle issues. Frank Case, the Algonquin's manager and a close friend to the group, did daily puzzles as his "before-dinner stimulus instead of cocktails," according to his daughter, a proxy drug for liquor in the days of Prohibition. Crosswords were also a stimulant and balm to the women members of the Round Table for the triumphs and disappointments of first-wave feminism. No figure better captures its function in these terms than Algonquin regular Ruth Hale.

HALE WAS THE COFOUNDER AND PRESIDENT OF TWO LEAGUES: THE Lucy Stone League, an activist group agitating for married women to keep their own last names, founded in 1921, and the Amateur Cross Word Puzzle League of America, founded in 1924. Wickedly smart but less playful than her peers at the Round Table, Hale used language as her principal tool for feminist activism. Organizing it—and organizing around it—offered her a sense of control and propriety as she attempted to redefine marriage for the New Woman of the 1920s. The namesake of her feminist organization, Lucy Stone, was born in 1818 and married in 1855. Stone maintained her birth name until her death in 1893, and when asked why she did so, she said, "My name is the symbol of my identity and must not be lost." Her credo became the motto for the Lucy Stone League.

There is no US law that dictates that a woman must take her husband's name upon marriage—a fact that submitted so-called Lucy Stoners to ridicule in dozens of newspaper columns about their crusade—but English common law held that "A man and his wife are one, and he is the one." To this, Hale replied simply that times had changed: "Any family begins and ends with two adult persons, one male and one female. These are two units of productivity, whether both work outside the home—as so frequently happens now—or whether one works outside the home and the other works within it." However cogent in theory and law, keeping one's maiden name after marriage posed practical and bureaucratic difficulties for Hale and other Lucy Stoners.

Hale married Heywood Broun in 1917, but when the young couple traveled to France that year to report on the war—Broun for the *New York Herald Tribune*, Hale for the Army Edition of the *Chicago Tribune*—Hale couldn't get a passport in her own name. She was instead issued the identifier "Mrs. Heywood Broun." When she tried to return to France again in 1920, she applied for a new passport, again in her own name, and was eventually sent one with a compromise (and, to her, compromising) half measure: "Mrs. Heywood Broun, otherwise known as Ruth Hale." On her third try, she asked to be identified as "Ruth Hale, wife of Heywood Broun," but her inquiry was denied. "When the verdict went against her," Broun wrote, "she decided she would rather remain Miss Hale in America than be Mrs. Heywood Broun in any garden spot of the old world. It would have spoiled the scenery for her." The sacred symbolism of her name—a mark of her fierce independence—had her returning invitations sent to Mrs. Heywood Broun and once redirecting curtains sent to that name to Broun's mother's home.

Hale spent many hours at the Algonquin and in her West 85th Street brownstone, a frequent after-lunch outpost of the Round Table, complaining about her passport verdicts and their significance for women's rights in the years after the ratification of the Nineteenth Amendment. Her conversations were often staged with Jane Grant, who did not take Harold Ross's name after their marriage in 1920. Ross is said to have tired of the women's plaints, telling them, at one point, "Aw, why don't you hire a hall?" And although they didn't hire a hall, they did institute their league, for which Grant was secretary-treasurer. They were joined by thirteen members of Heterodoxy, a Greenwich Village–based feminist debating group that Hale had been attending since its founding in 1912 and that included Fola La Follette, Charlotte Perkins Gilman, Crystal Eastman, and Zona Gale. These women and many other Lucy Stoners (Elsie Ferguson, Fannie Hurst, and Anita Loos among them) had already "made a name for themselves" before their marriages. This allowed dismissive journalists to accept that *they* should be allowed to retain their maiden names after marriage in the spirit of the "stage name"—but not, apparently, in the spirit of feminism. As a columnist in the *Philadelphia Inquirer* wrote, "The idea that a woman loses her individuality unless she retains her maiden name after marriage strikes many persons as rather silly. It is the manifestation of that restless, not to say turbulent, spirit that animates the 'new woman' in these days."

Hale was captured by that spirit and, like the women who pioneered the prefix *Ms.* in the early 1970s, she wanted to register her feminist politics in language. She was as militant about her civil rights as she was about proper usage, grammar, and syntax—both a crusader and a vigilant abider of language's norms. Unsurprisingly, she was the best crossword solver among her set. As founding president of the Amateur Cross Word Puzzle League of America, Hale worked to codify the rules of the grid, which, as of the league's founding, had only one rule: words must cross. After the league's first meeting, its rules were many more:

1. Pattern
   The pattern shall interlock all over.
   Only approximately one-sixth of the squares shall be black.
   Only approximately one-tenth of the letters shall be unkeyed. [That

is, connected only to one word, not two. By the 1930s, any "un-keyed" letters were considered flaws of construction.]

The design shall be symmetrical.

2. Words

Obsolete and dialectic words may be used in moderation, if plainly marked and accessible in some standard dictionary, such as *Merriam's Webster,* Funk & Wagnalls's, *Century,* etc.

Foreign words that are more or less familiar and are easily accessible may be used, and should be marked with the language to which they belong.

Technical terms that are found in a standard dictionary may be used.

Abbreviations, prefixes, and suffixes should be avoided as far as possible. When used, they should be plainly marked and must be legitimate.

3. Definitions

The only requirement is common sense.

Synonyms that are too far removed from the word should be avoided, and also what Gelett Burgess calls smarty-cat definitions.

If this sounds like all games and no fun, all rules and no play—and therefore a vast departure from the freewheeling spirit of the Round Table—it was. Hale was witty but never frivolous; she took herself and (for better or worse) her crossword puzzles very seriously. When a friend once accused her of lacking a sense of humor, she replied, "I thank God that the dead albatross of a sense of humor has never been hung around my neck."

In addition to formalizing the puzzle's bylaws, the Amateur Cross Word Puzzle League organized College Bowl–style crossword tournaments in which Hale was a judge. Pitting Harvard against Yale, Vassar against Bryn Mawr, the games were widely covered in the country's regional and national newspapers. The Harvard-Yale contest on April 31, 1923, had Broun and Robert Sherwood representing Harvard. (Newspapers reported that the Yale team "called foul" when Hale "came over and sat by Broun," as if he might absorb her crossword acumen through osmosis.) There was little trickery to the clues and low stakes to the game, but reporters seemed to enjoy anointing the humble grid with the inflated rhetoric of sports coverage: "Broun tackled a seven-letter word meaning 'a slight convex curve in the shaft of a column.' . . . The crowd roared. . . . Bryn Mawr roared soprano, and Vassar roared alto, and these, with the basso profundo of the C.C.N.Y.[,] made the scene one well worth hearing."

Papers also noted how odd it was that Broun and Sherwood were representing Harvard, as neither had actually graduated from the school. Sherwood dropped out in 1917 to fight in the war, but Broun had no excuse beyond his own shiftlessness. Having failed to pass his freshman French course after four years on campus, Broun never completed his requirements for the degree. His father refused to pay for an extra year, sending him to work for a friend at the *New York Morning Telegraph* instead. In temperament, then, Broun and Hale could not have been more different. He was loud and gregarious; she was assiduous and sometimes abrasive. He suffered from what his psychiatrist called "pantophobia," or a phobia of all things; she fearlessly approached her days as she did the

State Department that refused to grant her a passport in her name. She provided their marriage with the structure, conviction, and even intelligence that he admittedly lacked. As their son later recalled, "He liked that she didn't hide that she was smarter than he was. His mind was roving and creative but hers was sharper, and he liked that sharpness."

Broun was born in 1888 with the privilege of patrician Old New York: he attended the Horace Mann School before Harvard, and his father ran a successful printing business before becoming a no-less-successful wine merchant. His parents loved luxuries as much as the social rules that accompanied them—which wine paired with which meal, which cuffs for which occasion. By contrast, Hale was born in 1887 in the small rural town of Rogersville, Tennessee. Her family was well-off but not well-to-do, and when her father died, Hale was eleven and her mother was left without income or support in raising their three children. Hale resented her town's insularity and rigid proscriptions for "ladylike" behavior. As her son later described in his memoir about growing up with famous parents, Hale's upbringing required her to force her contralto voice "upward to the appropriately 'feminine' register"; she was only to read "genteel literature," which meant an inordinate amount of Sir Walter Scott; and sidesaddle was her only option when horseback riding. (She scandalized her town—"a basket of snakes," she called them—when she rode astride nonetheless.) Hale even deemed her birth name Lillie Ruth "squashily feminine" and trimmed it of Southern ornamentation as soon as she left Rogersville.

Both Broun and Hale were eager to depart from the strictures of their upbringings, and while Broun did so passively, through sheer indolence and slovenly dress, Hale worked her way from Rogersville to art school in Philadelphia to Washington, DC, where, in 1905, at age eighteen, she became a society reporter for the Hearst Bureau. Three years later, she returned to Philadelphia to work as a drama critic for the *Public Ledger*, where she occasionally covered movies and sports, becoming one of the nation's first female sports reporters and perhaps its first woman film critic. In 1910, she moved to New York and worked as a drama critic at *Vogue* and then *Vanity Fair* and then at the Sunday *New York Times*. In 1915, while still at the *Times*, she met Broun at a baseball game at the Polo Grounds. At the time, he was a sports reporter for the *New York Tribune* and was soon to be dumped by his girlfriend, the dancer Lydia Lopokova, who later married John Maynard Keynes. (Although Broun spoke of Lopokova frequently, she confessed, after his death, that she "[couldn't] remember anything of Heywood at all.")

When Broun and Hale married in 1917, Franklin Pierce Adams, Broun's best man, called them, in a typically clever inversion of cliché, "the clinging oak and the sturdy vine." Broun, the oak, was always fighting his weight and his fears; Hale, the slender but sturdy vine, "would have been who she was whether he existed or not," their son wrote, "but he was very much her creation." For their wedding, Hale wanted to skirt ceremony, preferring a trip to city hall with a handful of friends as witnesses, but Broun's mother insisted that her son marry in an Episcopal church, the fashionable St. Agnes on West 92nd Street. In a rare concession, Hale agreed to the ceremony but made provisions of her own: there would be "no goddamned music—no marching down the aisle to Mendelssohn"; nor would she promise to "obey" Broun in her vows; nor would she wear a wedding ring, which was, she later said, "as counterfeit as the custom that created it." Broun's mother agreed to these terms but nonetheless hired an organist who began playing the "Wedding March" at the ceremony's start. Hale didn't budge. She refused to walk down the aisle until the organist stopped, and when she did walk, it was reportedly

Ruth Hale, published alongside her interview, *"Has Modern Woman Disrupted the Home?"* Independent Woman *(1929).*

"the purposeful tread of the crusader as she marched toward the passive, perspiring man who was distributing placatory smiles to everyone in view."

Although Hale and Broun's mothers grew up in different social stations miles apart, they firmly agreed on a vision of matrimony in which a woman disguises her authority as deference, in which she is the "great woman behind the great man," "the neck that turns the head," and any number of other clichés that relegate her power to the anonymous, domestic sphere. The mothers' similarities ended there. Hale's mother, Annie Riley Hale, loomed large in her daughter's imagination as her political foil but her match in all matters of temperament. Despite her protestations, Riley Hale did little to disguise her authority, publishing half a dozen books to promote her numerous fanatical positions: pro-vegetarianism, anti-vaccinations, anti-Roosevelt, anti-Wilson, anti-feminism (in general), and anti–woman's suffrage (in particular). Phyllis Schlafly before her time, Riley Hale campaigned tirelessly against a woman's right to participate in the political sphere where she personally thrived. Her 1916 book—fittingly, for our purposes, titled *The Eden Sphinx*—promised to "get some light on the puzzle-picture" of the New

Woman. The women's movement, she claimed, "is marked by the same note of mystification and bewilderment that . . . [has led] other men in other lands and ages . . . to make [women] into an unsolved and insoluble riddle." Her book was meant to crack the New Woman's code, to discover her "true nature," and to reestablish her rightful political arena: the home.

With an enormously lengthy bibliography, featuring the works of British and American suffragists, poets and philosophers from Tennyson to Nietzsche, and "biologists and sex-psychologists," *The Eden Sphinx* offered five principal arguments against a woman's right to the vote. The first four are fairly conventional rehearsals of retrograde thinking: woman's suffrage is "futile" and "superfluous," and it threatens the marriage unit and the balance of power between public and private spheres. Riley Hale's final argument, however, takes a surprisingly psychoanalytic turn. "Woman-suffrage," she wrote, "is not a 'cause' but an *effect*; an eruptive misleading symptom of a deep-seated malady whose source is *not* political disaffection, and whose cure is *not* the ballot." In other words, the fight for woman's suffrage evinced a psychological displacement of women's true unhappiness.

It is here, in this last argument, that Riley Hale promised to solve the riddle of the suffragette sphinx, assuming the posture—and diagnostic—of the Freudian analyst. The last third of *The Eden Sphinx* amounts to nothing less than a group analysis of first-wave feminists, whose agitation for the right to vote, she suggested, was no more than a neurotic symptom of their penis envy and their inability to accept and gratify their sexual appetites, preternaturally more ravenous than those of men. The petition for suffrage, she wrote of feminists, was simply an effort to "scratch where it didn't itch."

Some of Riley Hale's books were reviewed in national publications, but they never offered her commercial success. As a result, she lived fitfully for many years with her feminist daughter and her socialist son-in-law on

West 85th Street, in a home that her daughter had purchased in her own name. With the backing of the Lucy Stone League, Ruth Hale was reportedly the first married woman in New York City to have done so. "Maiden Namers Score a Victory; Ruth Hale Gets Her Name on Deed Just That Way, Not as Mrs. Heywood Broun," read a *New York Times* headline about her achievement.

———

ANNIE RILEY HALE'S APPEARANCE IN HER DAUGHTER'S HOME WAS not its only source of acrimony. Hale and Broun's marriage was neither conventional nor exactly happy, but it was—like the clinging oak to the sturdy vine—functionally dysfunctional. After their wedding, the couple traveled to Paris, where Hale worked for the Army Edition of the *Chicago Tribune*. Hale's work there was unspecified, but the understaffed newspaper published fourteen columns a day, and though she held no bylines there, she worked tirelessly on its output. Alexander Woollcott wrote of Hale's time in Paris that "she has been far nearer the front than I and can tell you many things I have never seen and never may see." The couple returned to New York in the winter of 1917 when Hale was six months pregnant. Whereas Broun was able to pick up his drama column at the *Herald Tribune* and begin a new syndicated column there titled "Books and Things," Hale had fewer professional opportunities. She began working part-time in a theatrical publicity job for Broadway producers.

In 1921, Broun took a job at the *New York World*, where he launched the syndicated column that made him a national celebrity. As was clear to *World* editor Herbert Bayard Swope, Broun was a lazy reader but a lively writer about his own life, politics, and milieu. At the *World*, "Books and Things"—but mostly "things," as seen by Heywood Broun—was retitled

"It Seems to Me." Hale and their son, Heywood Broun III, who went by Woodie, made frequent appearances in the column under the pseudonyms "Miss X" and "H. 3d," respectively. But as Broun later confessed, Hale was more than just fodder for his daily musings:

A very considerable percentage of all newspaper columns, books, and magazine articles which appeared under the name "Heywood Broun" were written by Ruth Hale. I mean, of course, the better columns. And even those which I felt I was writing on my own stemmed from her. . . . I suppose that for seventeen years practically every word I wrote was set down with the feeling that Ruth Hale was looking over my shoulder.

It's a tragic irony that a woman so invested in her name would find her work subsumed under her husband's byline and her life anonymized as "Miss X." Her voice became known to the public as his; or, as Woodie put it, having honed his wit on the toughest of whetstones, "Ruth was conscience and Heywood was the voice of conscience."

In 1922, Hale was hired to write movie reviews for *Judge* in a column that lasted a little more than a year. Her freelance book and theater reviews appeared in the *New York World*, the *Brooklyn Eagle*, and the *Bookman*, but nothing stuck for long, and nothing had the popular appeal of "It Seems to Me." Hale was convinced that employers overlooked her because of her marriage to Broun, who, by 1926, was making $30,000 a year at the *World* (or half a million dollars in today's currency), reportedly bringing in fifty thousand extra readers to the daily paper. Throughout the 1930s, as the Depression deepened, his annual salary soared to $70,000, and Hale presumed that since employers knew she didn't "need" a job because of her marriage, they didn't think to offer her one.

The critic Percy Hammond once called Hale "the principal martyr to the Lucy Stone cause," writing that, as Broun's wife, "she might share more fully the joys of his prestige were she willing to sacrifice her own identity"—if she were willing to be Mrs. Heywood Broun—"but she will not. Rather than be vicariously glorified by another's headline, Miss Hale elects to lurk in the shadows of an independent obscurity." But this was not her election. Broun saw Hale's professional plight differently. Echoing Freud, he suggested that her biology determined her destiny: "I have never denied that Ruth Hale was the better newspaperman of [us] two," he wrote. "I think the things which held her back were biological. Brisbanes [Arthur Brisbane, famous newspaperman] don't have babies."

But Hale did have time to write. She had live-in help with her son, a woman named Mattie Wilson, who Woodie claimed "could have taken care of me lovingly and capably during whatever working hours professional demands imposed on Ruth." For whatever reason, then, whether bias or biology, Hale redirected her unflagging energy away from writing and toward political activism in the later 1920s. She helped then-famous Virginia Douglas Hyde secure the copyright to her poems and plays in her own name; she led the journalists' council of the National Woman's Party (although her work as a journalist was now scant); and she became increasingly involved in the fight against capital punishment in the wake of the Sacco and Vanzetti case, which sentenced two anarchist Italian American immigrants to death for a crime that they were widely believed not to have committed. When the American League to Abolish Capital Punishment was formed, Hale was elected its treasurer. And when Broun was asked why he continued coverage of the Sacco-Vanzetti case long after its conclusion—and long after his editors had asked him to stop—he replied that he did so "at the request of his wife."

When Hale sat at her writing desk in those days, she spent most her time not at her typewriter but with crossword puzzles. Her puzzle of choice was the diagramless crossword, invented in 1925, when the editors of the *New York World*'s crossword puzzle were said to have brought clues to edit to lunch but forgot their corresponding grid; as a result, they drew a blank grid at the table and reverse engineered a crossword based on the clues, figuring out where the black squares went as they plotted the puzzle's answers. The diagramless puzzle, still featured in the back pages of many *New York Times Magazine* issues, looks like a blank fifteen-by-fifteen-square grid. But it is no tabula rasa. Instead, it has already been imprinted with black squares and answers that have been erased (or, if you prefer, repressed). The solver needs to discover the answers and the placement of the black squares in order to bring the latent puzzle to the grid's surface. What looks like a wide-open grid, an expanse of freedom, is rigidly, but subliminally, rule-bound.

Woodie once said of his mother that "she wanted me to be a free soul who never broke any rules." He wrote of both his parents, "Vigorous and articulate rebels against the rigidities of their times . . . they conducted their battles by the rules they didn't believe in, the rules of the enemy, the rules woven right through them when they were children." Like the diagramless grid, Hale honored order, even as she resisted its appearance as the stuffy conventions by which she was raised. Despite her standardization of the puzzle with the Amateur Cross Word Puzzle League, her efforts to codify in law a woman's tacit right to keep her own name, and her devotion to "proper English," Hale's love of rules was not always evident on the surface. Like many of her peers at the Round Table, she believed in free love, never committing herself or Broun to monogamy; and the pair often lived in separate homes, despite their codependent working relationship. Nevertheless, she strongly believed that her rigidity

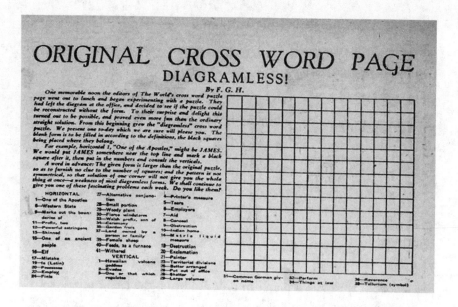

Diagramless crossword puzzle, the New York World, *December 26, 1926.*

and righteousness—what she would have called her ideals—enabled her commitment to freedom.

Hale claimed that she "disliked her mother so much . . . because we're so much alike." This stunned Woodie, as he struggled to see past their surface differences: his mother's progressivism and his grandmother's bigotry, Hale's flapper fashion and Riley Hale's Victorian dress. But both women championed their antithetical political causes with unyielding ferocity, both read incessantly, and both believed that freedom could emerge from within the structures of responsibility—to the traditional home or the modern one.

———

AS BROUN'S SUCCESS CLIMBED, HALE DUG DEEPER INTO HER DIA-gramless fixation, but she continued to do his work too. When the

Book of the Month Club was founded in 1926, Broun was asked to join its five-person selection committee. The judges met monthly to decide on the club's next selection, which was sent to subscribers around the country. But Broun rarely read—and when he did, he liked sentimental pulp fiction—so he offloaded the work onto Hale. She prepped him before each meeting, offering him points in support of her book of choice and rebuttals to the others. In return, he gave her his $5,000 annual salary from the job, but the work and prestige remained in his name. As Woodie wrote:

If all this had happened in Rogersville, Ruth might have been quite happy, steering her husband to eminence . . . but she had left all that behind—or perhaps not quite all—as the tables covered with jigsaw pieces and ruled pads for diagramless crosswords had a heartbreaking resemblance to the petit point frames and needlework gear that traditionally dulled the knife edges of feminine frustration.

To Woodie, in taking up the crossword puzzle with such dedication, Hale had merely replaced an old-fashioned sublimation ritual with a modern one. Was she a victim of the crossword craze, or did the crossword mitigate her fury that her marriage, as she understood it, had sabotaged her career? In Woodie's mind, at least, his mother's diagramless puzzles were overdetermined symbols of the failures of her career, her marriage, and her politics. Diagramless puzzles became a useful heuristic, for example, as he worked to parse his parents' inscrutable relationship and their political disagreements: as a socialist, Broun worked for the common man, ultimately sacrificing his newspaper column to cofound the American Newspaper Guild; as a feminist, Hale believed women's rights preceded workers' rights. Her militancy ultimately isolated her from collective politics, from her husband, and from her peers. She was left alone with her puzzles. As Woodie described it, "The really big gap [between Hale and Broun] was on a really big issue, her absolute and occasionally antisocial individualism. . . . They argued endlessly about this but in the argument, in the interplay, she was for a time pulled out of the emptiness that is the ambience of individualism, the emptiness that was as diagramless as the crossword puzzles that dotted it."

Hale's individualism led her to leave Broun's side in more ways than one. In 1923, she purchased, with her own money, a ninety-four-acre plot of land outside Stamford, Connecticut. She named the property—which featured an eleven-acre lake, two deteriorating houses, and no indoor plumbing—Sabine Farm, after Horace's villa in Licenza, Italy. To Woodie, "it looked as Horace's place must have looked after the Goths, Gauls, and Vandals had passed over it several times." Despite the farm's inhospitable lodgings, Round Table guests were frequent visitors during summers, so Broun, perhaps jealous of Hale's popular retreat or simply unable to function without her, bought a nearby property of his own. In 1928, the couple had sold their 85th Street brownstone and had purchased nearby apartments in the West Fifties. With four properties between them, never severing their Gordian knot but loosening its grip slightly with real estate, they still spent most of their time together. Broun needed Hale's help with his column, and both needed the support of Mattie Wilson, their housekeeper, and her husband, Earl, who had become their "houseman." More often than not, the five of them—Hale, Broun, Woodie, and the Wilsons—shuttled between farm properties or apartments, maintaining the fragile conceit of Hale's independence.

Hale's second attempt to separate from Broun was a shock to him and to the newspapers that zealously covered the couple's unconventional marriage. In the fall of 1933, Hale asked for a divorce. As she explained to Woodie, who was then sixteen, "Nothing . . . would change in their relationship with [him]. Nothing would change in their own relationship [with each other]. It was just that [she], wishing to take up again her journalistic career, felt that this could be better accomplished if she were not operating in the shadow of Heywood Broun." In 1926, Hale had gone on record in the pages of *Forum* as a proponent of divorce—not because she didn't value the sanctity of marriage but because she did. She was a champion of new marriages for newly socially and financially independent women. She wrote, "We have a marriage form which is unsatisfactory and is steadily becoming more so; we have women in the position to repudiate it if they cannot reform it; we do not want to live in a mateless state if we can help it; and we must have divorce—preferably cheap, easy, collusive divorce and nobody's business why—not only to get marriage on its good behavior but to keep it there."

But Hale's divorce, secured in Mexico in 1933 precisely because such "new" and faultless divorces didn't yet exist in New York, neither repudiated nor reformed her marriage to Broun. When she returned from Mexico, Broun picked her up at the airport, and they went home together to bed. When newspapers asked Hale about the separation, she replied that she had elected to be an "old maid" and "spinster." She told them, "Ruth Hale, spinster, that appeals to me, and soon I shall retire to our Connecticut estate and enjoy it to the fullest." Meanwhile, Broun merely assured reporters that "we weren't mad at each other." She wanted to be "Miss Ruth Hale," and with no "Ms." prefix available to her at the time, she got to be a proper "Miss" in the end.

If there were no material changes as a result of the Hale-Broun divorce, there were psychic costs. Even though Woodie had been commuting between his parents' homes for five years, he was asked, in the wake of their divorce, to choose which parent he would prefer to stay with. In keeping with Hale and Broun's philosophy that their child, at any age, was as much of a free agent as they were—a free soul, that is, who never broke the rules—this request was meant to empower him. "We were free adults consulting together as we so often had in the past," Woodie wrote. "They were too mature to turn this into a whom-do-you-love-the-best proceeding, and they assumed that I was mature enough to treat this matter as a simple business not of where do I put my heart, but where do I put my clothes and books." Thinking that he had found a rational, harm-reducing solution, Woodie suggested that he stay with his father, who had an extra small bedroom in his apartment. Everyone consented, but Woodie later learned from his uncle that his decision had left his mother heartbroken—that she had "wept inconsolably for days."

This, of course, injured Woodie too, and he blamed himself for Hale's sudden death the following year. In her *New York Times* obituary, Hale's cause of death was reported to be "intestinal fever," or typhoid—likely contracted from the impotable water at Sabine Farm and her aversion to vaccines, contracted from her mother. But Woodie insisted on describing her death as a "mysterious final illness." Or, if not a mystery, a symptom of a disease that he felt he had induced.

When Woodie was five years old, his mother disciplined him for the first and only time. He refused to go to bed, preferring to stay downstairs with his parents and their Round Table guests, and Hale spanked him. The following day, she apologized for letting her emotions overcome her. The Hale-Broun household, as Woodie described it, wasn't fit for hot emotions, which were to be reserved for political causes, not interpersonal relationships. After receiving his spanking and his "confusing" apology, Woodie "burst out" at his mother, invoking a "magic" wish for her harm that "seemed to be working." In the following days, Hale came down with a case of diphtheria, which Woodie, believing in the omnipotence of his own thoughts, as five-year-olds and paranoiacs are known to do, assumed was his fault.

When his mother died in 1934, Woodie recalled this earlier event—and his crushing self-implication—writing, "I held the doors against feeling. Feeling would mean looking at the causes of this mysterious illness, and I wasn't ready to hold up the weight of my guilt." Guilty for being born, for making his mother return from Paris where she had thrived professionally. Guilty for strapping her to a marriage that perhaps she didn't actually want, for exacerbating the pain of a divorce that never achieved its goal of liberating Hale from her life's choices. But of course, they were her choices, not Woodie's, and his guilt was a sign of his devotion to his mother as much as his narcissism, which, as a believer in Freudian analysis, he would be the first to concede. Woodie wanted his devotion to his mother registered in language, just as she wanted her devotion to herself, to her independence, registered there too. As a young child, he announced to his parents that he would be changing his name. No longer Heywood Broun III, he was Heywood Hale Broun, an homage to his mother and a release from his birth name's aristocratic performance. Changing his name, a gesture of his love for Hale, was perhaps as close as he could get to its saccharine display, which she might have ridiculed.

In his memoir, Woodie describes a home environment of emotional repression that stood in contrast to the Round Table's cultivated libertinism and the era's free-floating Freudianism. But Hale and Broun were Freudian enthusiasts too. It surprised Woodie to learn that at the very first meeting of the Algonquin Round Table, Hale dominated the conversation, describing the benefits of her sessions with her analyst: "Ruth seems to me to have been a very unlikely prospect for successful analysis," he wrote. "The opening of doors to the cellars and attics of memory requires the removal of locks you put there yourself, and I do not see the proud and stubborn Ruth Hale letting anyone much past the front porch, let alone into the sealed rooms." But Hale loved solving puzzles, and the enigma of her unconscious—and the collective unconscious of her milieu—was one that absorbed her. In a 1922 review of four new books on Freud in the *Bookman*, Hale wrote, "Psychoanalysis is valuable because, and only because, the thing it analyzes is no longer an x quantity. No more is it an impotent quantity. It is the great source, and the only source, of emotion—that strange rush of blood somewhere that makes men git up and git." In identifying with Freud, and in identifying the libido as the function that can "solve for x"—for emotion, for behavior, destructive or otherwise—Hale was still no master of her emotions. For them, she apologized. They lay dormant in her body, even as they captured her mind.

BOXED IN BY HER COMPETING DESIRES TO FOLLOW AND FLOUT rules, Hale was similarly trapped by the fantasy of immaculate and impossible autonomy. In defining herself and her politics in the name of independence, she frequently negated her emotional need for others—her son most of all—denying herself the sustenance of the relations that made her most human. Although she only ever published one crossword puzzle of her own (featured in 1925's *The Celebrities Cross Word Puzzle Book*), Hale's devotion to diagramless puzzles comes close to my teenage practice of writing crossword puzzles for no one. The diagramless crossword, after all, allows the solver to create the very puzzle that she solves—to place the black squares, fill in the grid, and solve its clues in one sitting. It allows her the conceit that she has created the enigma that she has also decrypted. She can imagine herself as constructor and solver, patient and analyst, operating under the frictionless fiction of total self-reliance. Hale clearly harbored regrets about her life's choices—choices that tied her to others—but was she, like her son, filled with guilt for their spillover effects on her dependents?

"Guilt is not a productive feeling." These words, spoken by my first therapist, have become something of a maxim to me and my mother. "The only good thing that ever came from her," my mom will sometimes say. Although my therapist told us that guilt would only compound hurt, not release us from it, guilt consumed us both. However resentful my mother was of my deception and my cruelty, I imagine that she was also plagued by the possibility that she had enabled them. My guilt, meanwhile, felt inevitable and insurmountable. When we reassured each other at the time—"Guilt is not a productive feeling"—I don't know that these words actually alleviated guilt's potency. They did allow us to communicate our love for each other, however indirectly, and to acknowledge that we didn't want to be exerting such throttling emotional force on each other's lives. We wanted each other to be free, but much like the Hale women, our understanding of freedom could only take root within a set of preexisting rules and responsibilities.

I was constantly negotiating between the rules of my eating disorder and the rules of my family, which were mostly tacit. When our shared familial values and the rules that they implied were articulated to me, they were voiced as "the blah blah blah speech." This was my father's clever coinage. Before we left the house to see extended family or family friends, he would pull me and my sister aside and say, "Remember the blah blah

blah speech." It was clever because of course we knew what it meant—be respectful, be kind, be generous—but it allowed him to bypass those clichés and the sentimental register of feeling. Guilt, however, operated in an emotional idiom that my family did speak. When I expressed guilt about my anorexia and the damage it wrought on our family unit, I was understood and, I think, appreciated. I was expressing my commitment to "the blah blah blah speech" and its underlying moral code, even if I couldn't abide by it with my actions. In this way, at least, guilt was productive for us; it was a feeling that communicated so much more than a request for absolution.

Freud wrote minimally about guilt. In his discussion of obsessional neurosis from 1907, he described the neurotic subject, whose behavior would today be recognized as consistent with obsessive-compulsive disorder, as someone whose ritualized behaviors are motivated by guilt—much as the religious observer's rituals stem from a compulsive performance of guilt and atonement. In 1929, in developing his writing on the death drive, or the masochistic desire to return to an inorganic state, the theme of guilt again emerged. He wrote, "Guilt is the expression of the conflict of ambivalence, the eternal struggle between Eros and the destructive or death instinct." This conflict that produces the subject's guilty conscience can, according to Freud, be staged between the young child's contradictory attachment to and resentment of its first love object (the mother); or, as the superego develops, it can turn inward, expressing itself as an internalized ambivalence—a feeling of guilt for wanting to love and destroy oneself.

Did I want to die? Was this the simple solution to my puzzle: A desire to destroy myself, to relinquish my right to organicity and return to the earth, a desultory heap of bones? I never thought about death when I was systematically planning my starvation. I know, at least, that I wasn't trying to starve myself *to* death. But I thought about death frequently as my anorexia became increasingly intractable, after years of ambivalent participation in my own recovery. I used to tell my mom that I felt trapped, and that was a true feeling—not a theory or an idea meant to impress. I twice acted upon that urgent sensation—*I'm trapped*—running into traffic or sprinting up the stairs of our apartment building, committed to throwing myself off its roof. I was afraid to take the subway, unable to trust myself that I wouldn't jump onto its tracks, waiting for the oncoming train to release me from my tedious food thoughts and from my "unproductive" guilt.

I once told my mother that I wanted to die, and she responded with three words that stain my memory: "Suicide is contagious." I understood her message—*If you die, I die*—but her words were less a guilt trip than a theory. If guilt was an emotional language that our family could parse, theories were the true building blocks of our communication system. "Suicide is contagious" was expressed as a theory, but beneath its menacing surface was a true feeling of maternal love. In fact, it was a theory and a feeling that has saved my life on more than one occasion.

I have been told that anorexia, among its many paradoxes and perils, is a comorbid disease. It is always masking and manifesting another mental illness, whether depression or OCD or psychosis. When I was told this, I was still very ill, and I didn't believe it. I was a "pure" anorexic, and if I could just figure out why and how, and how to recover, I would be fine. Our vocabularies are social and familial inheritances, and I am still more comfortable with ideas and theories than with feelings and so can now speak freely about my secondary diagnoses, those that have been "unmasked" by my recovery. Now that I have climbed out of the well, untangling myself and my eating habits from anorexia's thought patterns and rules, I can tell myself and others when I'm depressed (sometimes, sure) or hypomanic (absolutely). I can fit these medicalized terms more confidently into my vocabulary than sadness or elation.

I wonder what would have happened if, in the very first days of my self-imposed starvation, I had come to my parents and said, "I'm really sad. I'm so sad that I need to change my life. I want to become a brand-new person. I want to become an exceptional person, a better person than I am." I think that's what I was feeling. I think, in other words, that by starving myself, I wasn't trying to die but to speak. I wasn't suffering from aphonia; not all words had become "dangerous and unwanted commodities" for me, but I wanted to speak in a register of feeling that skated along frequencies beneath my family's hearing. And so, like so many hysterics before me, I used my body to speak instead.

I'm not sure that my family would have known what to do with those feelings of self-loathing and sadness if I had expressed them. I'm not sure that they could have said or done anything that would have changed the course of my personal history or would have prevented me from falling into anorexia's well. Such counterfactuals are tempting— *What if I had just said what I felt? What if I knew what I felt and how to say it?*—and my mother and I have worked through others, fairly systematically, over the past fifteen years: What could we have done to avoid this? Should I have changed schools? Should I have been hospitalized in high school before the disorder threatened to become chronic? What if she had insisted that I eat a more diversified menu from the start (I was a picky eater as a young child)? Would I still have been tempted by food restriction as a teenager? Would a better therapist have helped? These theories tend to compound our collective guilt, if not disperse blame, and we still try not to traffic in those hostile feelings.

But if guilt is not productive—productive toward healing, toward accepting the ambivalent relays between ego and superego, Eros and death—what fills its absence? What feelings are productive, and why am I still repelled, like Hale, by their "squashy femininity"? I don't know when this happened or why, but I no longer feel guilty about my anorexia, about my lies or my viciousness. I don't think that I've "forgiven myself," but I feel proud of the relationships I've built and healed in my recovery and as its function.

When I was a teenager, my father used to speculate that my life would become so rich and so full that it would crowd out my eating disorder. I'd have no time, no use, and no desire for it. This, as I understood it, was how he coped with the vicissitudes of psychic life: just stay busy. But he didn't understand that the busier I got, the busier my anorexia would get, finding new tricks to maintain its coercive power over my actions and thought. He didn't understand that starvation had changed me and that, as a result, I wasn't a rational actor, but a desperate child caught between conflicting imperatives: to be good and to be anorexic; to excel and to starve; to be functionally independent and a person in need of care. In brief, his theory was wrong. At the time, it couldn't have been more wrong or more well-meaning. It was just a theory, his way of expressing a true feeling of love.

III

Margaret Farrar and the Domestication of the Crossword

TO CALL ANYTHING A "PUZZLE," "RIDDLE," OR "ENIGMA" IS TO INCITE intrigue. Each word contains the promise of a solution, perhaps even a dramatic reveal. In 1978, the German-born psychoanalyst Hilde Bruch published *The Golden Cage: The Enigma of Anorexia Nervosa*, a composite portrait of anorexia pieced together from the testimony and observation of seventy of her patients. Bruch outlined the many "contradictions and paradoxes" of the "puzzling disease" more lucidly than any analyst before her—and perhaps anyone since. She acutely captured the distortions of anorexic thinking, so much so that it feels like a personal invasion when she so often gets it right and a personal betrayal when she gets it wrong. My copy of the book is studded with check marks and the rare, marginal X—as if to say, that wasn't *my* experience—as if she had any right to stray from an otherwise perfect rendering of my teenaged life and thoughts.

Bruch's solution to the "enigma of anorexia"—dramatically revealed, right at the book's start—emerges from the very conditions of starvation itself. The starving mind thinks differently from the satiated one: it becomes rigidly obsessed by food and food ritual, relentlessly preoccupied with feeding others and imagining the "right" and "wrong" conditions of eating. Perhaps because of her close proximity to World War II and Holocaust internment—a Jewish émigré, she only just escaped it, adopting one of her nephews whose parents hadn't—Bruch was highly aware that the starving mind would take over like "a dictator" (as her patients reported) whether the tyranny of famine was imposed from within or without. In other words, the solution to anorexia couldn't, or couldn't only, be found in psychiatry and psychopharmacology. It lay in eating. Cognition, self-image, and psycho-familial dynamics could be repaired only in a patient with a medically healthy weight.

This is not a solution that anorexics want to hear, and Bruch's patients didn't. They were certain that they could live their lives according to the "relentless pursuit of excessive thinness," even as their doctors, families, and friends offered them copious evidence to the contrary. It wasn't until they gained weight, Bruch countered, that they could apprehend all the evidence and begin to imagine their lives outside of a punishing preoccupation with weight and with food.

But Bruch took her composite portrait with a shallow lens. The social backdrop against which her patients are finely rendered is muddy and abstract. Why "starving minds" were proliferating in the households of "well-to-do, educated and successful families" in the 1970s is a puzzle that Bruch didn't really pretend to solve. When she approached the social factors that could be contributing to the "new disease," as she called it, Bruch minimized the role of diet culture, "the enormous weight that Fashion places on slimness," and their patriarchal implications. (These are now well-known social forces that contribute to eating disorders, and admonishing them has become cant among prevention activists and health care providers.) Instead, Bruch alarmingly suggested that the victories of second-wave feminism—the "justified claim of women to have fuller freedom to use their talents and abilities"—were contributing to the preponderance of anorexia among her white, "young, rich, and beautiful" patients.

"Growing girls experience this liberation as a demand to feel that they *have* to do something outstanding," she wrote. "Many of my patients have expressed the feeling that they are overwhelmed by the vast number of potential opportunities available to them which they 'ought' to fulfill, that there were too many choices and they had been afraid of not choosing correctly."

Unmarried and celebrated in her field, Bruch was not suggesting, as Annie Riley Hale had two generations earlier, that the "enigma of anorexia," like the "puzzle-picture" of the New Woman, could be *solved* with political retrenchment. She wasn't advocating that well-off women should stay at home with the children. She was, however, observing that her anorexic patients, women whose backgrounds offered them the greatest possible opportunity to benefit from feminism's political victories, were instead sabotaging their futures, finding their affordances an unbearable burden. New sexual freedom, Bruch ventured, only compounded their anxieties. Her patients couldn't reconcile their vast ambitions with conflicting social demands. How could they be Great Women when the social definition of a woman's success was shifting beneath their feet?

In the years since the publication of *The Golden Cage*, the reported demography of eating disorders has changed dramatically: anorexia is now recognized as the third most common chronic illness among all adolescents, regardless of gender. It no longer afflicts only the daughters of rich, white families—if it ever did. But the image of the anorexic teen as a member of this elite class has since circulated far beyond Bruch's portrait. Rich white girls have always occupied an outsize space in the cultural imagination, and masochistic rich white girls—rich white girls who present an *enigma*—are too precious a headline to fade from the news cycle. This was how I imagined anorexics to look and be seen when I began fasting.

I wanted to be anorexic. It was an identity and a diagnosis that I stumbled upon just when I was trying to imagine how I could be a Great Woman myself. My ambition had always been vast but unfocused. My mother kept a list that I wrote when I was five years old of the jobs that I aspired to, including president of the United States, taxi driver, and cashier. I think I saw these positions as seats of power: these were the people operating the machines that seemed to control the world around me. By the time I started high school—a private school in Brooklyn Heights—my understanding of power was only slightly more refined, even if my appetite for it hadn't waned. Like all teenagers, I knew where power resided in my school's social field, and I wanted all of it: I wanted to be both the hottest girl in school and a boy.

As puberty approached, these twinned goals were increasingly impossible to square. In ninth grade, my friends started drinking, smoking, and having sex, initiation rites that took on typically regional forms: mostly white, all rich, my peers sat on stoops in Cobble Hill and drank 40s and smoked spliffs, overidentifying with Brooklyn rap history before returning to their Park Slope brownstones. I abstained from these rituals, and not because I had a developed critique of cultural appropriation but because I was scared. I was too risk averse and too invested in being a Good Girl to excel at the Bad Girls' game. I feared that my desire to be competitive and even domineering in the classroom would register as a social demerit, especially since I wasn't willing to compensate for it with drugs and sex. Even though my female friends were still doing well in school, their academic success wasn't their social currency, as I understood it. The boys seemed to have more latitude: they could be academically arrogant and socially credible. They would brag about acing a math test while being stoned out of their minds; they used the same dumb, blustery language to describe their academic and extracurricular triumphs: they smashed; they hit; they crushed. Being Good (in school) and Bad (out of it) seemed like a frictionless negotiation for them—or no negotiation at all.

I remember asking my sister why I didn't have the social credit I craved and how to get it. Anyone asking this question probably doesn't deserve it, but she patiently tried to reroute my thinking away from a shallow aesthetics of Good Girls and Bad and toward an ethic. She told me not to be an asshole. More precisely, she said, "When the teacher hands back your test with the grade face down, don't flip it over for the class to see." She was telling me not to flaunt my As, but I didn't take her advice; in fact, I took affront to it, protesting that the boys in my class with whom I was in explicit academic competition—a competition we sometimes called friendship—always told everyone their test scores. Why shouldn't I have done the same?

It seemed that I couldn't be the hottest girl in school and that I couldn't be a boy, and so, as if scanning the dramatis personae of a high school comedy, I found a new social role. I would be a nerd. But a very thin nerd. A very thin, very nerdy, very Good Girl. I didn't say a curse word throughout all four years of high school; I straightened my naturally curly hair; I played principal flute in my school's woodwind ensemble (I didn't particularly like the flute, but it did seem like something a Good Girl would play); I had a 4.0 grade average; I began fasting; I began writing crossword puzzles. I was self-consciously building a character that I considered my social protection and my pride. It consisted of a hard, reactionary turn against my classmates—a turn encoded in self-righteous antagonism, internalized misogyny, and unconscious racial bias.

At the start of my rapid weight loss, my friends cornered me on the bus to a basketball game and staged an intervention. (I came home elated, as if they had thrown me a surprise party. I was clearly desperate for their attention.) I don't remember most of what they said, except that one of them asked me if I wanted to look like another girl in our class—a tall, skinny, slow-to-develop girl. "Guys aren't into that," she assured me. But I did want to look like that girl. Even though I hadn't yet read her work, I wanted to look like the kind of girl who Bruch described, the kind of girl that my health class textbook said was predisposed to anorexia: high-achieving, perfectionistic, or as I heard it, very thin, very nerdy, very Good.

In the introductory essay to the 2001 reprint of *The Golden Cage*, clinical psychologist Catherine Steiner-Adair described another solution to the enigma of anorexia's rise among ambitious, privileged American girls in the 1970s. She wrote:

How ironic that just at the historical moment when women were demanding to be freed from the cultural cage of gender restriction and to "throw their weight around" in the world dominated by men, an image of beauty appeared that is completely unnatural for adult women—the weightless waif. Although young women's bodies were still the primary measure of their desirability, the location of worthiness shifted from sexuality to weight.

Steiner-Adair noted that the same language that was once used to discipline a woman's sexuality could, in a post–sexual revolution world, still be used to discipline her weight: *She has no self-control, no self-respect. She's a loser.* Like a wayward symptom of patriarchal might, "thinness," she wrote, "replace[d] virginity as the key to feminine value, and the assessment of a woman's moral character shifted from when she was sexually active to what she ate." In Steiner-Adair's words, we can see the Freudian equation (food = sexuality) that marked early case histories of anorexia. But the equation, she suggested, was now playing itself out in the cultural unconscious, not in the latent desires of individual neurotics.

As I began to hone my ambition around the shape of the anorexic girl, I narrowed its focus onto infinitesimally small measures of so-called success: my grade on an upcoming test, how a certain pair of pants loosened at the waist, whether I could get the words in the corner of my graph paper notebook to interlock. Just as my weight loss had no end goal—simply by losing it, I was proving my new identity and self-worth to myself—my good grades didn't have purpose beyond getting them; and I didn't think that my puzzles would ever be published anywhere, let alone in the *New York Times*. I didn't have ambitions; I had ambition. Grades, weight, and crosswords were three incidental outlets for its drive.

When I began taking time off from school to regain weight at the behest of my doctors and parents, I started sending crossword puzzles to my high school newspaper as dispatches from my sick bed. I have no idea if anyone ever solved them—no one ever said so—and as I look back at them now, they're full of errors and are maybe even unsolvable. Each puzzle indexed the preoccupations of my starving brain. They referenced early aughts politics: one was titled "Wea-Puns of Mass Destruction" and included clues like "Dubya's favorite Hemingway novel" (answer: THE SON ALSO RISES). Another riffed on "midterms," which I took alone after school, my private school accommodating my illness, and featured words with *term* in their "middle": DE*TERM*INED, MAS*TERM*IND, WA*TERM*ELON. A particularly strange one included the following clues and answers:

19-Across: "It was worn around Billy Bob's neck in a vial"
    Answer: ANGELINA'S BLOOD
47-Across: "Wellesley College's first student commencement speaker"
    Answer: HILLARY CLINTON
35-Across: "What 19-Across and 47-Across have in common"
    Answer: THEY'RE BOTH TYPE A

If this puzzle theme isn't exactly an outright condemnation of the feminist vacuum of the early aughts, it does reveal my own limited sense of what a successful woman could be when I was hitting puberty. The hottest girl in school or a desexed, power-hungry nerd.

The ugly implication of Hilde Bruch's hypothesis that some rich white girls were anorexic collateral of the feminist second wave is that these women would have "had it easier" when their options were narrower. They might have thrived in a world where to be a successful woman meant to be the great wife of a great man. They might never have gotten sick when to be a successful woman was to be a successful housewife. I never aspired to be a wife, to say nothing of housewife, but my options felt narrow enough.

THE EVOLUTION OF THE CROSSWORD PUZZLE IS INDEBTED TO women who lived with a very clear sense of what it meant for them to be successful. They were wives, mothers, and homemakers. They have largely been forgotten—perhaps because the puzzle's inventor was a man—but as we have seen, Mrs. M. B. Wood can claim the first crossword ever published under a byline (in 1914). In 1924, Mrs. Helen Haven, the founding puzzle editor of the *New York Herald Tribune*, pioneered the crossword contest; and in 1934, Mrs. Elizabeth S. Kingsley invented the double-crostic puzzle. These early innovators of the crossword form were followed by Bernice Gordon, who, in 1965, was the first person to include a "rebus" in a crossword puzzle (in which more than one letter or a symbol occupies a single square of the grid); and Frances Hansen, who, in 1968, began putting her own limericks in her puzzles. In her *New York Times* obituary in 2015, Gordon is said to have "reinvented herself as an artist and crossword puzzle constructor after raising three children." After her death in 2004, Hansen was named a "self-described housewife who marshaled imagination . . . to make crossword puzzles."

For these white, mostly college-educated women, the crossword puzzle was an intellectual outlet, providing escape from the relentless routines of childcare and the doldrums of an empty nest. A housewife doesn't exactly have "leisure time"—she is never really off the clock—but she produces the comfortable conditions under which others can enjoy their off-hours. Like knitting and quilting, the construction of a crossword puzzle may look like a leisure activity, but it is only another way of filling the home (or the commuter train) with pleasures for the worker in his downtime.

The word HOUSEWIFE has only appeared twice in the *New York Times* crossword. In 1981, it was clued with deliberately misleading trivia: *Nine letters for* "Small container for sewing articles." (See the portable "housewife" sewing kit, which derived its name, in the eighteenth century, from the women who used it—those who mended the clothes and knit together the fabric of domestic life.) The puzzle that featured this archaic definition of "housewife"—skirting its obvious connotations in a post–*Feminine Mystique* world—was written by Sara V. Tuckerman, who constructed dozens of puzzles for the *Times*. But the clue very likely came from the *Times* crossword editor in the 1980s, Eugene T. Maleska, who was infamous for his merciless rejection letters and who privileged knowledge, maybe even especially esoterica, over wordplay and timeliness. Thus "small container for sewing articles."

In 1988, HOUSEWIFE appeared again in a Maleska-edited grid as part of a three-entry theme: 40-Across (DIARY), 43-Down (OF A MAD), and 33-Down (HOUSEWIFE). The three answers were collectively clued "Homemaker's memoirs," an almost impossibly flat translation of the theme entries, making no reference to the 1970 film *Diary of a Mad Housewife* that, along with *Wanda*, *A Woman Under the Influence*, and *An Unmarried Woman*, divorced the image of the housewife from domestic bliss on the silver screen.

Although this 1988 puzzle appeared under no byline, it was constructed by Jane S. Flowerree. In a 2014 interview, she recounted, "I was a full-time homemaker, and mother of toddlers, in dire need of intellectual stimulation, so for my first effort, I chose a theme I could identify with." One wonders what her original clues were, untamed by Maleska's pen. What else—besides "Many a crossword constructor, e.g."—could stand in for HOUSEWIFE as a crossword puzzle clue? *Nine letters for—*

"You needn't be married to be one, on a hit Bravo franchise, e.g."
OR
"Capital created it to 'service the male worker,' per Silvia Federici"
OR
"Word from which 'hussy' derives, paradoxically"

Like so many constructors before me, I turn first to the dictionary when I write clues. By the middle of the sixteenth century, the *Oxford*

English Dictionary reports, *housewife*, "a (typically married) woman whose main occupation is managing the general running of a household," took on a sour second meaning: "a frivolous, impertinent, or disreputable" woman. By the seventeenth century, the meaning of the term depended on the pronunciation of its first syllable: *huss-wife* (negative), *house-wife* (positive). There's something at once uncanny and reassuring about seeing the history of a concept—in this case, woman—embedded in the evolution of a word. It's linguistic proof of a truth universally unacknowledged: that the housewife and the hussy are one—cleaved from one another to discipline women with language, to establish the stark terms of a woman's "success." Her reputation clung to a single vowel sound.

———

MARGARET PETHERBRIDGE FARRAR, THE FOUNDING EDITOR OF the *New York Times* crossword, wasn't exactly a housewife. The daughter of a wealthy licorice manufacturer, she was born in Brooklyn in 1897. She raised three children—Curt, Alison, and Janice—in Scarborough, New York, thirty miles north of Manhattan, taking enormous pride in their development and in the illustrious career of her husband, publisher John C. Farrar. She did the family taxes and organized their social schedules; bought John's seersucker suits; organized book drives at their church; and cared for Kewpie, the family dog. She eagerly identified as a mother and wife, even when she was working outside the home. During World War II, when John was stationed in Algeria, Margaret attended board meetings at Farrar & Rinehart—the publishing house that he founded before Farrar, Straus and Giroux—and after a day in his shoes at the office, she wrote to him:

I have wanted to tell you how much I have learned and am learning

about a commuter's life, how I will never more think you extravagant be-
cause you use taxis! Nor fail to understand the way you feel when you've
climbed up the hill after a strenuous day that doesn't seem to have accom-
plished much of anything! And I'll never cease to wonder how you got—and
will get—all the telephoning done, and the arranging, and the work accom-
plished. Every wife should have this training!

She echoed the sentiment in a letter two weeks later: "I have learned
so much about your business life and have thought so much about our
home life that I'll be a much better wife for you during the rest of our
years together!"

But Margaret Farrar wasn't exactly a housewife because, as much as
she preened over house, home, and the career of her husband, she tirelessly attended to her own job as a crossword puzzle editor. By the time of
her death in 1984, Margaret had edited 134 crossword puzzle books for
Simon & Schuster, more than 7,000 crosswords at the *New York Times*,
28 collections of *Times* puzzle books, and dozens of crosswords for the
Los Angeles Times syndicate. Her education at Berkeley Institute (now
the Berkeley Carroll School) and Smith College offered her a glimpse of
the life of the mind that ultimately prepared her for a life at home. Like
many graduates of the Seven Sisters colleges, she was a clerical worker
after graduation—first in a bank and then at the *New York World*—
presumably stops on the way to finding a suitable mate and moving to
the suburbs. In many ways, she followed this template. Upon marrying
John in 1926, she quit her job at the *World* and moved to Scarborough,
but she continued to write and edit puzzles after the children were asleep:
"After the phone stopped ringing was the best time to think of that
magical definition," she said.

When Margaret started at the *World* in 1919, she was the assistant to

John O'Hara Cosgrave, the paper's Sunday editor and the stepfather of
her Smith roommate. Published by Joseph Pulitzer, the *World* was the
New York paper whose sensibility most reflected and fueled the blowing
changes of the Jazz Age. Home to the ostentatiously, playfully erudite
columns of Franklin Pierce Adams and Heywood Broun, it was also a
pioneer of yellow journalism. In keeping with its imperative to sell newspapers at any cost—stretching the truth to do so—it was one of the first
newspapers to include comic strips and the very first to feature a crossword. The flexibility of the new puzzle form fostered creativity and
disorder. There were no rules about the shape or symmetry of the grid;
the number and placement of black squares were arbitrary; and some
puzzles featured the same word multiple times. After two months of writing puzzles himself, the puzzle's creator, Arthur Wynne, opened up the
"word-cross" to outside submissions, and the already loose conventions of
the word game became looser still. By 1915, when a typographical error
permanently turned the *word-cross* into the *crossword*, Wynne claimed to
be receiving as many as twenty-five new puzzle submissions a day. "Every-
where your eyes rest on boxes, barrels, and crates," he wrote, "each one
filled with crossword puzzles patiently awaiting publication . . . the present supply will last until the second week in December 2100." Wynne
hadn't expected the puzzle to attract the following that it did; nor did
he tend to the weekly puzzles with the care that its fans expected. There
was little copyediting and no fact-checking: the nascent crossword was
not just unwieldy; it was oftentimes unsolvable. This is where Margaret
intervened.

Margaret had not fallen prey to the crossword craze that Wynne had
ignited. Although she worked next door to Adams and Broun—and
probably dined at the Algonquin—she was a half generation younger

than they and presented a gentility and gentleness that was unwelcome at their Round Table. When Cosgrave assigned Margaret the task of editing the *World*'s puzzle in 1921, she was unenthusiastic. Having never solved a crossword before, she chose puzzles for print based on their appearance—how pleasing they would look on the page—and sent them to the typesetter without testing them first. Unsurprisingly, she was barraged with mail from frustrated solvers, whom she first dismissed as "cranks," but Adams convinced her to take the job more seriously. She recalled:

I began trying to do one and thus experienced the throes of acute agony that come to all solvers of puzzles on discovering definitions left out, numbers wrong, hideously warped definitions, words not to be found inside any known dictionary, foreign words—very foreign—and words that had no right to be dragged out of their native obscurity.

If today's crossword solvers are often frustrated by the uncommon initialisms that still fill puzzle grids—OBE (Order of the British Empire), SBA (Small Business Administration), APO (army post office)—they at least don't have to contend with those of the earliest crossword puzzles, including, as Margaret later remembered with horror, GPJU (Grand Potentate of the Johnstown Union).

Taking Adams's reproach to heart, Margaret became the grid's duty-bound custodian: "Then and there," she wrote, "with my left hand reposing on a dictionary and my right raised in the air, I took an oath to edit the crosswords to the essence of perfection." She didn't lack a sense of humor, but she did lack the Round Table's atmospheric arrogance and humbled herself before the grid. In 1924, she instituted the rules adopted by Ruth Hale's Amateur Cross Word Puzzle League of America, becoming the arbiter of their guidelines, especially their last: "The only requirement [for a crossword clue] is common sense."

"I am the essence of common sense," she used to say with determined frequency. But if *common sense* was her byword, so too was *fun*. "This is just for *fun*," she'd say to May Dikeman, the assistant she hired late in her life, as she dictated a letter to a constructor or fan. Between common sense and fun was where her puzzles took root—straddling the self-improvement ethos of American liberalism and the libertine sensibilities of American modernism. If the crossword puzzle began as a disorderly form, Margaret, a product of a Victorian home, was well-suited to tidy it. She never left home without silk white gloves, and her wardrobe was full of patterned dresses and skirts, never pants. As she continued to hone the parameters of the crossword, her sense of decorum informed the puzzle's rules. A standard letter she sent to new constructors featured the following stipulations:

The concerns and foibles of life are almost always good for puzzle fodder. Try to keep the puzzles bright and entertaining, and moderately instructional. Remember that there is a certain element of pleasant relief from daily cares involved in puzzle solving. So try and steer the puzzle away from unpleasant news and grave diseases. Best to avoid all references to drinking, illness, profanity, violence. Entertainment is the watchword. Matters of religion have to be treated delicately.

This set of precepts has been succinctly reduced to the aforementioned "Sunday morning breakfast test," the rule that a crossword puzzle must not upset the sensibility—or stomach—of a morning solver. This is to say that despite her initial indifference to the puzzle, Margaret became its standard-bearer.

———

"CIVILIZATION IS AT THE CROSS-WORDS," WROTE RICHARD SIMON and Max Schuster in a preface to a special edition of their puzzle book series in 1925. "Ten million men and women, according to conservative estimates, are daily devotees of the tantalizing black-and-white word-squares in the United States alone." The enterprising pair had launched the nation's first crossword book the year prior, hoping to capitalize on the puzzle craze. Not only was it the first ever book of crossword puzzles, but it was also Simon & Schuster's first publication. Crossword lore has it that the idea for the book came from Simon's Aunt Wixie, who proposed it over dinner on the day they incorporated their business. If apocryphal, this story is in keeping with the publishing team's eagerness to distance themselves—and their new company—from the faddish pastime around which they ultimately built their business. Their peers had dissuaded them: Adams called the puzzle book the "worst idea since Prohibition," and booksellers couldn't imagine it a success. They charged ahead, tapping Margaret and two of her colleagues at the *World*, Prosper Buranelli and F. Gregory Hartswick, to edit fifty puzzles for the first book for $25 each.

Simon & Schuster's ambivalence about the project can be traced to the first edition's front cover: instead of using their eponymous imprint, they published the book under "Plaza Publishing Company," a name they took from the exchange of their telephone number, Plaza 6409. They weren't the only men of letters looking to distance themselves from the early puzzle's publication in book form: Adams was asked to write a foreword for the book, but he declined, as Simon & Schuster put it, "thinking it beneath his dignity." The foreword was also turned down "for similar reasons" by John Farrar, Margaret's soon-to-be husband, then editor of the *Bookman*. After graduating from Yale in 1919, John worked briefly at the *World* before moving to the *Bookman*, a monthly literary journal responsible for publishing H. L. Mencken,

Robert Frost, and the country's first bestseller list. Although crosswords didn't produce sufficient cultural capital for John and other literary men of the time, Simon & Schuster's puzzle books went on to underwrite some of the country's most celebrated cultural institutions.

Their first crossword book sold for $1.35 and came equipped with a "life-saving pencil and eraser" and a postcard that solvers could mail in to receive the puzzles' answers in return. The cost was high for books at the time, but book buyers were undeterred: the first run of 3,600 copies sold out in twenty-four hours. By October 14, 1924, when Simon & Schuster was ten months old, it lay claim to four of the five bestsellers in nonfiction. All were crossword puzzle books—and after the first run of the very first book, all were published by Simon & Schuster, not Plaza Publishing. In a single day in December, they sold almost 150,000 copies, and by the end of the year, they had sold half a million. There's reason to believe that Margaret did the bulk of the editing on these early books, even though she shared the byline. Her *World* colleagues were older men whose reputations in journalism had helped legitimize the venture, but by book 44 in 1938, Farrar's name stood alone on its cover.

In the first five years of working for Simon & Schuster, Margaret earned $8,000 in royalties (roughly $125,000 today), money that her father invested in US Steel and Standard Oil. The dividends provided seed money for Farrar & Rinehart and, later, Farrar, Straus and Giroux. She liked to say that the latter company was a product of "John's brains and Roger [Straus]'s money," but the truth is that the company that came to be FSG was at least partially built on the back of Margaret's puzzles.

John and Margaret's marriage bridged the two strata of Manhattan's publishing world—the commercial and the literary—revealing the division between the two to be not so neat. Prosper Buranelli introduced

Margaret and John in 1922. "Pros," as he was called, was a features writer at the *World* who wrote short stories and "looked like an unmade bed," as was also said of Heywood Broun. That year Buranelli collaborated with John on *Gold-Killer*, a murder mystery novel about organized crime in New York City. The duo published the novel under their first names only: again John, who had won Yale's prestigious Younger Poets Prize, used subterfuge to distance himself from mass-market publishing. The year after he declined to introduce the first puzzle book, however, he participated in Simon & Schuster's *Celebrities Cross Word Puzzle Book*, edited by Margaret, in which fifty celebrities—from Irving Berlin and Al Jolson to Emily Post and Harry Houdini—all tried their hand at cross-word construction. (Both Heywood Broun and Ruth Hale also had puzzles published in the collection.)

John's puzzle, titled "The Gossip Shop," is studded with literary people and terms, including 18-Across: "A certain literary magazine" (answer: BOOKMAN) and 52-Across: "Name of a publisher" (answer: DORAN). John had just accepted a position at George H. Doran Company, publisher of P. G. Wodehouse, Arthur Conan Doyle, Sinclair Lewis, and John Dos Passos, among many others. Less a "gossip shop" than a wink at those already in the know, John's puzzle, like all puzzles, represented the concerns of its maker.

The news of John's new position ran as a squib in the very first issue of the *New Yorker* in 1925: "John Farrar didn't have enough to do lately editing the *Bookman* . . . so he's taken on acting as general head of George H. Doran and Company, which may manage to keep him busy enough during week days." Twelve more pages into the issue, its "Jottings About Town" section noted, "Judging from the number of solvers on the subway and 'L' trains the crossword puzzle bids fair to

*Caricatures of John C. Farrar,
Ruth Hale, and Heywood
Broun by Herb Roth in Simon
& Schuster's* Celebrities Cross
Word Puzzle Book, *1925.*

become a fad with New Yorkers." Although John had been dating Gloria Swanson when he met Margaret—"Gloria wouldn't have fit in at all," Margaret confessed to Dikeman late in life—their paths had inevitably crossed in New York publishing society, and they wed in June 1926.

"EDITORS TO MARRY," THE *NEW YORK TIMES* ANNOUNCED ON ITS wedding page that April, but the headline was more egalitarian than their marriage. John was an editor and publisher; Margaret edited the Simon & Schuster books, yes, but it wasn't until John left for Algeria that, like many wives during World War II, Margaret assumed a larger role in the workforce. The attack on Pearl Harbor resulted in two monumental changes in the dynamics of their marriage: John enlisted with the Office of War Information overseas, and Arthur Hays Sulzberger, publisher of the *New York Times*, asked Margaret to become the paper's first puzzle editor.

The *Times* had held the crossword craze at bay during the 1920s and '30s, fearful that it was a gateway to other debased forms, like classified ads and comics. A 1924 column in the paper titled "A Familiar Form of Madness" couldn't have been clearer: crossword fanaticism was nothing more than the latest iteration of "mob mentality," and the paper wouldn't enable it. When the first Simon & Schuster puzzle book appeared, the *Times* book review ran a headline with funereal overtones: "Cross Word Puzzles Embalmed Between Covers." But just as the first crossword craze had metastasized during the First World War, a new demand for puzzles emerged at the start of the Second. "We ought to proceed with the puzzle, especially in view of the fact that it is possible there will now be bleak blackout hours," Lester Markel, the *Times* Sunday editor, wrote to Sulzberger two weeks after Pearl Harbor. Attached to Markel's memo was a note from Margaret: "I don't think I have to sell you on the increased demand for this type of pastime in an increasingly worried world. You can't think of your troubles while solving a crossword."

Sulzberger didn't need convincing. The rumor circulating at the *Times* was that he had been buying the rival *New York Herald Tribune* to solve its daily crossword puzzle since the war had begun. Sulzberger hired Margaret in 1942 to start a weekly puzzle in the Sunday magazine with "a flavor of current events and general information." In keeping with the paper's reputation, the *Times* crossword puzzles would be topical and sophisticated, including only words "fit to print." Margaret took to the task with characteristic diligence. She coopted an address book, with tabs A to Z, and began filling its pages with timely words and clues for the *Times* puzzle:

Alexi—New Patriarch of Moscow
Bulganin—Soviet no 2 man, deputy Prime Min. of Russia
Cybernetics—science of machinery to replace brains + nerves

She didn't shy away from new coinages or trendy tokens of common usage, and her definitions became looser and more playful over time:

Gobbledygook—pompous polysyllabic verbosity; disease of bureaucracy
Hutzpa—Defendant murderer of his parents pleads for mercy on grounds he's an orphan
Hype—The process of inflating careers and reputations by almost any means

She amended the palm-size book with new words up to 1983 [Jedi—Star Wars role], and the resulting compendium reads like Borges's Chinese encyclopedia—lists of words and things organized only by letter and the caprice of Margaret's active imagination: Academy Award winners, airports, butterflies, ballets, cheeses, dress designers, dogs, ducks, dames, flies, grapes, hats, horses, languages (and how many speakers globally), two pages of different kinds of missiles, music genres, Nobel laureates, pen names, Rembrandts, Seven Dwarfs, submarines, salads, Spanglish words, signs, trees, tennis players, similes, and winds. The last pages of the address book are filled with recipes for crab soup and veal shoulder, the desiderata of the housewife's mind.

Margaret's dual imperative at the *Times*—escapism and timeliness—often left her at cross-purposes. Were solvers to think of the war or not? Although the bulk of her work was editing crosswords, not constructing them, she often reworked corners of submitted grids to fit current events into the puzzle page. In November 1943, she wrote to John about an editorial predicament that resulted from her intervention:

I seem to have created an international incident on Nov. 7th by defining Gomel as "recaptured Russian city"! It was duly noted in the New Yorker *Talk of the Town that the crossword puzzle had scooped the news pages! The definition is all right now, thanks to the Russians, but my face was red going into the* Times *last week. However everyone seems to think it was good publicity!*

The temporary mistake was a result of Margaret's optimism about the Eastern Front, not any privileged information from John, whose letters from Algeria had to pass through War Department censors before reaching New York. In January 1944, Margaret sent a photo of herself to John—"Will you wear it next to your heart, please?"—and described

Margaret Farrar at her desk on East 96th Street, with her "suitcase full of puzzles" (date unknown).

CREDIT: John Chipman Farrar Papers. Yale Collection of American Literature, Beinecke Rare Book and Manuscript Library. Used with permission.

her appearance for both her husband and his V-mail censor: "You can see that I have had my black coat relined and it looks as chic as ever . . . but you can't see the suitcase full of puzzles (*note to the Censor—I really am a crossword puzzle editor, of all things*) that is my weekly companion."

While Margaret was producing a kind of propaganda in New York—a way to distract and develop patriotic feeling in the Sunday *Times*—John was editing the army magazines *Victory* and *America*. As part of the Psychological Warfare Division of the Office of War Information, he was also involved in radio and leaflet campaigns with the explicit purpose of undermining German morale. As none of this work could be divulged to Margaret while he was abroad, John's daily letters to her are filled with sociological portraits of his workplace, especially the women working in his midst:

Feb. 15, 1944

I am surrounded, completely surrounded, by women. They are all over the place. And I'm lonely, in spite of all. I like some of them very much, but I can't even start getting romantic. It's a complete bore. I love you.

Mar. 9, 1944

The whole picture of the women in this business is something. I think your sex is amazing. But I don't believe I really ever began to be aware of its complexities until I began to see this situation unfold. I'll try to write a letter on the subject soon.

Mar. 15, 1944

I respect enormously the English girls who are here. We have more of them than Americans. The Americans are nice, but it so happens that our better ones are British. Oh no, not better, cleverer, I'd say. And even that's not fair because I was forgetting our WAACS [Women's Army Auxiliary Corps]—of whom we have several excellent examples, both intelligent, and, I must confess, shapely.

———

TOWARD THE END OF HIS SERVICE, JOHN BROKE HIS ANKLE AND required an operation. His fixation on the women at war even informed his hospital stay:

May 28, 1944

I am told by the doctors and nurses that under anesthetics, I am extremely discreet, and never mention the affairs of the office, but that on one occasion I delivered a somewhat trenchant address on "Women in the Theatre of War." It added to the Farrar legend at the hospital.... Apparently everyone agreed with my sentiments.

What was it about women at war that so captured John's imagination? It's tempting to read his persistent declaration that he can't imagine "getting romantic" as protesting too much. But the letters are no less filled with adoration for Margaret and lengthy descriptions of where he would take her in Algeria were she there with him.

As World War II brought women of all ages out of the home and into professional life, perhaps John was adjusting, however neurotically, to the change in gender norms that was taking place abroad and in his own home. It is not as though his wife didn't work before the war, but the "pleasure of your mind . . . of your voice and yes the sound of your typewriter downstairs" that he longed for in his war correspondence somehow differed from the sensibilities of these women in the field.

Apparently unfazed by his obsession, Margaret responded: "You are wonderful and very sustaining to your 47-yr-old-and-don't-look-it-wife, even if you are surrounded by WACS." Her letters are filled with updates on the children, especially Curt who was excelling at Andover, and board meetings at Farrar & Rinehart. Her own work at the *Times* and Simon & Schuster is tucked in—sometimes unceremoniously, sometimes coquettishly—between her daily updates:

Feb. 21, 1944

"Just a short one from me—it's a day off from going into town and I'm trying to accomplish a thousand things left undone—get my clothes ready for this big weekend ahead, get my puzzle into shape so I can skip the final proofreading, tend to steaming Jan out of a mild cold so she'll be ready to go to Sonja's on Friday, dry Kewpie every time she comes in out of the wet with très muddy paws, do some ironing for Curt and get his laundry off, a mite of button sewing and house cleaning, etc. etc.

May 28, 1944

I went to church proudly wearing my orchids [which John had sent to her]. In fact, I have them on now, aslant on my bosom, and they look extremely fetching (I've just looked that word up in the big dict. at my elbow—I'm sure you'll be glad to know it means pleasing, attractive, fascinating, alluring!) The children had guests for lunch—Ella's best fried chicken—and I have been sitting on the porch finishing up the proof reading and thinking of you between the horizontals and verticals.

The portrait that emerges from these letters is of a woman who, with all the privileges afforded to her station—a housekeeper, a handyman, and children in private schools—is grasping for a concept that crystallized decades later: that unholiest of hyphenates, work-life balance. The one hint she gives of the evolving dynamic of her household appears in a letter from January 7, 1944: "It is good that you are a puzzle editor's wife, with the problems that must come to you daily—I wish I could help you solve them," she wrote. A slip, unconscious or teasing, Margaret's epithet for John ("a puzzle editor's wife") signals her evolving self-image as both breadwinner and caretaker.

This division of labor, or lack thereof, persisted when John returned home, only to learn that he was being pushed out of Farrar & Rinehart. In letters addressed to Hervey Allen, one of the firm's bestselling authors, Margaret defended John's wounded honor: "The question is simply this," she wrote to Allen, "how can it happen that John, who is a great and gallant man, can come back from the wars to find that his three oldest and closest friends . . . have prepared for him a reception as ethical—as brimming with integrity—as a miniature Pearl Harbor?" To Fay Rinehart, the publisher's wife, Margaret took a more diplomatic tact, writing, "We are bound to meet occasionally. . . . We should be able to speak to each other casually, for the ease and comfort of our friends." Neither letter was mailed. Margaret and John returned to Manhattan to start a new life after the war—and, together, founded a new publishing company.

FARRAR, STRAUS LAUNCHED IN 1946, WITH MARGARET AS A founding board member. Between her copious puzzle work, she also copyedited manuscripts for the new firm and worked with aspiring authors on their submissions to John. Having joined the Upper East Side Episcopal Church of the Resurrection, John and Margaret began a writers' group in its lower parish hall, where the novelist John Speicher, historian James Chace, and poets George Dickerson and Edith Dobell, among others, shared works in progress. The group was nominally John's writers' group, but Margaret was its organizer and a moderating presence in the often-contentious meetings. When May Dikeman joined the group, Margaret was mindful that, as a single mother, she had a sitter at home. Dikeman, who became Margaret's assistant after John's death, remembered, "She always asked me, at the start of the meeting, 'How's your time, May?' . . . [and] I was always one of the first to read."

Meanwhile, the institutions that Margaret helped build had blossomed. In 1955, John and Roger Straus brought on Robert Giroux—and his stable of writers from Harcourt, including T. S. Eliot, Robert Lowell, Jack Kerouac, Flannery O'Connor, and Bernard Malamud—and FSG emerged as one of the nation's preeminent publishers of American fiction. In 1950, the *Times* began running a daily crossword in addition to the Sunday puzzle. Margaret was as surprised as anyone that the crossword took root at the *Times*. "The longest flash in the pan in history!" she called it. The new puzzles multiplied Margaret's workload and her opportunities to stretch and reform the conventions of the crossword.

She had already made dramatic changes to the Sunday puzzles that she later applied to the daily grids: she abolished all two-letter words (gone were the days in which the sun god Ra appeared in every solver's lexicon) and instituted the rule that puzzles must have 180-degree symmetry—they must look the same when held right side up and upside down. Both changes were cosmetic, but they vastly increased the pleasure of solving and the difficulty of constructing. Like the work of so many mid-century formalists—from the art criticism of Clement Greenberg to the New Critics at Yale—Margaret's changes at the *Times* culled away all excesses of the puzzle form, a stripping away that unleashed its creative possibilities. As a result, the puzzle became an iconic modernist form. As Margaret described it:

The 1950s were remarkable for the most important of innovations—

the freedom to use phrases, full names, book and song titles, quotations or parts of quotations. . . . In the 1960s, experimentation was the thing. The EMU-MOA-ROC era was far in the past and the stage was set for fresh ideas, new ways and means of enhancing the puzzlement.

In those years, Margaret encouraged constructors to load their grids with new words and novelties to capture the zeitgeist in language. The war no longer had a stronghold on her vocabulary: "I can find a funnier clue for 'bulge' than 'World War II battle,'" she confessed. But only up to a point. "We have to hold the line," she'd say when, for example, a constructor wanted to clue LSD as "psychedelic drug" instead of "British currency," referencing the abbreviation for "pounds, shillings, and pence."

Margaret credited constructor and adman Harold T. Bers with one of the most profound changes to the 1950s crossword: the introduction of "themes" into the daily grid, or, as she called them, "inner clue" puzzles. In his 1958 grid titled "Catalogue," Bers included multiple cat-themed answers, including KITTY ALLEN, KRAZY KAT, PUSSY WILLOW, and THE CATS MEOW. This theme will seem rudimentary to any regular solver of the daily *Times* crossword, where Monday-through-Thursday grids are required to have more elaborate and high-concept "inner clues," but Margaret was eager to foster constructors' creativity, challenging herself as well as the solvers whom she catered to daily.

Deemed "the most important person in the world of the crossword puzzle" in the *New Yorker* and "the Queen of Crosswords" in *Good Housekeeping*, Margaret developed a following beyond New York publishing circles. When she rode the bus to the *Times* office, test-solving puzzles in her lap, she was frequently recognized and engaged in the usual caviling over definitions that has always appealed to solvers—and that occupied much of her professional correspondence. As Dikeman recalled:

Occasionally a nitpicker launched a campaign of real harassment, as was the case with Mrs. Bodenheimer, evidently a multilinguist, who lived to pounce on any arguable form. . . . No communication ever went unanswered. . . . There could be several exchanges on a single word. . . . [Margaret] never shied from the most onerous ("Dear Mrs. Bodenheimer: Thank you for taking the time to write me . . . ").

Margaret never received more mail than when the *Times* announced her retirement in 1969. Dedicated solvers and the constructors she had mentored wrote eulogistic letters, a handful of which included poems in her honor. One came from Frances Hansen, the self-described housewife who frequently put her own limericks in her Farrar-edited grids:

> O Margaret! Dear Margaret!
> I am forever in your debt;
> Of all the editors I've met
> There's none so rare as Margaret;
> I'd rhapsodize, but etiquette
> Forbids. Besides, my eyes get wet,
> And Margaret, words fail me yet.

Margaret didn't leave the paper of her own accord. The Newspaper Guild held a mandatory retirement age of seventy, and Margaret was seventy-two when she was told, "Here's your hat; what's your hurry," as she put it. Upon her seventieth birthday, Margaret was offered a freelancer's contract so she could continue editing, but this workaround didn't satisfy the guild, which, Margaret believed, harbored a grudge against her because she had crossed the picket line during the newspaper strikes of the early 1960s. Fighting for higher wages and against the automation of the paper's printing presses, which promised to cut jobs, the Newspaper Guild joined the New York Typographical Union on a strike that lasted 114 days between 1962 and 1963. Margaret worked right through it. Socially conservative but not anti-labor per se, she never identified as a worker, so much as a wife. The roles were not fungible in her imagination, and despite her wage and her royalties, which proved instrumental to John's success, she considered her editing extracurricular to her work at home. "There is certainly nothing like a crossword puzzle job for keeping a gal busy and out of trouble!" she wrote to him in Algeria.

Margaret coped with her departure from the *Times* just as she coped with John's "ousting" at Farrar & Rinehart twenty-five years prior. Her papers, held in boxes among the attics of her grandchildren, include handfuls of furious but unsent letters to the *Times* editorial board, but her abiding sense of etiquette had her keep the intensity of her emotions to herself and her typewriter. In a letter that she did ultimately send to the *Times* board, she conceded to the terms of her departure and concluded: "The trick is to never get to be seventy, and NEVER NEVER NEVER to cross a picket line."

The board was apologetic but added to Margaret's frustration by asking her to find and train her replacement in only three weeks. It was a nearly impossible task, she protested, writing, "A really special skill is required, and it will be difficult to find someone who is free from other commitments; and who has the experience, the stamina, and the *good taste* needed." Ultimately, Margaret was satisfied with the choice of Will Weng, chief of the Metropolitan news desk. Weng had worked with

Margaret as a constructor since the early 1960s. She kept in touch with him and his successor, Maleska, writing to the latter on September 30, 1981, when she was eighty-four:

> 1-Across on September 20th! SCAB defined as "Strikebreaker" is something I thought I'd never see in a Times Magazine Puzzle. It's an ugly word, and I think you'd agree. . . . I hope you'll decide to put it on the NO-NO-NO list. . . . Yours as ever,

Margaret worked just as tirelessly after leaving the *Times*. She continued to edit the Simon & Schuster books and collections of *New York Times* crosswords, in addition to freelance puzzle jobs at *Good Housekeeping*, *Seventeen*, and the *Los Angeles Times*. After John's death in 1974, she received his manuscripts from Farrar, Straus and Giroux, working with young writers in her Upper East Side apartment. She dictated letters to Dikeman, as her hands grew stiff with arthritis; she began attending the American Crossword Puzzle Tournament, launched by Will Shortz in 1978, her face flushed with a rosiness that many attributed to her vitality but which she knew to be a symptom of lupus. On the day that she died, she dictated sixteen letters to constructors, nitpickers, writers, and friends. "Retirement," she wrote to her friends and fans after leaving the *Times*, is "a 10-letter word not in my vocabulary!"

IF THE HOUSEWIFE IS ALWAYS WORKING—HER LEISURE TIME IN-distinguishable from her working hours—she embodies a condition known to many workers in the current economy. Ours is a culture

committed to constant work and work by other names: gamified training, content-creating, the ghastly portmanteau "prosuming." Unlike
these forms of so-called leisure, which make you feel like you're *not* working even when you are, solving crossword puzzles makes you feel like you
are working, even when you're not. The puzzle's production of a "work
feeling" in times of leisure shouldn't be so pleasing. But the sensation of
intellectual labor that it offers is discrete and immediately rewarding, unlike the conditions of endless work that mark so many other arenas of the
waged and unwaged economy.

Perhaps the puzzle's peculiar status as "work that's not work" allowed
Margaret to minimize its significance and her status in her household.
She could be the wife of a "great and gallant man," the sign of a successful
woman within the terms of her world, and also have a job. Put otherwise,
crosswords gave her work to do without making her a "career woman."

Margaret's commitment to conservative norms allowed her to
thrive as the *Times*'s first puzzle editor. It was also what led to her unexpected dismissal from the paper, having failed to find solidarity with
other workers. The crossword puzzle, under Margaret's stewardship—
and today, according to her legacy—is a conservative cultural product.
Conservative in both senses of the word: *traditionalist* (few create or
solve crosswords to change the culture but to assert their fluency in it)
and *self-preserving* (a crossword is a coping mechanism, a way of feeling
in control of the culture, even when you've lost it or could never lay
claim to it to begin with).

In 1974, five years after Margaret retired from the *Times*, the author
Jean Stafford wrote an essay for *Esquire* magazine titled "The Crossword
Puzzle Has Gone to Hell!" Although Stafford won the Pulitzer Prize in
1970 for her collected short stories, by 1974 she had mostly stopped writing

fiction and had become something of a pariah in New York City's literary scene, where her first husband, Robert Lowell, was a fixture. Her social isolation was often self-imposed: when Robert Giroux, her longtime friend and editor at FSG, took on Mary McCarthy as an author—a well-known friend to Lowell and his second wife, Elizabeth Hardwick—Stafford insisted that Giroux choose between them. He chose McCarthy, passing off Stafford to his subordinate, Denver Lindley.

Between rehabilitative institutions and bouts of mandatory bed rest—for alcoholism, for depression, and, as one biographer has speculated, for anorexia—Stafford took to the pages of *Esquire* to chastise Margaret's successor at the *Times* for his bastardization of the crossword, a proxy battle against the debasement of language she saw all around her:

Mr. Weng moves in circles I do not: I do not receive people with standards so low. I do not believe that a mycologist would accept edible as "A mushroom variety" . . . nor would the dumbest of quacks diagnose anemia as "Weakness," as does doc W.W. The interns, cocky and authoritarian, whom I have known throughout my valetudinarian life, would not take kindly to being called "Hospital aides," and would, I am sure, if they met him in a saloon, ask Mr. Weng to step outside.

Stafford started the essay with the confession that she began solving crossword puzzles at age eight; they inspired her with a thirst for knowledge, especially classical knowledge, which she pursued as a philology student at Heidelberg University in 1937. Now infirm, and unwilling or unable to "begin my day with a few passages from Pliny the Elder," she both comforted and tested herself with the *Times* puzzle. After paying her respects to "the meticulous and honorable Margaret Farrar," Stafford launched her attack on Weng's work with the contempt of a society snob:

The unattractive people—those we do not choose to know socially—have taken up the word "area" as an omnibus to carry almost anything on land or sea or in the heavens. I present a few samples of the way it has appeared recently in the puzzles:

City area = park

City area = slum

City area = boulevard

City area = subway

Pertaining to the area of a city = urban

(That one takes the cake and beats the band and beats the Dutch)

STAFFORD'S ESSAY WAS ONE OF MANY SHE WROTE FOR WIDE-circulation magazines (*Esquire*, *Vogue*, *Cosmopolitan*, and *McCall's*) to earn a living at the end of her life. At the time, she pictured herself "spinsterish," even though she had married three times and was widowed by her last husband, *New Yorker* writer A. J. Liebling, in 1963. In all of these late, journalistic essays—whether they're about travel or hosting a dinner party or crossword puzzles—Stafford's principal focus was the depreciation of the English language. Each essay's topic was a vehicle for her to express her prejudice against "jargon," "solecisms," "mongoloid bastards," and "knock-kneed metaphors." Meanwhile, diction became the vehicle for her prejudice. Each essay lists the many colloquialisms du jour that she found distasteful, if not nonsensical—words prepackaged and sold to American consumers by "the sociologists and the psychologists and the sociopsychologists and psychosociologists, the Pentagon, [and] the admen." Words like *generation gap*, *job situation*, *lifestyle*, *think pieces*, *feedback*, and *gut feeling*. When describing the language used at a sensitivity training seminar that she covered for *Horizon* magazine, she wrote of her fellow seminar participants, sensitivity far from her mind, "They said 'simplistic' when they meant 'simple,' 'formalistic' when they meant 'formal'; they said 'home' when they meant 'house.' . . . They used 'structure' as a verb and 'construct' as a noun. . . . There seems to be an action, quite inscrutable, known as 'psyching out.'"

Throughout these essays, Stafford's tone is acidic but self-ironizing: she was actively cultivating the image of a stuffy, pedantic grammarian (or, more properly, a linguistic morphologist, as word choice, not grammar, was the object of her fixation). But self-parody can be self-determining. In many ways, she became the "spinsterish" conservative that was her public mask; and as the manners, if not the morals, of the culture loosened in the 1970s, she found herself protesting its liberationist movements. She took particular aim at what she called "fem lib," writing an impassioned screed against the new prefix *Ms.* and deeming *sexism* "the most teratoid coinage so far." The adjective *teratoid*, meaning monstrous and malformed, was common in her vocabulary—a word she used with greater frequency as the patterns of American life became increasingly monstrous to her and her self-image. It wasn't that she didn't believe in equal rights and equal pay for women (she did), but she used language to cut herself off from the feminist movement, subordinating its righteous values to its protest aesthetics, which were not hers. As for *sexism*, she wrote, "It is difficult to get a purchase on the exact meaning of the word, but it is pejorative, make no mistake."

The spinsterish recluse was the last of many personas that Stafford adopted throughout her life—including country rube, Mrs. Robert

Lowell, New York sophisticate—but each, according to her performance, was also a new iteration of the suffering artist, a role she never relinquished. In 1988, David Roberts's sensationalist biography of Stafford prompted Joyce Carol Oates to coin the term *pathography*: a work that foregrounds the author's tortured life over her celebrated writings. But Stafford was a complicit coauthor of her pathography, allowing her psychic antagonisms—between country and city, traditional and radical, normative and teratoid—to stifle her career, her health, and ultimately her alliances with other women and other writers.

The structuring antinomy that Stafford wrestled with all her life was that of "woman" and "writer." She found the terms wholly incompatible. Before her marriage to Lowell, she wrote many letters to her friend and romantic prospect James Robert Hightower on this theme, protesting first that she could not be "his woman" because she had to be a writer; then just as quickly she reversed course, insisting that she was a "woman," which is to say, a suitable wife:

> It is that I love both you and my novel, and for the time being any marriage of the two is out of the question.

> Sometimes I feel that I really *do* have a masculine mind. I cannot otherwise explain how it is that loving you as I do, I can separate myself from you for the sake of my book.

> I have been afraid to tell you before, but I will tell you now: thinking of myself as your wife, my daydreams have been those of a woman who had sloughed off all but the essence of womanliness.... I know I am a woman.... One thing I can promise you is this: I am a woman.

Before she had published anything, Stafford was scouring the landscape, surveying its power centers. Her ambition was vast: she wanted to be the essence of womanliness, and she wanted to be a man.

In 1947, after the publication of two bestselling novels, after her divorce from Lowell and the hospitalization that was its direct result, she wrote to Lowell, again holding her identities as a writer and a woman at discrete and irreconcilable remove:

Why should it console me to be praised as a good writer? These stripped bones are not enough to feed a starving woman. I know this, Cal, and the knowledge eats me like an inward animal: there is no thing worse for a woman than to be deprived of her womanliness. For me, there is nothing worse than the knowledge that life holds nothing for me but being a writer.

In Stafford's imagery, skeletal bones, "being a writer," and her own desexualization form the triptych of her tragic fate. Unlike Margaret Farrar, whose way with words apparently posed no conflict to her decorous embodiment, Stafford presented language as fleshless, if not frigid. In her 1948 lecture "The Psychological Novel," she described words as a "familiar set of bones"—bones that jargon and neologism could merely make "unusual" or "out of joint." But always the lay philologist, Stafford reminded her audience that "'out of joint' is synonymous with 'inarticulate.'"

Two years after she wrote "The Crossword Puzzle Has Gone to Hell!" Stafford suffered a stroke that left her without the ability to talk. Her friend Nancy Flagg Gibney wrote to her in the hospital, "You can't speak because you find everything unspeakable. You can't talk because you see no one fit to talk to." This wasn't far from the truth. Stafford's aphonia was not psychosomatic, but the speech pathologist who worked with her after her stroke suggested that Stafford's speech was "frustrated" because she was "inclin[ed] to search . . . for polysyllabic words rather than [the] common colloquial word which is easily within [her] grasp." Her condition could have been stolen from one of her image-dense novels. She was the writer-invalid, thwarted by the words she cherished most—big words, big words used precisely.

While Stafford was in the hospital, Lowell read new poetry at New York City's 92nd Street Y, including "Jean Stafford, a Letter," a poem addressed to his first wife. "You wrote outlines for novels more salable than my poems. . . . *Roget's* synonyms studded your spoken and written word." These are cruel compliments, meant to diminish Stafford's talent as rote and academic, and her taste as commercial and bourgeois. He wasn't granting her the high praise of an artist so much as conceding to her the pedestrian tools of a crossword puzzle solver. Having already stripped her of her womanhood, as Stafford described it, Lowell left her with words only. Only to use them against her.

But words were her weapons too—against others and against herself. Wanting so much to become a Great Woman, and finding Great Writer of little compensation, she couldn't be common or succumb to common usage. Instead, in her last years, Stafford asserted her social authority, with the dictionary as her truncheon, in the pages of *Esquire*, *Vogue*, and *McCall's*. "The Crossword Puzzle Has Gone to Hell!" is a conservative screed: reactionary, yes, but also a symptom of her increasingly unsuccessful efforts at self-preservation. (As Stafford liked to remind her students in the early 1970s, "'conservatism' and 'conservation' . . . have the same mother.") Like the housewife, Stafford worked to maintain a tradition and a set of values that nonetheless subjugated her. This too was Margaret

Farrar's work—tidying and reproducing a culture that was properly the domain of her husband—though neither woman would have seen it in those terms.

Crossword puzzles are already a minor form of cultural production. To write or solve one, when your labor is already considered minor (un-waged, underappreciated), may be a form of self-care. In accounting for the experiences of these women who were so integral to its innovation, and who were so devoted to its upkeep, we may also see the puzzle as a form of cruel optimism—an attachment, as the late theorist Lauren Berlant described it, to the very object or thing (work, decorum, a need for control or success) that is one's undoing.

THE SEXUAL
POLITICS
OF
WORDPLAY

IV

Do Crossword Puzzles

ADVICE TO A YOUNG PSYCHOANALYST

ALTHOUGH THE CROSSWORD PUZZLE, IN ITS EARLY YEARS, WAS associated with social disruption—with the New Woman and the indecorous wit of the Algonquin Round Table—its social role was conservative. Crosswords tested the solver's knowledge of preexisting words, often arcana culled from entries buried deep in *Webster's International*, reproducing language norms and the expectation that to be smart was to know old or esoteric things. This was a function of its form: crossword clues from the 1920s through the 1960s were mostly definitional. They were not, as devoted cruciverbalist Stephen Sondheim wrote in 1968, the product of a "devious mind" but of "encyclopedic memory."

Sondheim's essay, published in *New York* magazine, was not only a rebuke of American puzzles; it was also an impassioned endorsement of British crosswords, or cryptics, as they're often called in the States. "There are crossword puzzles and there are crossword puzzles," his essay began. And the British crosswords that he preferred featured clues that needed to be decrypted before their answer could be plotted in the grid. Each cryptic clue has an internal logic that directs the solver to the type of wordplay required to discover its solution: anagrams, inversions, deletions, and homophones among them. The result, as Sondheim wrote, are clues that share "many characteristics of a literary manner: cleverness, humor, even a pseudo-aphoristic grace."

Since the 1990s and the installment of Will Shortz in the seat once occupied by Margaret Farrar, American-style crosswords have included cryptic-like clues in their harder iterations. Wordplay is now increasingly required to play this word game. But if the American puzzle began as a conservative form—rewarding fluency in a canon of Western knowledge—is there a politics that inheres in cryptics? Put more broadly, is there a politics to wordplay?

The question risks a double embarrassment: trivializing the serious stuff of politics or, maybe worse, taking trivialities too seriously. It was first posed to me during an oral exam for a modernist literature course that I took in college, and I wasn't prepared for it. The examiner had introduced the weight of politics into what, to me, had been a playful conversation about the word games of James Joyce and Samuel Beckett. Thinking nothing of politics, I had been working to demonstrate my fluency in what Joyce called "litteringture"—recycled sounds, chance homophones, and frankly stupid portmanteaus mixed together on the page like so much rubbish. "You complain that this stuff is not written in English," Beckett said to Joyce's critics, "It is not written at all. It is not to be read—or rather it is not only to be read. It is to be looked at and listened to." In other words, it was meant to be puzzled through.

The college I attended made a pageant of final exams. Notoriously lacking in athletic ability, my classmates and I prepared for finals with the intensity of varsity athletes. I spent weeks tracking down Joyce's allusions, solving his puzzles, and cross-referencing them with my edition of *Ulysses Annotated*. I enjoyed my study in "litteringture"—a language not so much composed as composted from the dregs of English-speaking life. If puzzling through *Ulysses*'s 700-plus pages was an obscene task, it was no less depraved than much of the book's content. Joyce's protagonists fart, masturbate, and come; they piss into the sea ("flop, slop, slap . . . floating foampool") and into a commode ("Chamber music . . . Acoustics that is. Tinkling.") It's not hard to see why a young crossword constructor would enjoy these word games—and would delight, especially, in the elevation of the lowest forms of comedy to the heights of high modernism. But is there a politics to all this literary shit-stirring?

In response to my professor's question, I stumbled into an answer about *defamiliarization*, a byword for the artists and writers of the early twentieth century who disrupted their reader's common sense of the world by making familiar elements of a text seem strange. This estrangement is meant to have political effects—to challenge the reader's encrusted expectations and jar their bourgeois sensibilities. *Make It New*, the title of Ezra Pound's 1934 essay collection, became the political imperative through which this literature was meant to be read. Make language new, and you could make the world anew, presumably.

This was the "right" answer to my professor's question, but it didn't feel right. My college courses were expanding my vocabulary, a project that offered me marks of distinction in the name of intelligence and pried open new neural pathways, new ways to think abstractly about the world through language: the most comfortable way for me to think about anything at all. But *defamiliarization*, a technical term overburdened with suffixes, didn't capture the eros of Joyce's language, and it certainly didn't account for the power I felt in asserting some mastery over his famously un-masterable prose. I was drawn to modernist literature just as I was drawn to crossword puzzles: it was hard, and it flirted with control over the unwieldy body of language. It teased the reader, tempting her into believing that, with enough mental effort, its feral syntax could be brought to submission.

Joyce and Beckett poked holes in the pretensions of literary taste and the flailing pretensions of the human body. They matched the unruliness of the body—its insatiable appetites, its psychosexual disappointments—with an unruly use of language. Joyce inflated his characters' inevitably flaccid dicks and filled their gaping hunger holes with a material glut of words; Beckett matched the foolishness of embodiment with the fool-hardy project of trying to capture it in prose. They didn't seem to despair over these various disappointments: bodies fail us; words fail us. They laughed, and they made me laugh too.

Although I couldn't find humor in my own failing body—couldn't even accept that it might be fallible—I could access a vicarious pleasure through Joyce and Beckett's power play with language. More, I discov-ered a form of social power in the disconnect between my diminished body and the robustness and crudeness with which I could talk about Joyce's ecstatic Molly Bloom or the abject body of Beckett's Molloy. With no secondary sex characteristics of my own to display, I exulted in perfor-mances of masturbatory language and chamber pot music. The gap be-tween how I looked and what I could do with words, I imagined, was the source of my power. To me, the politics of wordplay were sexual politics.

I understood my way with words to be sexy, and its sexual power, I thought, was contingent upon my extreme thinness. I devoted my brain-power to verbal seduction: innuendo and double entendre of the highest order. I had, at least, seduced myself. "You talk like a virgin," my college boyfriend told me. At this point, he wasn't yet my boyfriend, and I was. By talking a big game, I was flaunting a sexual power that I didn't have and that I wasn't really sure I wanted. In high school, as my friends experimented with sex, drinking, and drugs, I retreated into a social identity that I understood "Good Girls" to embody. As for sex, drinking, and drugs, as with food, I abstained.

In the years that I was in college, the clinical discussions of anorexia nervosa shifted from the paradigm of the "Good Girl" to that of the "Perfect Girl." Courtney E. Martin's 2007 book *Perfect Girls, Starving Daughters* is largely responsible for identifying this shift in the anorexic imaginary. According to Martin, the Good Girl gets straight As and follows rules; she is polite and defers to authority; she is chaste to the point of asexuality. The Perfect Girl has all the ambition of the Good Girl—she excels in school and extracurriculars—but instead of being polite, she is brash and unsentimental; instead of being chaste, she fucks. To use a clumsy but potent shorthand, if the Good Girl is a Charlotte, the Perfect Girl is a Samantha.

The Perfect Girl is the product of good intentions and chronically mixed messages. The inheritor of second-wave feminism's civil rights victories and the sex positivity of the 1980s, she is told that she can do anything that she puts her mind to. And she should have anything she desires—career, family, sexual gratification—but her desires have been shaped in a culture of anti-feminist backlash. The contours of this culture's contradictory demands are, by now, familiar: the Perfect Girl should make her own money (but not be strident); she should be sexually uninhibited (but not a slut); she should look fabulous (she should be thin). As Martin wrote, "We are not . . . 'Good Girls.' We are 'Perfect Girls,' obsessed with appearing ideal. We aren't worried about doing things 'right.' We are worried about doing things 'impeccably.'"

It's humbling, if not humiliating, to see one's psychosexual trajectory captured by these neat monikers, but my evolution from high school to college followed this course: I stopped modeling myself on a Good Girl and cultivated the persona of Martin's Perfect Girl. Where I grew up, girls were supposed to become Perfect by the time they reached puberty, if not before. Our particular brand of perfection was highly localized— overdetermined by 14th Street, the dividing line between uptown and downtown Manhattan. Uptown was square, downtown cool. Our inflated sense of coolness was another inheritance from our parents, the bourgeois bohemians whose creative spirit and generational wealth turned SoHo, Chelsea, and Tribeca into gallery spaces, artists' studios, and residential lofts. Our Perfect Girls were high on pubescent sexual energy, recreational drugs, and literary pretension. It wasn't until college that I began to consider this a mantle that I might reasonably claim as my own. "I only date girls who grew up below 14th Street," someone told me in my freshman year. I was ready to assume the role, and like so many posers before me, I began with talk—sex talk, routed through the works of high modernist acrobats whose implicit sophistication, I thought, could mask the very explicit fact of my virginity. If I couldn't quite be a sexual sophisticate, I could at least talk like one and read like one.

The belligerently indecent humor of Joyce and Beckett was only my starting point. I honed my model for the Perfect Girl that same semester in a class called "French Critical Theory." Every word of the course title was a seduction, promising access to a cerebral brand of sexuality that needed to be translated (from French) and decrypted (from Theory) in order to be enjoyed. It was here that I was introduced to the so-called French Feminists: Hélène Cixous, Luce Irigaray, and Julia Kristeva, women whose writing from the 1970s and early 1980s promised a revolutionary sexual politics based on the manipulation of language. A sexual politics, in other words, of wordplay.

———————

THE FRENCH FEMINISTS WERE ONLY KNOWN AS SUCH ON AMERIcan campuses, where, in the early 1980s, their writings landed on American syllabi alongside works by Jacques Derrida, Jacques Lacan, and Michel Foucault. In France, they were obviously not called the French Feminists. They weren't even called feminists, a label and a movement that they repudiated for its reformist tendencies (its willingness to sustain patriarchal institutions, so long as women had access to them) and for its anti-intellectualism. Instead of agitating for abortion rights and equal pay—causes they no doubt believed in—the French Feminists' ambitions were to rewrite the history of Western thought, undoing its entrenched logic, which subordinates woman to man. Cixous delineated the terms of this prevailing patriarchal logic under the heading "Where is she?"

Activity/passivity
Sun/Moon
Culture/Nature
Day/Night
Father/Mother
Head/heart
Intelligible/sensitive
Logos/Pathos

She, it will come as no surprise, is hidden in the subordinated terms of these binaries. (We might add Laura Mulvey's "Gazer/gazed at" to the list. Her essay defining the "male gaze" emerged from the same intellectual milieu, albeit in England.)

"Traditionally," Cixous wrote, "the question of sexual difference is coupled with the same opposition: activity/passivity." Man is active, and woman is passive. The fight for women's liberation, then, isn't simply a fight for rights. It's a project, shared by Mulvey, of "inscribing femininity" in new terms, of "writing women" in a new language. In her 1975 essay "The Laugh of the Medusa," Cixous called this new language *écriture féminine*. Sometimes translated as "feminine writing" or "women's writing," *écriture féminine* is more often than not left untranslated in the English-language versions of French Feminist texts—its referent apparently incommensurate with Anglophone experience.

Though their books spanned a range of topics and approaches, the French Feminists can be understood to have shared a broad, two-fold project:

1. Write to disrupt the "phallocentrism" of Western philosophy—the masculine bias of Western intellectual and institutional traditions.

2. Write to disrupt the "logocentrism" of Western philosophy—the fantasy of an authentically whole "self," an independent subject who can locate himself in time and space through the power of his reason and his speech.

In Greek, *Logos* variously means "speech," "reason," and "discourse." It became, in the post-structuralist tradition to which the French Feminists were committed, a shorthand for the philosophical presuppositions that had grounded the history of Western philosophy, from Plato to Heidegger. The project to disrupt phallocentrism and logocentrism could not have been more radical; it could also not have been more theoretical and often alienating to those on the ground who were agitating for equity and access to power. Alienation was, to some extent, the point. Their project was a defamiliarizing one: a revolution of the *world* predicated on a revolution of the *word*.

According to the French Feminists, the first of these goals (an attack on phallocentrism and patriarchy) could not be achieved without the second (an attack on logocentrism and Western philosophy). Collapsing the two norms that they sought to disrupt into one Joycean portmanteau, they directed their written attacks at Western philosophy's "phallogocentrism."

In English, such bloated compound words have assumed the forbidding allure of theoryspeak. To think of them as word puzzles is not to diminish their intellectual heft but to restore them to the acts of wordplay that motivated their creation. I'm not sure that I would have continued writing crossword puzzles in college if I hadn't found the French Feminists. I was beginning to think of my puzzles as simple nerd-work and a vestige of my Good Girl eagerness to impress authority. But through the writing of Cixous, Irigaray, and Kristeva, I discovered a theory of wordplay that strategically linked playing with language to anti-patriarchal defiance and feminine attraction. Their writings continue to guide my thinking about contemporary efforts to "diversify" the crossword puzzle: What does it mean to introduce "women's language" into the puzzle? Can wordplay be used to undermine the pervasive maleness of mainstream discourse? There are other, perhaps more intuitive, entry points into these questions, but I began here—with *écriture féminine*.

Although Cixous, Irigaray, and Kristeva marshaled different textual strategies in the name of *écriture féminine*, each imagined that playing with language could disrupt its hegemonic forms. In "The Laugh of the Medusa," Cixous's puns abound. She writes: "Flying is woman's gesture—flying in language and making it fly." Here *voler*, she points out, could equally mean "to fly" or "to steal." In the spirit of utopian feminism, the theorist-practitioner of *écriture féminine* steals patriarchal language to free herself from it. As Cixous wrote, her goal was to "break up the 'truth' with laughter."

The source of this laughter is always in excess: the excessive power of language to mean more than we think it does, and—in a pervasive metaphor that returns over and over again in French Feminist texts—the excessive pleasures of a female body that can feel, enjoy, and produce so much more than it is thought to. The French Feminists drew a grounding analogy between the erotic surfeit of language and what they often called the *jouissance* of the female orgasm. In any French-English dictionary, *jouissance* will be defined as enjoyment or pleasure. In the French Feminist tradition, the word alludes to the extravagant, extralinguistic pleasure of coming. Like *écriture féminine*, it almost always remains untranslated in English texts, baiting the Anglo-American woman into a familiar position of mystified jealousy: French women don't get fat. They don't just come. They experience *jouissance*.

The excess of the woman's multiple orgasm and her multiply erogenous body—finding pleasure all over, not just in genital stimulation—is accessed in *écriture féminine* through puns. Wordplay unleashes the multiply signifying, disruptive body of language. By contrast, Cixous wrote, "masculine language" operates through an economy of "thrift": the meanings of words are stabilized through a "rigid" structure of laws and norms. One word, one meaning. Man's "libidinal economy," as Cixous put it, is equally "thrifty" with meaning:

Rigid = turned on
Soft = turned off

In "masculine language," the meaning of words is like the meaning of an erection: it's singular, crystal clear. And the French Feminists were not above dick jokes. Cixous, for example, demoted this great, stable sign of masculine authority to a "little pocket signifier," telling you exactly what it means. The dick, in other words, is a pocket dictionary of desire. In contrast to the male writer's linguistic and libidinal economy of thrift, the woman writer spends and wastes. Cixous wrote, "Woman un-thinks the unifying, regulating history that homogenizes." Here, the word "un-thinks" (*dé-pense*) is a pun on *penser* (to think) and *dépenser* (to spend). The French Feminist is profligate with language and sexual energy.

Irigaray most sensationally developed this contrast between women's language and "masculine thrift" in her second book, *This Sex Which Is Not One*. Hers is an anatomical metaphor that remains, perhaps, the most infamous paragraph in French Feminist thought. She wrote:

Women's autoeroticism is very different from man's. In order to touch himself, man needs an instrument: his hand, a woman's body, language.... And this self-caressing requires at least a minimum of activity. As for woman, she touches herself in and of herself without any need for mediation, and before there is any way to distinguish activity from passivity. Woman 'touches herself' all the time, and moreover no one can forbid her

131

to do so, for her genitals are formed of two lips in continuous contact. Thus, within herself, she is already two—but not divisible into one(s) [un(e)s]—that caress each other.

If second-wave feminists in the United States worked to redirect women away from the pursuit of an apparently mythical vaginal orgasm and toward a sexual revolution of the clitoris, Irigaray rejected the dichotomy altogether. Clitoris/vagina, active/passive—again, we are trapped in a phallogocentric regime of either/or. "Female sexuality has always been conceptualized on the basis of masculine parameters," she wrote, "Thus the opposition between 'masculine' clitoral activity and 'feminine' vaginal passivity." Instead of succumbing to these "masculine parameters" by choosing an active clitoris over passive vagina, Irigaray skipped over the obvious choice—why not "both/and"?!—opting instead for "neither/nor." She redirected readers outside of the dichotomy altogether, devising a sexual politics of the labia. The "lips," she suggested, that "speak together."

I will venture that the vulva-having people reading the above paragraph will find it, at best, unrelatable: that my labia minora are constantly touching does not get me off. Men should know this. But the image does provide a cerebral pleasure, more akin to self-satisfaction than autoeroticism. The verbal and visual puns of the paragraph enhance this pleasure. Lips (*labia*, in Latin) have a double meaning: women speak from their lips; *écriture féminine* emerges from their other lips.

But Irigaray did not stop there. She arrived on the lips as a governing metaphor for *écriture féminine* precisely because of the plurality of their form. They are not divisible into "one(s)." This pun requires some parsing. Irigaray is not only saying that lips are indivisible into one lip, and then another lip. She is also saying, in French, that the labial lips are not divisible into *uns* (the masculine pronoun) or *unes* (the feminine pronoun). The awkward parenthetical in the original French—*un(e)s*—not only signals this grammatical resistance to gendering but also visually manifests the lips () on the page.

The reader would be forgiven for wondering here: *Is she joking?* By pushing language to the limits of its signifying power, the French Feminists were high-wire rhetoricians, willing to risk the dual embarrassment with which this chapter began: Aren't they making a joke of feminist politics? Aren't they taking wordplay a little too seriously?

———

IN COLLEGE, I COULDN'T HAVE BEEN MORE PERSUADED BY THE French Feminist project. Nor could I have been more anorexic. If I struggled with my examiner's question—"Is there a politics of word-play?"—I was just as confounded by the question "Is there such a thing as an anorexic feminist?" Could I consider myself a feminist at all, French or otherwise?

Feminist literary critics of the 1990s were attracted to the Victorian anorexic as a figure of anti-patriarchal protest. Hysterics who refused to eat, they suggested, were rejecting a culture in which their value was bound to their ability to bear children. Although my eating disorder had denied me a postpubescent woman's body, I couldn't, by the time I was in college, identify it as an act of feminist protest. Far from it. I wasn't rejecting patriarchal values; I was committing to them.

My blooming identification with a smug French Feminist sensibility only isolated me further from anything like sisterhood. To men, my small-frame-big-brain act seemed to work. I got the impression that I was physically unthreatening and could therefore be as outspoken as I wanted to be while remaining diminutive and cute in their eyes. To women, my preoccupation with male attention, coupled with my self-punishing relationship to my own body, could have easily been interpreted as an act of war.

There is a common belief that anorexic women are highly competitive with other women and that we treat other women's bodies with the same contempt that we have for our own. Dozens of studies from the early aughts consider eating disorders as forms of female competition, with one even hypothesizing that bulimics are more likely to be "competing for mates," while anorexics are "competing for status." Woefully reductive, these studies can't capture my experience. This isn't to say that I wasn't comparing: I constantly compared what I ate with what others ate and compared my body to other women's bodies. But I wasn't just trying to beat others at anorexia's losing game. I was trying to reaffirm my own eating disorder as a foolproof social code. With every bite not taken, I recommitted to anorexia. It made me feel strong and sometimes superior ("I have such willpower!") just as often as it made me feel deficient and inferior ("How do other women live their lives so freely, so comfortably, so playfully with each other?").

I was terrified of what other women thought about me. Perhaps they could see right through me—could see the effort that went into my French Feminist masquerade and the lack of joy, to say nothing of *jouissance*, that informed my daily choices (what to eat, what to wear, what to say). Straight men, I knew, couldn't tell the difference. Or didn't care to. But my estrangement from women plagued me. I wanted to tell them, "It's not personal; it's pathological!" But maybe in the case of anorexia, the pathological is the personal is the political.

———————

WOMEN WERE SOME OF THE FRENCH FEMINISTS' HARSHEST CRITICS. By insisting on alienating their readers—instead of bringing them together in sisterly solidarity—Cixous, Irigaray, and Kristeva prompted some women readers to ask:

1. Aren't they elitists?

2. Aren't they essentializing the woman's body, entrapping her in the same sexualized prison that would men?

3. Far from creating writing for women by women, isn't their theory-speak, derived from the works of Derrida and Lacan, just propping up a new patriarchal code?

It's worth taking on these criticisms one by one to show how seriously the French Feminists and their defenders took their critics—and to show how determined they were to use wordplay to defend their project and insist, above all, on *its* seriousness. They would not be embarrassed.

The hardest charge to defend was that of elitism. Having rebuffed other factions of the French Women's Liberation Movement for their anti-intellectualism, they were, for lack of more feminist words, "asking for it." But despite its encrypted puns and robust theoretical apparatus, Cixous's "Laugh of the Medusa" essay was a call to all women: "Write!" she implored. "Writing is for you, you are for you, your body is yours, take it!" *Écriture féminine*, she believed, exists within all of us. But lest you think she'd gone all touchy-feely—all *Our Bodies, Ourselves*—she proceeds to explain why more women don't write. And true to form, her hypothesis is a charmingly debauched metaphor, a provocation, if not an outright joke:

I know why you haven't written. (And why I didn't write before the age of twenty-seven.) Because writing is . . . reserved for the great—that is for "great men"; and it's silly. Besides, you've written a little, but in secret. And it wasn't good because it was in secret, and because you punished yourself for writing because you didn't go all the way, or because you wrote irresistibly, as when we would masturbate in secret, not to go further, but to attenuate the tension a bit, just enough to take the edge off.

The will-to-crudeness with which all of the French Feminists wrote was, in fact, a function of their anti-elitism. Theirs was a call for an insubordination of the body held forth in writing. The French Feminists enjoined women to be "not proper" and "not property."

If this defense of *écriture féminine* as a collective project—one mobilized on behalf of *all women*—doesn't quite exonerate the French Feminists of elitism, it only compounds the most prevalent critique of their writing as essentialist. The concern here was not exactly that all of this textual vagina worship was biologically essentialist—reducing the definition of a woman to her anatomy and therefore excluding trans women—though it certainly was that too. Instead, critics of the French Feminists who accused their writing of essentialism were concerned that *any* attempt to define woman's writing necessarily required a definition of "woman," reducing her to "essential" parts, be they anatomical, psychological, or metaphysical. Is there a definition of "woman" that doesn't double down on the "right" side of Cixous's binaries—woman is *passive*; woman is *sensitive*; woman is *mother*? This is a problem for all feminists (and all members of socially marginalized groups) seeking to base a politics on something other than the very terms by which they are subjugated. But the French Feminists, with their insistence on a poetic equivalence between a woman's body and her self-inscription in writing, courted the problem instead of retreating from it.

American defenders of Luce Irigaray insisted that the language she used to describe *écriture féminine* was figurative and, in its very nonliteralness, resisted a neat equation between women's writing and women's bodies. The literary critic Diana Fuss, for example, described Irigaray's "lips" not only as evidence of her wily, subversive language-play—her way of thinking outside of Logos without sliding into pathos—but also as a metaphor for language itself. For Fuss, Irigaray's "lips" become a metaphor for the slippages that occur between words in their perpetual proximity to each other. As we saw with both Freud's symbolic displacements (forest = vagina) and the forms of play that inform every crossword clue ("not fast" = EAT), words exist only in relation to other words. Despite what a dic(k)tionary might lead you to believe, they cannot be isolated from each other. Like lips, words are always touching.

Fuss's defense of *écriture féminine* as fundamentally metaphoric—and not literally corresponding to the anatomy of cis women—is, to me, persuasive. Julia Kristeva's work can't quite be defended in similar terms. No less invested in the woman's body as a prism for a new kind of language, Kristeva didn't write about *écriture féminine* per se. Instead, she described women's emancipatory relation to language in terms of what she called the "Semiotic."

Like Irigaray, Kristeva was trained as an analyst under the tutelage of Jacques Lacan, the psychoanalyst responsible for a resurgence of Freudian thought in France in the 1950s through the 1970s. Kristeva's notion of the "Semiotic" was defined in direct opposition to the Lacanian category of the "Symbolic." (The terms proliferate: theories and words beget more theories and more words. What better way to articulate the world anew?) Lacanians modified the Freudian progression of childhood development—oral phase, anal phase, phallic phase—to account for the child's entrance into language. What happens when a child first learns to recognize himself as "me"? What are the psychic and social mechanisms that allow for this naming of the self, this first apprehension of one's self-hood in language? Lacan called the psychic dimension that allows one to locate oneself as a subject of speech the "Symbolic." Shaped by the laws and institutions that dictate the rules of communication and ultimately desire, the Symbolic is, according to Lacan, the paternal function of language. It is underpinned by the Name-of-the-Father: the "name," *nom*, but also, punning on its French homophone, the "no," *non*, of the father—the various prohibitions and restrictions of language that help make us legible to ourselves and others. Using the same logic that Cixous used to account for the "thrift" of masculine language, Lacan called the term that stabilizes language's meaning in the Symbolic "the Phallus." Playfully, of course, Lacan also insisted that his use of this term was figurative. It is nothing more nor less than a symbol for the rules and norms that knit language into meaningful forms of communication and identification. Although it invokes the father whose social prescriptions give shape to the Symbolic, the Phallus is *not* the penis. The Phallus is not literal.

Like Irigaray and Cixous, Kristeva was looking for a path outside of the Symbolic, outside of the Phallus, outside of "masculine language." She found this path in what she called the Semiotic, which referred to language's "more archaic dimension"—including rhythm, tone, color—and all of language's melodious effects that do not directly serve the project of representation. The Semiotic can be witnessed in the pre-verbal infant's "goo-goos" and "ga-gas," but Kristeva posits that it is always present in language, always working to disrupt the authority of the paternal Symbolic.

In Lacanian analysis, the child's prelingual sounds are associated with the mother-child bond. The child babbles before he "enters" the Symbolic, at which point he can understand himself as separate from his mother. (We can see the governing binaries that Cixous posited—active/passive; father/mother—emerging in this entrance into the Symbolic.) By investing the so-called Semiotic with revolutionary, anti-patriarchal energy, Kristeva risked identifying woman's liberation with the figure of the mother. And not just any mother: a mother who exists outside of language, outside of culture, in the politically marginalized and imaginary realm from which many feminists would like to liberate her. If an inherent relationship to the "Semiotic" is woman's essence—even a potentially disruptive essence—it's hard to find it an image of political freedom.

Even Kristeva's most sophisticated defenders conceded the point. The British academic Jacqueline Rose wrote, "As soon as we try to draw . . . an image of femininity which escapes the straitjacket of symbolic forms, we fall straight into that essentialism and primacy of the Semiotic which is one of the most problematic aspects of [Kristeva's] work." For Rose, Kristeva's writing points to the central problem of all French Feminist writing—and to a certain extent the problem of all identity politics. Rose asked, "What does it mean to construct a political identity out of processes heralded as the flight of identity itself?" To completely escape the Symbolic would be a form of madness (the figure of woman's liberation would be "the mad woman in the attic"); to submit to its terms would be a retreat to reformism (the figure of woman's liberation would be a woman who "acts like a man"). Both moves are political nonstarters; both can be construed as reactionary. The feminist is trapped in a double bind of male-generated social roles. How, then, can marginalized subjects fight to be released from their subjugated identities without doubling down on those identities in the process?

Rose found an answer, unsurprisingly, in a bit of wordplay. Kristeva often used the verb *traverser* (to pass through) in relation to the Semiotic. Women have to *pass through* the Semiotic and get to what Rose called "the other side" of identity. As Rose pointed out, if *traverser* means "to pass through" it must also mean "to go out." Rose suggested that Kristeva's work required *passing through* the male-constructed ideal of a sensualist, maternal, and maybe even "mad" woman—precisely in order to get out of it.

But did the French Feminists really get out of "masculine language"? Especially since their ideas so depended on the work of men, this question has been yet another stumbling block for feminists approaching their prose. Jacques Derrida and Lacan were the French Feminists' most influential interlocutors. The very terms *phallocentrism*, *logocentrism*, and *phallogocentrism* were coined or popularized by Derrida. And the idea that the unconscious is structured like a language, foundational to the French Feminists' investment in wordplay, is a central tenet of Lacanian analysis. How, then, could they lay claim to "women's writing" if their works were so indebted to men?

To answer this question, one needs to *pass through* two of Lacan's central contributions to psychoanalysis. It's a knotty detour, but a tremendously rewarding one for those willing to take language games seriously. These interventions in Freudian theory were, first, to account for the role of language in the unconscious; and second, to return to Freud's perennially deferred, though obsessively considered, question: "What does Woman want?"

The first item on Lacan's post-Freudian agenda can be cleverly and appropriately summed up in three words: *do crossword puzzles* ("*faites des mots croisés*"). This was his recommendation to young psychoanalysts in training in his field-defining essay of 1953. It's a rare bit of practical advice in an otherwise wickedly cryptic set of writings, but the advice itself is a clue to Lacan's psychoanalytic theory and its departures from Freudian gospel.

Freud had imagined the unconscious as an ever-evolving rebus puzzle, transforming the words of everyday speech into images and projecting them onto the blank screen of dreams. Puzzle solvers will know that a rebus—derived from the Latin expression *non verbis, sed rebus* ("not by words, but by things")—is a puzzle composed of images that stand in for words. Think of the T-shirt slogan "I ♥ NY." The heart is a rebus, an image standing in for the word *love*.

In advising young analysts, Lacan twisted Freud's puzzle metaphor: the unconscious, he suggested, is not a rebus, full of dream images that the analyst must translate into words, but a crossword puzzle. He described the unconscious as a "chain of interlocking signifiers," connecting at arbitrary but nonetheless generative cross sections in an endless play of word games, chance, and desire.

In truth, the crossword puzzle is a fairly limited analogy for Lacan's understanding of the unconscious. The development from Freud to Lacan—from the unconscious-as-rebus to the unconscious-as-crossword—can best be understood by reference to an image from Lacan's 1957 lecture "The Instance of the Letter in the Unconscious." It is an image, not surprisingly, that engages with the Freudian problematic of sexual difference, a riddle that Freud could never quite solve.

LADIES   GENTLEMEN

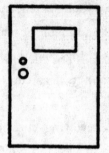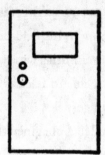

Although these two doors look identical, their difference is heavily circumscribed by the words that hover above them. The relationship between the doors and their labels, however, is not a simple one-to-one correlation (as in a rebus). Rather, the doors and their labels only gain meaning in relation to each other (as the words in a crossword puzzle exist only through their crossings with other words). "Gentlemen" only gains meaning when contrasted to "Ladies." And they only really gain meaning in relation to the entire interlocking "chain of signifiers" that comprises the Symbolic. Lacan related his theory of language in the form of bathroom humor: "A train arrives at a station," he wrote.

A little boy and a little girl, brother and sister, are seated in a compartment face to face next to the window through which the buildings along the station platform can be seen passing as the train pulls to a stop. "Look," says the brother, "we're at Ladies!" "Idiot," replies his sister, "can't you see we're at Gentlemen?"

Each child mistakenly thinks that they can determine what things "mean" based on what they see. Their mistake is a result of their partial view: once seen together, and in relation to one another, "Gentlemen" and "Ladies" can be understood not as station stops, but as bathroom signage.

Although Lacan didn't make it explicit, it's significant that the "little boy" and "little girl" can only see the signs of the opposite gender. By sitting in "one compartment" of the train or another, each child is placed in a linguistic and ideological structure, but neither can see the structure as such. As Lacan wrote, "Ladies and Gentlemen will henceforth be for these children two countries toward which each of their souls will strive on divergent wings." This seems like a theory of gender at once biologically and socially determined. Biology places them in their train compartments, and language is the train, whisking them off to separate countries.

But Lacan, like the French Feminists whom he inspired, insistently disrupted these determinisms in his writings—and, more seductively, in his speech. Those present at his lectures in the 1960s and '70s described the classroom as libidinally charged. Innuendo, humor, and the free-floating eros of Lacanian wordplay saturated the space. Jean-Michel Rabaté described the "heavy billows of smoke coming from the participants' mouths," which "allegorized the cloud of ideas released, a dense mist from which Lacan alone could extract meaning." Women scholars attested to the intensity and the opacity of the experience. Catherine Clément wrote that "one understood nothing . . . nothing, for several years; but a familiarity began to form in the ear, by necessity." Jacqueline Rousseau-Dujardin confessed, "What was said passed, *hélas!* resolutely over my head."

Breaking the spell of Lacan's high-class nonsense, the writer and feminist theorist Jane Gallop asked the obvious question: Why did everyone keep attending? "Why would anyone subject herself to this sort of berating?" Arguably the sharpest American reader of the French Feminists, Gallop insisted that the women students devoted to Lacan were not just masochists, his intellectual submissives. No, Lacan's charismatic, cryptic grandstanding, Gallop maintained, was not ultimately a demonstration of his masculine authority. He was not just performing male chauvinism; he was also undermining it. She wrote, "To designate Lacan at his most stimulating and forceful is to call him something more than just phallocentric. He is also phallo-eccentric. Or, in more pointed language, he is a prick."

Gallop played Lacan's game against him: if he could reduce an entire cultural order to a symbol of the penis, she could too. Phallus: meet the prick. She elucidated her theory of the prick—Lacan's prick, as it were—with teasing endearment and startling lucidity. If, in Lacanian theory, the Phallus bears the authority of law and order, the prick subverts it. Where the Phallus claims to stabilize language's meaning around a system of rules and norms, the prick subverts those too. The Phallus must mask desire—Daddy can't show his hand if his word is to become law—but the prick unveils his desire. His cards are on the table: he wants you, and he's pretty sure you want him too.

Gallop had another term of endearment for women Lacanians, including Irigaray and Kristeva. Drawing on Irigaray's claims that "what [woman] emits is flowing, fluctuating," Gallop called them "floozie(s), flowing and oozing." Perhaps Gallop was just *passing through* the stereotypical images of women—like the floozie—to *get out* of them. Or perhaps she just liked to transgress for transgression's sake. "You can't trust a floozie," she wrote. "Not only is she unscrupulous, she's not level-headed." Turning these vicious female stereotypes on their head,

Gallop triumphed the floozie for her lack of (phallogocentric) sense. You can't "extract meaning" from her. You'll "understand nothing." She'll go "over your head." Gallop finished her essay with praise for Lacan "and his stable of floozies," for "these principled women and that shameless floozie Lacan."

The feminist who rolls her eyes at this bluntly transgressive, sometimes reactionary, and always abstract method of anti-patriarchal "play" will share good company. In her 1985 film *The Man Who Envied Women*, for example, Yvonne Rainer pictured the French Feminist as the male chauvinist's naive accomplice. In the hallway outside a Manhattan cocktail party, Jackie, a woman with a thick French accent and a plunging neckline, encircles Jack Deller, an American professor of French critical theory. Studded with quotes from Cixous and Foucault, their words cross for a languorous, puzzling ten minutes, culminating in an inevitable French kiss. Theirs is a game of linguistic conquest: she, a "feminist" femme fatale; he, a "feminist" misogynist. Though they both profess a feminist project, Rainer seems to be suggesting that we shouldn't take them at their word. A dick is a prick is a phallus. And playing with it won't set you free. *Écriture féminine*, Rainer implies, is wordplay in the service of nothing more than heterosexual foreplay.

Rainer juxtaposed the hallway seduction scene with footage from a Board of Estimate hearing in New York's city hall, where artists are lobbying for government housing subsidies. The juxtaposition makes a clear, if lightly anti-intellectual, point: city hall is a political space; a cocktail party among sexually charged professors is not.

In a voiceover, Jack's ex-wife tries to reconcile the politics of the home (her divorce, her eviction) with the politics of abroad (American imperialism in Guatemala and El Salvador). These are political issues, and they,

Rainer suggests, are the true terrain of feminism. But the final voiceover announces:

Lately I've been thinking again, I can't live without men, but I can live without a man . . . something is different now. Something in the direction of un-womanliness. Not a new woman, not non-woman or misanthropist, or anti-woman, and not non-practicing Lesbian. Maybe unwoman is also the wrong term. A-woman is closer. A-womanly. A-womanliness.

Rainer's protagonist is grasping for a new language for feminism, a way to escape the antinomies male/female, active/passive, same/difference. Despite her tragicomic satire of the French Feminist, Rainer concluded her film by reproducing the French Feminist project: a new language for women. And a bit of wordplay.

———

THE FRENCH FEMINISTS I STUDIED IN COLLEGE OFFERED ME A WAY to act out a transgressive form of sexuality that was more conceptual than it was physical. My own sex life could be variously profligate, "mad," oozing, and somehow also strictly metaphoric. The actual figure of my body was almost incidental to the figurative forms of womanliness I imagined I could possess through words alone. I began to feel that I didn't have to engage my body to access sexual power—or the power of sexual difference—at all.

By my sophomore year, I had become a site of irreconcilable contradictions: an anorexic, Francophile feminist without a woman in my life, save my desperately worried mother. Even my therapist broke up with me—something I didn't know was possible. She called me "manipulative," to which I wanted to reply, "What did you expect?" Anorexics are notoriously calculating, saying and doing anything they can to protect the sanctity of their relationship with the disorder. Still playing the Good Girl for my therapist, I had been telling her that I wanted to recover and that I felt trapped. This was a partial truth. It wasn't a lie to confess that anorexia was eroding my relationships, hampering my freedom of thought, and limiting my movements. What I didn't confess was that I loved my eating disorder—that I couldn't and wouldn't imagine my life without it.

At the start of my junior year, my boyfriend moved to Brooklyn, and I scheduled my life around studying and seeing him. In practical terms, that meant finishing my schoolwork without really eating during the week and going to New York on the weekends, where I allowed myself to eat, have sex, and role-play the Perfect Girl. To the horror of my parents, I was beginning to imagine myself as an anorexic adult. Not a Good Girl, not even a Perfect Girl, but a grown woman with a maximally expressed, and now chronic, eating disorder.

My boyfriend was under no illusion that I was anything other than very anorexic. Even though I tried to keep my disordered behavior from him, I didn't keep the fact of it from him. I couldn't have. There were two restaurants in his neighborhood we could order from; I ordered the same thing each time. I passed out on the one vacation we took. Unable to negotiate the challenge of eating in a foreign country, I chose not to eat at all. We talked about whether he would love me if I weighed more—a fear that stemmed mostly from my therapist and mother, who were understandably but unjustly concerned that he desired me for my emaciated figure, not despite it. I imagined that my anorexia, held at some remove from our weekends together, allowed him to idealize me in the very terms that I hoped he would. I was so capable but also so wounded. So strong-willed but also strongly in need of his attention if not exactly willing to submit to his care. In truth, I don't know what he thought of my anorexia beyond its relentless inconvenience. He never shamed me or lost patience or interest. Instead, he pretended with me that the half-measure of a life that I was living was okay, for now. Okay, and maybe even a little sexy.

During the Thanksgiving break of my junior year, I was told by my parents, the school's health center, and my doctor that I needed to reenter therapy. I walked into my new therapist's office prepared to sell her on my Perfect Girl life: straight As, a crossword puzzle published in the *New York Times*, a devoted boyfriend with whom I had romantic weekends and multiple orgasms. She was unconvinced. She told me that she wouldn't see me unless I committed to residential treatment first. I lobbied: I couldn't go to treatment for plain logistical reasons. I, a junior, had been selected to join the advanced modernist literature seminar that spring. The course was usually only offered to seniors. Her face remained placid. Yes, I had already taken a course in modernist literature the year prior. And yes, I could theoretically take this advanced course for seniors, as a senior, the following year. Placid, and maybe a little pitying.

I worked to convince her that this "life of the mind" I had chosen for myself was, in fact, a choice: I was living my dream, if she could just take me at my word. I had a buoy for my future—sheer brainpower—and an altar at which to worship—some abstract notion of linguistic "play." Her eyes said in so many words: *You're playing yourself; don't try to play me.* If the scene was, in fact, a power play, in her near silence she was winning. When she did speak, she told me that I was ill, that my life was unsustainable, and that she was pretty sure I knew it.

By the time the hour was up, I had committed to residential treatment. When I called my sister, on my way home, I told her that I was going to treatment to heal my relationships, especially my relationships with women. There was truth in this, but I was also lying to myself. I was using the pretext of feminist sisterhood to shield myself from the possibility that anorexia just wasn't working for me anymore—that my life wasn't perfect—and that I was going to crack under its punishing regime.

The treatment center I attended—located in Paradise, Utah—couldn't take me for two weeks, so my first day there would be New Year's Eve. Between committing to treatment and arriving in Utah, I refused all food. It wasn't a hunger strike but a last hurrah, like someone making a New Year's resolution to diet and bingeing before the new regimen started. I wanted to be at my lowest weight before recovery began, and I got what I wanted. The center was concerned that I would have to be hospitalized and fed through a tube before I entered their program—they were equipped for long-term recovery, not urgent care. Thankfully, they spared me that fate and humiliation.

Despite—or, in my mind, because of—my final weeks without food, I was truly committed to recovery. In fact, I was certain I was going to ace it. I knew that this was just rerouted perfectionism: the Perfect Girl would have the perfect recovery. But neither I nor my family was particularly interested in thwarting my momentum.

When I left for treatment, I packed for something more like school. In addition to the advanced modernism seminar, I was also missing an American literature course that semester, and I brought with me the syllabus—books by Hawthorne, Stein, Hurston, and Roth among them—to compensate for the classes I was missing. Our days in Paradise were highly structured: three meals, and three snacks, between which we would practice a diverse set of therapy models (individual, group, art, music, and animal). We also had unstructured periods in which to read, talk, or play board games. For the first two months of my six-month stay, I only read. I read during many of the therapies and even brought books with me on our periodic outings—trips to the bowling alley, the movies, Walmart, and the local mall.

My therapist, a Mormon man in his mid-thirties with three children and a pregnant wife, told me that he saw my reading as a defense—a wall constructed between me and the other women in treatment. He also told me that because of my prolonged starvation, I was technically "cognitively impaired." I took this as a challenge. I assumed that he was encouraging me to stop reading—and to stop thinking at all—in order to submit to his will. I tried to impress him in the very same terms that I had worked to impress the men on campus, hoping too that my verbal seduction would be all the more destabilizing because of his Mormon upbringing. I began filling our sessions with pseudo-intellectualized discussions of my anorexic sex life. I asked him, for example, how to reconcile my fear of food with my voracious sexual appetite. But he consistently redirected me away from sex, away from my boyfriend, and toward my other relationships. I was certain I had won this round: he was a prude, a puritan, a phallocrat. Who was impaired now? What's more, I told everyone: I complained that my *therapist*, in *rehab*, for *anorexia*, wouldn't let me talk about *sex*. As a result, I was given a separate therapist with whom to discuss sex in particular, and to my surprise (but probably not hers), I had nothing to say. Sex wasn't the point. Sexual transgression through language was.

My therapist had been right twice over. I was using books as a defense. I wasn't prepared to affiliate with the other women in treatment, and reading was just one way I was trying to distinguish myself from them. I became particularly attached to the work of Philip Roth, whose writing, though not as formally dense as that of Joyce or Cixous, shared a sensibility that I craved while in Paradise: Roth was a consummate prick. He shared the French Feminists' libertine spirit—the provocation of unbridled sexuality on the page—and more than anything, his wit was a wel-come antidote to the sometimes solemn, always earnest, ethos of group therapy. It was also a wedge between me and the women with whom I ate three meals and three snacks a day—with whom I couldn't, crying at the snack cabinet, panicking over dessert, be otherwise invulnerable.

Roth's novels sustained me through the first stage of treatment, a stage unfortunately called "refeeding." The term seemed better suited for livestock and therefore cruel for a group of women whose greatest fear was to be considered a "pig." But we had to confront the animal urge to eat—the urge we wouldn't acknowledge as a need, the need that Roth described as a bestial compulsion—and so we had to be refed. Over the course of two months, with an increasingly calorie-rich diet, I restored my body to a healthy weight, as determined by a team of doctors and nutritionists. Throughout this period, I was expected to participate in group activities that didn't require physical exertion. Meant to simulate "real life" after treatment, many of these activities were more like stress tests for our recoveries. They ranged from the quotidian ("Surprise! Doughnuts for breakfast today") to the surreal ("Group therapy will be done in bikinis today!"). I complied with the program's demands, all the while wondering, *What would Roth say?* These words echoed in my head with the davening rhythm of liturgical prayer:

A Jewish patient confessed that when she decided to enter treatment, her mother replied, "Really? But you're nowhere near as thin as your sister was when she was anorexic."

What would Roth say?

Our bathroom trips were monitored and recorded (B for bowel movement, U for urination) to prevent purging and to track the health of our digestive system.

What would Roth say?

A patient and I made a recovery goal together: to swallow, instead of spit, when we returned home to our boyfriends.

What the fuck would Roth say?

As my weight crept up to my "healthy range," I found myself connecting with the other women, both the patients and the mostly Mormon staff who supervised our meals, snacks, and sleep. Many eating disorder treatment centers have Christianity baked into them like the sacrament. My therapist in New York recommended Paradise to my family, specifically because it didn't have a religious affiliation (I was required to accept Lexapro, not Jesus, for my sins), but because of its location, the facility was staffed almost entirely by Mormon women. With them I shared a mutual fascination: I wanted to know about their lives as young mothers, what it meant to be a Mormon feminist, and the constraints of Mormon underwear on their fashion choices. They wanted to know what beer tasted like, to which I answered, "I don't know. I'm an anorexic."

With the other patients, I talked about the things our anorexia didn't want spoken: our fatphobia, the smallness of our worlds at home, our fears of relapse, our desires for relapse. They told me how much my arrogance about recovery had wounded them. For most of them, this was not their first time in residential treatment. It was their second or third; for one woman it was her seventh. I had stridently entered rehab, insisting that I was going to fully recover then and there. I believed that this confidence was—and has been—essential to the maintenance of my recovery, but I could have kept it to myself. Determined to have the perfect exit from anorexia, as willful as my entrance into it, I hadn't been thinking of them at all. I began to.

That these connections were formed when I was no longer clinically underweight is, I think, no coincidence. The facility "treats to outcome," which means that its treatment teams only recommend that you leave once you have sustained a healthy weight for many months. They care for you until they can reasonably expect you to care for yourself. This process can be exorbitantly expensive, despite a team of employees whose full-time job is to battle with insurance companies. By contrast, many hospitals that supervise "refeeding" for anorexics discharge patients as soon as they meet 90 percent of their designated "healthy weight" (a percentage and a weight based on the abstract calculations of a faulty body mass index paradigm). Nevertheless, when a patient meets 90 percent of her supposed "healthy weight," insurance companies stop paying, and hospitals release patients. The treatment center's model required us to sit in the discomfort of our "refed" bodies. It prioritized recovery maintenance. The hospital model, by contrast, prioritizes physical safety but doesn't support the anorexic's behavioral and emotional recovery after "refeeding." It also lets the anorexic patient remain technically underweight. I have always suspected that the 10 percent difference—the difference between a patient clinically underweight and not—is fuel for relapse, a way for the patient to signal to the world and, most importantly, herself: I am still anorexic. I am not like other women.

I WONDER IF THE FRENCH FEMINISTS, DESPITE THEIR THEORETICAL identification with the womanly body, identified with other women. The question is both too banal and too earnest for them. I am not asking whether they identified with Woman as an imaginary concept or with its constitution in and through language. Those questions are heady and hard and, I believe, worth wrestling with. Instead, I am asking if they believed in sisterhood.

After a string of books about the scandalous writing of Lacan, Cixous, Irigaray, and Kristeva, Jane Gallop wrote one that truly scandalized her readers. The title was *Feminist Accused of Sexual Harassment*. It was 1997, and she had been so accused. Two women graduate students had filed harassment complaints against Gallop, alleging that she had retaliated against them after they rejected her sexual advances. In some way, Gallop's book, and her case, contends with the predicaments that I faced in recovery: Can you be a feminist and still flaunt your power over women? Can you be a feminist and wound other women?

To a certain extent the obvious, if disappointing, answer to these questions is yes. Feminism does not preclude being a messy human. It does not preclude the desire for sex and power. It does not preclude expressions of sex and power that emerge from a woman's relation to her own body (her desire to tame it or expose it, for example) or her relation to other women's bodies. Feminism allows for psychic contradictions. Gallop would be the first to defend this position. Nevertheless, she began her book by insisting that "a feminist sexual harasser seems like a contradiction in terms."

She explains what she means here by returning to 1986, when "sexual harassment" was added to the legal definition of discrimination on the basis of sex or gender. This was a feminist victory. But language, as Gallop knows as well as anyone, is not static. By 1992, the year of her case, the term *sexual harassment* had migrated to mean all sorts of things that Gallop wanted to say are antithetical to feminism. Sexual harassment had come to be affiliated with any expression of sex in professional settings.

As a result, a once-feminist term had been appropriated by feminists' political foes: puritans, those promoting "family values" in the workplace and home, and, by extension, those suppressing women's sexual desire.

One way to think about this changing definition of *sexual harassment* in public discourse is to return to Lacan's psychic crossword—the interlocking chain of signifiers that comprise the Symbolic, shaping desire and modes of relation in our social worlds. Sexual harassment had slipped down the signifying chain, confounding Gallop's expectations and perhaps even her sense of herself as it was reflected back to her by her students, colleagues, and the Name-of-the-Father, which is to say the bureaucratic apparatus of Title IX.

The literal crossword puzzle is a remarkably sharp instrument for gauging these oscillations in language—the way words move away from us, from what we thought they meant. SEXUAL HARASSMENT would have been clued differently in 1992 than in 1986, if it were clued at all. Like an ephemeral expression of the *Oxford English Dictionary*, the puzzle marks the minor and major changes in the vernacular, changes that can have dramatic effects on how we live and relate to others. The evolution of linguistic norms, the raw material of the unconscious in Lacanian terms, is the fount of puzzle history.

Against her accusers and this new definition of *sexual harassment*, Gallop defended herself. She argued that she was being charged with allowing any form of sexuality to invade the realm of pedagogy. This was not, she insisted, a form of discrimination per se. Even the university administrators conceded the point: she had not discriminated, but she had harassed. She was guilty of making her students uncomfortable—of introducing "amorous relations" into the scene of instruction. But wasn't that precisely the point of feminist pedagogy? Wasn't the goal of feminism to disrupt rigidity, to challenge norms, to defend women's desire? You can imagine how a career immersed in the works of the French Feminists might have led Gallop to hold these beliefs deeply.

In the course of her book, Gallop vividly described her own sexual affairs with professors in graduate school, and those she had with students when she was a younger professor, for which no known complaints were filed. She wrote: "Sexual harassment creates an environment that is hostile to a student's education. My experience was the opposite. I was in an environment extremely conducive to my education, a heady atmosphere where close personal contact intensified my desire to learn and my desire to excel. I learned and I excelled; I desired and I fucked my teachers." She conceded that "not all such liaisons are so empowering for the student." What she didn't concede was that the two students who accused her of sexual harassment might have felt harassed. Or that her displays of sexualized power made them feel not just uncomfortable, but exploited or unsafe. She may have been playing the floozie, transgressing social norms through her verbal and physical seduction, but she was also, undeniably, being a total prick.

In writing her book, published in 1997 by Duke University Press, Gallop was continuing to wield her authority over her accusers. The book went into five printings. And with this demonstration of intellectual and professional force, she was not only being a prick. She was picking up the Phallus and exercising a form of symbolic power that intensified the subordination and humiliation of her accusers.

I am not suggesting that Gallop doesn't believe in sisterhood. I believe that she does. Her intellectual and sexual transgressions brought her *closer* to women—and to feminism—in the "heady atmosphere" of the American and French feminist second wave. But in the 1990s, the same strategies of seduction drove a wedge between her and her women students. As I understand it, she wanted her repartee and innuendo to say not just "I like you," but "I *am* like you." That is not, evidently, what her students heard. I don't think this is a structural inevitability: students might have been able to hear what Gallop was meaning to say with her come-ons. But language is volatile, and she couldn't control it. She could, however, have been more empathetic to her students, young women intimidated by their brilliant professor, who held their professional fates in her hands.

There is no doubt in my mind that Gallop injured her students. Nor do I doubt that I injured the women in my life by defining myself in the very terms by which women are judged so harshly under patriarchy: their weight. I suspended my ethical relationships with other women to pursue my own desire. I wanted women's equality and wanted to be better than other women; I wanted women's liberation, but I entrapped myself in an image I thought would be unthreatening to men. A feminist politics can contain the contradiction "feminist sexual harasser," just as it can contain the contradiction "feminist anorexic." We can all be seeking, through language and through activism, a way out of patriarchy. But perhaps a feminist ethics can't contain these same contradictions. Perhaps, in order to connect to women ethically, you need to get off your high horse—drop your displays of power, your 10 percent underweight—and just be willing to identify as one(s).

V

Julia Penelope, Cunning Linguist

SINCE LEAVING PARADISE, I'VE MAINTAINED THAT, OF ALL THE therapies I practiced there, group therapy was the most essential to my recovery. In my early weeks in treatment, that conclusion was unimaginable. The tenor of group therapy, as I first encountered it, was simply too earnest. Those participating practiced a studied form of sensitivity and enforced vulnerability. Where was the irony, the tension-breaking self-deprecation?

Many of the women in the group spoke of feeling like elephants or cows, trapped in enormous bodies that bore no relationship to those that sat before me. It wasn't as though I didn't experience body dysmorphia, obsessing over the smallest sensations of bloat and magnifying them into referenda on my self-worth. But when I felt like an "elephant" or "cow," I'd call it my *What's Eating Gilbert Grape* syndrome, half-facetiously identifying with the mother in that 1993 film who had to be crane-lifted from her house, in her bed, because her morbid obesity had paralyzed her movement. *Gilbert Grape* became a codeword between me and my boyfriend: I was feeling "crazy"; body dysmorphia had paralyzed me; he shouldn't expect me to leave my bed. I liked to think that my cultural reference could diffuse the tragedy of my mental illness. If I couldn't escape it, I could at least make fun of myself.

I fixated on my petty differences from the other women in group therapy, at least in part to repress the very painful differences in our backgrounds. Many of them detailed experiences of sexual abuse, of parents with eating disorders, of gymnastics and ballet, professional and personal commitments that mandated their extreme thinness. My eating disorder, by contrast, seemed to have no legitimate excuse: no developmental, institutional, or sexual trauma could justify my insanity. Perhaps I wouldn't allow myself to indulge in the sentimental vulnerability of group therapy because I felt like my eating disorder was itself an "indulgence"— the highest of anorexic crimes—and something that my personal history simply didn't warrant. Better to dismiss group therapy's clichés than engage with the other women's trauma or my own insecurities. Better to be a snob than an imposter.

In my second week in treatment, my therapist instructed me to share "my story" with the group. His directions were vague because presumably self-evident. "Telling one's story" was a ritual act—a written self-narration that each of us read aloud at some point in treatment—but I chafed against the assignment. How could I recount my history without falling into the sanctifying register that repelled me? I had been trained in my French Critical Theory course to resist all grand narratives and to see any act of self-narration as a stultifying fiction, scripted by external expectations rather than internal truths. I'd learned that therapeutic descriptions of the self were modes of social discipline, inherited from the confessional imperative of Christianity. This is Foucault 101.

Like a good postmodernist, I wrote, instead, a meta-confession. I told "my story" as a list of the various stories I'd been told about myself. In my six years of therapy, I had collected a number of "selves" and a number of explanations for my eating disorder. Recounting my story through the words of my various diagnosticians allowed me to share it with the group in ironic, distantiating air quotes.

My first therapist was convinced that I was a daddy's girl, eager to please my impressive father. If he expected perfection (did he?), my eating disorder offered me a form of protest in his terms: I wielded perfectionism against myself. Perhaps too I was so eager to shape myself in his image that at the onset of puberty, when my gender difference from him had become most glaring, I was trying to stay his "little girl," or maybe even the boy he'd always wanted.

My second therapist, the one who dumped me, was more focused on my mother, whose bond with my sister filled me with jealousy. I had always been told that I was more "like my dad" in temperament and talent. Perhaps my eating disorder was a plea for my mom's attention. Or a way to signal, on the body, that I was truly different from the women in my family, who delighted in each other's company and seemed to have no ambivalence about being born female.

My second therapist also encouraged me to describe my eating disorder in the third person: "she" (anorexia) was not "me." I understood my therapist's suggestion as a means of alleviating my guilt: "she" was destroying the integrity of my family unit; I wasn't. "She" exalted thinness over freedom, self-control over self-fulfillment. Not me. I began to think of "her," my eating disorder, as a parasite, a colonizer. This mode of thinking released me from guilt but also responsibility. I could blame all my sins—deception, inflexibility, free-floating assholery—on "her." Externalizing the disorder also allowed me to think of it as an addiction, something that had deprived me of free will. There are limits to this analogy—the alcoholic can stop drinking, the drug addict can stop using, but the anorexic has to eat. Cessation is very much not the point. But this last framework for my eating disorder, however limited, provided a neat telos to "my story": I had lost control over my eating disorder—"she" was now controlling me—and I needed treatment, so here I was.

I presented my anorexia to the group as a kind of psychological puzzle, guiding my audience through the different framings and psychotherapeutic skills that I had developed over years of thwarted outpatient recovery. I concluded my presentation with one act of confession. I feared that my anorexia was not, after all, a puzzle to be solved—maybe it, and I, just weren't that interesting—but a compulsive behavior that had to be broken. Implicit in my confession was the idea that I didn't need any more psychotherapy. I didn't need the group. I just needed to learn how to eat again, and that was the promise of Paradise. The women protested—and not to tell me that I was, in fact, interesting—but to insist that in telling them "my story," I hadn't actually told them anything about me at all.

———

THE IMPERATIVE TO "TELL YOUR STORY"—AS A POLITICAL AND therapeutic tool—emerged from the consciousness-raising groups of second-wave feminism. Popular in the late 1960s and '70s, consciousness-raising groups took place in women-only spaces, often a living room, in which participants shared and discussed their experiences as wives, mothers, sisters, and workers. For those involved, personal experience was the foundation of political activism. The group sessions were earnest means to subversive ends, although they were often mocked by men in the New Left as "hen parties" or "bitch sessions" masquerading as politics. Those participating, however, were drawing on other revolutionary movements, specifically the Chinese Communist Revolution and the Black civil rights movement, where "speaking pain to recall pain" and "telling it like it is" were seen as essential steps on the way to action, not small talk that stood in its way.

The spirit and method of consciousness-raising groups could not have been more different from that of the French poststructuralists, who took for granted that political liberation was predicated on a liberation from Logos and the conceit of an authentic speaking subject. In the same years that Foucault was proposing a radical "critique of the subject"—one that would demonstrate the constitution of "subjecthood" as a set of historical and rhetorical processes—women and people of color in the United States were finally gaining recognition *as* subjects, legal subjects with civil rights. This would seem conspiratorial. Why would women want to critique, deconstruct, or decenter "the subject" without ever having reaped its political rewards?

Dismissed as chatty by the American New Left and naive by terms of the French one, the women who took part in consciousness-raising groups were not, after all, waging an attack on *logocentrism* or *phallogocentrism*. Their political target was *phallocentrism*, or, in terms more meaningful to most English-speakers, they were fighting the patriarchy. *Visibility*, *solidarity*, and *recognition* were their bywords, and telling their stories was one strategy toward these ends. As Julia Penelope wrote, consciousness-raising "referred very specifically (and exclusively) to the resulting process of change in how we perceived ourselves, our situation in the world, and our relationships to men. . . . [It was] a profound, mind-altering experience that impelled us to change our lives."

Penelope was a self-described "lesbian who couldn't pass," an English and linguistics professor (or a "cunning linguist," as she liked to say) who repeatedly solicited other lesbians to "tell their stories." She edited six volumes of lesbian coming-out stories, stories about lesbians and class, lesbians and culture—and contributed to many more. She was also a talented crossword constructor, publishing *Crossword Puzzles for Women* with a small, independent press at the end of her career in 1995. Penelope's puzzles, like her anthologies, extended the project of consciousness-raising to the page.

It would, in fact, be impossible to complete her crosswords if your feminist consciousness hadn't already been raised. They were filled with references to Penelope's peers in the radical feminist and lesbian separatist movements. Her political commitments—and her "story"—emerge from nearly every entry:

Fourteen letters for "Name of the group that disrupted a NOW (National Organization for Women) convention to protest Lesbian invisibility"
    Answer: LAVENDER MENACE
Four letters for "Pornography is the theory, ___ is the practice"
    Answer: RAPE
Four letters for "Prolific woman writer, abbr."
    Answer: ANON

Many of the answers in Penelope's puzzles related to the cisgender woman's body. BREASTS, CLIT, CERVIX, and PAP [smear] all found their way into a puzzle titled "Our Bodies, Our Selves." Other clues used Penelope's training as a linguist to mislead: VAGINA, for example, was clued as "Sheath" (its Latin etymon), and a whole puzzle called "Venereal Terms" referred not to sex or disease but to "terms of venery," the technical term for collective nouns. Answers included a SWARM of bees, a SCHOOL of fish, a CRIB of writers, and a TRIP of hippies.

Penelope received her PhD in English, with a subfield in linguistics, from the University of Texas at Austin in 1971. For twenty years she taught at the University of Georgia, the University of South Dakota, the University of Nebraska, Washington University, and Amherst College. If *Crossword Puzzles for Women* was an activist's tool, it was also a pedagogical one. Having taught some of the first women's literature courses in the country, Penelope filled her grids with the names of novels and poems by women from Radclyffe Hall to Toni Morrison. Each of her puzzles also included footnotes to the material that inspired them, especially the feminist dictionaries that second-wave academics compiled in the 1970s and '80s: Suzette Haden Elgin's *A First Dictionary and Grammar of Láadan* (1985), Monique Wittig and Sande Zeig's *Lesbian Peoples: Material for a Dictionary* (1979), Cheris Kramarae and Paula A. Treichler's *A Feminist Dictionary* (1985), and Mary Daly's *Websters' First New Intergalactic Wickedary of the English Language* (1987). Like the work of Cixous, Irigaray, and Kristeva, each of these projects took as foundational the idea that language has been indelibly shaped by men to their own advantage. Each imagined the dictionary as a site of patriarchal power and therefore a battlefront in the feminist movement.

Suzette Haden Elgin's dictionary, which was the subject of many of Penelope's clues, outlined the rules of Láadan, her invented language meant to capture the experience of women in its grammar and lexicon. In the Láadan dictionary, *láa* means "to perceive," and *dan* means "language." *Láadan* therefore means "perception language"—or a language equipped to express the perceptions of a woman. As Elgin wrote, Láadan was designed for women all too accustomed to saying, in the language we've inherited from men, "I know I said *that*, but I meant *this*." Láadan's pronouns are gendered, but they are also inflected by feeling: "she" (with a neutral inflection) is *behizh*; "she" (a beloved one) is *bahizh*; "she" (an honored one) is *bihizh*; "she" (a despised one) is *lhebehizh*. Every subject and object pronoun can assume these moody registers. Láadan also accounts for the breadth of a woman's experience in its lexicon, including three distinct words for menopause (*zháadin*, menopause itself; *azháadin*, when it's uneventful; *elazháadin*, when it's welcome) and seven words for menstruation (*osháana*, menstruation itself; *elasháana*, menstruation for the first time; *desháana*, when it's early; *wesháana*, when it's late; *husháana*, when it's painful; *ásháana*, when it's joyful; and *zhesháana*, when it's in sync with other people).

With Láadan, Elgin filled in the gaps of what Wittig and Zeig called, in their dictionary, "lacunaries"—male-made tomes that catalog a partial language written by and for men. Their book, *Lesbian Peoples*, served as another corrective to lacunaries: its lexicon, A–Z, is full of Amazonian tribes and invented lesbian lovers of antiquity whose lives are no more or less true than those lost to history as collected and preserved by men. Wittig was a French Feminist who crossed over into American feminist activist spaces—not just academic ones—although, like Cixous, Kristeva, and Irigaray, her political investments took root in language. In her essay "One Is Not Born a Woman," first presented at New York University in 1979, Wittig departed from the other French Feminists, who found a sexual politics of language in the woman's ecstatic body. Instead, Wittig rejected the category of woman as a "natural" phenomenon, having anything to do with biology. She defined women as a "class . . . [a] political and economic categor[y], not [an] eternal one." More radically, she suggested that only *lesbian* was a term (and a social identity) that could exist beyond the stultifying categories "man" and "woman." A lesbian, she claimed, "is *not* a woman, either economically, or politically, or ideologically." She exists outside of "economic obligation" to men, escaping "forced residence, domestic corvée, conjugal duties . . . by refusing to become or to stay heterosexual."

Penelope wasn't willing to depart from the category of woman, biologically defined, as a platform for feminist activism. But she shared Wittig and Zeig's project in *Lesbian Peoples*, looking for traces of women and lesbians in the vestiges of human history. The entries in their dictionary even served as themes for three of Penelope's crosswords—"Lesbian Peoples," "Amazon Nations," and "Companion Lovers"—that are hardly solvable without recourse to Wittig and Zeig's companion text:

Seven letters for "Valeska and ＿＿＿ (companion lovers of the Bronze Age)"
    Answer: LIBUSSA
Six letters for "＿＿ and Melita (companion lovers who lived in Pelasgia)"
    Answer: THALIE

In her work as a linguist and activist, Penelope also looked for evidence of women and lesbians who might have existed in a mythical world before patriarchy, turning to Old and Middle English to extract them from the buried history of language. Penelope's academic publications focused variously on the overt sexism of early English grammar books; their bogus justifications for the "neuter" pronoun *he* (instead of *she* or *they*); the evolution of words that describe women, which, no matter their origin, inevitably became pejoratives (*crone*, *virago*, and *harpy*, for example); and the standardization of the words *woman* and *female* to make the "fairer sex" a linguistic and social appendage to *man* and *male*.

In a 1979 essay, for example, Penelope attributed the development of the term *woman* to the tenth- and eleventh-century influence of the Christian Empire on the British Isles. Around that time, the term *man*, once a gender-neutral term like *human*, began to be used exclusively to describe the male half of the population. So too did a word specifying women (*wer*) drop out of favor, replaced by the term *woman*, a lexical and social extension of the increasingly dominant gender. Penelope also demonstrated the parallel descent of the term *female* from Old French in the fourteenth century. From *femelle*, the Old French term for "young woman," the English term *female* became standard, on the assumption that its second syllable was, or should be, the term *male*.

In addition to recovering these false cognates and distorted etymologies, Penelope also accounted for the Láadan-like terms that were lost to English in the wake of Christian invasions, writing:

As the range of social opportunities for wimmin continued to narrow, so, too, did the available terms which designated female participation in social activities outside the home. Witness the loss of lócbòre *"free woman,"* guocwena *"battle woman," and* maedenheap, *"band of female warriors."*

Wimmin, instead of *women*, recurred throughout her writings and crossword puzzles. *Wimmin, womon, womyn*—these were popular coinages of the feminist second wave meant to rewrite and, as Penelope argued, restore women to a place in language beyond the subordinating prefix *wo-*.

Philology offered Penelope access to the evolution of patriarchy. Her scholarship led her to the firm belief that "English is a mongrel language," and as a result, she dismissed prescriptivism—the dos and don'ts of twentieth-century English—as a conservative effort to preserve a "heteropatriarchal" world order. Penelope coined this last term—*heteropatriarchy*, or the cultural bias toward men and heterosexuality—in 1982. She was one of its finest elucidators and most vociferous opponents. As a cofounder of New York City's Lesbian Herstory Archives in 1974—a robust institution that collects lesbian books, letters, and ephemera—Penelope not only championed such feminist neologisms (*herstory, wimmin, heteropatriarchy*); she activated them.

The term *herstory*, first used in print in the feminist anthology *Sisterhood Is Powerful* (1970), was relentlessly mocked for its corniness and its etymological fallacy. The English term *history*, from the Greek *historia*, meaning "finding out" and "narrative," has nothing to do with man or "his-story" per se. *Herstory*, however, wasn't a philological intervention; it was a pun. Penelope defended the archive's use of the term in one of its earliest newsletters:

Some women have objected to our use of herstory because they think it is based on a "false" etymology of the word history. We are using herstory because it is our term and no one else's. Frankly, we are not at all interested in the etymology of history, and we are aware of its derivation. But that is not the point. Male etymologies of male terms are irrelevant to our task and its accomplishment; we are interested in constructing our own vocabulary for our purposes and expressive needs.

Because of the very earnestness of their project—less ironic and more activist-minded than the language games of the French Feminists—Penelope and her peers left themselves vulnerable to ridicule. And as Penelope noted, many of those mocking the practitioners of *herstory*, the celebrants of *wimmin*, and the critics of *heteropatriarchy* were women themselves. The comedy writers Deanne Stillman and Anne Beatts, for example, parodied the work of the new feminist lexicographers in their

1976 book *Titters: The First Collection of Humor by Women*. Loosely based on the Whole Earth Catalog, *Titters* included raunchy comics, mock advertisements, mordant "household hints," and a "Feminish Dictionary." Lampooning the feminists who would have English-speakers use *herstory* instead of *history*, *chairperson* instead of *chairman*, and *spokesperson* instead of *spokesman*, Stillman and Beatts pushed the neologisms further, suggesting that *person* should also be stripped of its second syllable (*son*) and replaced with the "truly nondiscriminatory *one*," so that *person* becomes *perone*. Thus *chairman* should be replaced with *chairperone*, *spokesman* with *spokesperone*. "Even," they wrote, "the word *female* must be altered to the more fair and meaningful term *feperone*, which rhymes with *pepperone*." Taking the logic of feminist renaming to its illogical extreme, *Titters*'s "Feminish Dictionary" implicitly asked: Where do the feminist language games end? Was it worth sounding stupid—or worse, self-serious—for the sake of political correctness?

Such lightly reactionary humor was accompanied by genuine resistance from feminist linguists. Robin Lakoff and Mary Ritchie Key, pioneers of the new field of sociolinguistics, which studied the social forces that shape language use, considered coinages like *herstory* and *wimmin* quixotic at best, and more often counterproductive. Lakoff's *Language and Woman's Place* (1975), for example, documented the differences in women's and men's vocabularies and syntax. Women, she observed, tended to use polite euphemisms, whereas men traded obscenities; women softened their statements with "tag-questions" ("It's time for dinner, isn't it?"), whereas men felt no need to soften the blow of their demands. (The exceptions to Lakoff's generalizations, she claimed, were "the effeminate homosexual, the anti-capitalist hippie, and the effete male professor," whose exclusion from institutionalized male power, as she perceived it, allowed them to traffic in stereotypical female discourse.)

Lakoff argued that discourse shaped the social roles that women were allowed to assume and have therefore oppressed them. With this, Penelope would agree. But Lakoff ultimately defended linguistic norms and sounded a warning to feminist wordsmiths. That the neuter pronoun in English is *he*—in the sentence, "If a person wants to change the world, *he* should start by changing language," for example—caused her no consternation. Conceding that "this lexical and grammatical neutralization is related to the fact that men have been the writers and the doers," Lakoff didn't think it necessarily relegated women to second-class status in language. Efforts to change such evidently benign tics of usage, she thought, were "futile"; worse still, trying to replace words like *history* with *herstory* or *women* with *wimmin* was "both ludicrous and totally fallacious." She lamented, "If this sort of stuff appears in print and in the popular media as often as it does, it becomes increasingly more difficult to persuade men that women are really rational beings."

Lakoff's conservatism—and her insistence that her project was merely to describe the sexism of common usage, not to prescribe its reform—inspired Penelope's disdain. She saw Lakoff and others of her ilk as inheritors of a patriarchal double bind: men were allowed to innovate in language (see: *litteringture*), while women, as grammarians, librarians, and school marms, were meant to uphold man-made linguistic norms. The better that women were at mastering English's rules, the more they would be ridiculed for "stifling the linguistic creativity of generations of little boys." By this logic, Lakoff was no better than Miss Fidditch, a pedantic stereotype meant to relegate women to the position of language's custodians, not its innovators.

Penelope had no interest in accommodating English speakers' reflexive use of sexist words and grammar. Instead, she spent her life agitating against what she called, in a clever shorthand, *PUD*, appropriating the slang term for penis as an acronym for the "Patriarchal Universe of Discourse." But her break with Lakoff and other sociolinguists who shared Lakoff's relatively moderate feminist politics was only one of her very public repudiations of a feminist faction. As Penelope's friend Kathy Munzer wrote in her obituary, "Julia could be either your best friend or your worst enemy, with no in between." Interpersonal and political ruptures with other feminists eroded Penelope's participation in the women's and lesbian liberation movements, until she formally broke with them in 1994, the very year in which she wrote her separatist crossword puzzles—her final effort at consciousness-raising.

PENELOPE WAS BORN JULIA PENELOPE STANLEY IN MIAMI IN 1941. (In 1980, she dropped the patronym Stanley, "for the obvious reasons," she wrote.) If there is one theme that emerges from her prolific body of work—essays and polemics, academic articles, memoirs, and crossword puzzles—it is the power of language to shape identity and to wound. Between 1941 and her death in 2013, she—a cisgender woman—successively identified as transsexual, homosexual, butch, a radical feminist, and a lesbian separatist. But when she picked up a new term with which to understand herself, she did not just drop the old one; she repudiated it—and those who still used it—with righteous venom. To tell Julia Penelope's "story," then, is to tell the story of her evolution in language, her willingness to use words as political and interpersonal weapons, and her unyielding belief in the potency of naming.

Julia Penelope at her home in Lubbock, Texas.
CREDIT: From the documentary *Lesbiana: A Parallel Revolution*
© 2012 Myriam Fougère. Used with permission.

"Since before I can remember, I've been at war with my body," Penelope wrote in an unpublished essay she titled "My Life: A Cartesian Dilemma." Born with her umbilical cord around her neck, Penelope considered this fact a portent of her "mind-body problem"—the constant betrayal of her body, always attacking her robust mind. "I never wanted to be female," she wrote. "Intuitively I knew that being female was a 'bad' thing. . . . I couldn't accept the weakness, passivity, and powerlessness that such 'femaleness' required." When she was four years old, Penelope told her mother that "God had made a mistake," that she was meant to be a boy. After what she described as a "thorough physical examination" by a doctor, Penelope was assured that no mistake was made, but she was not reassured. Upon seeing a story in *Confidential* magazine about Christine Jorgensen's 1952 "sex-change" surgery in Denmark, the first of its kind to be publicized in the United States, Penelope pleaded with her mother to take her to Copenhagen to undergo surgery and fix God's "mistake."

"I am not, nor have I ever been a 'transgendered person,'" Penelope wrote in 1995. "I consider my belief that I was a male 'trapped' in a female body as one among many theories I constructed to account for the fact that I, a female, wanted to love only other females." Being told repeatedly that only boys could love girls, Penelope constructed a syllogism to explain her difference:

Only men can love women.
I love women.
∴ I am a man.

Penelope's childhood was transient and traumatic. Her father died in a plane crash when she was five, and her mother sent her to live with her grandparents and then her godparents. From there, she was sent to an orphanage in Miami for six months until her mother was solvent enough to take her home. Upon returning, Penelope found that her mother had a new boyfriend, Penelope's soon-to-be stepfather, who began molesting her when she was ten. His assaults intensified Penelope's alienation from her body: "I began to gain a lot of weight," she wrote. "Although the strategy was not conscious on my part—I didn't say to myself, 'I'll gain a lot of weight to make my body repulsive to him'—looking back, I understand that my need to repel him made growing larger a useful way to exist under the same roof with him." As anorexia functioned for many of the women in Paradise who had been sexually assaulted in their childhoods, Penelope's fatness, as she described it, facilitated her psychic disembodiment. At war with her body, she retreated into the abstract realm of language, taking refuge in her brain.

When she was nine, Penelope encountered the word *homosexual* in the stacks of her local library. She described the scene of reading as a site of revelation:

Few of [the books] mentioned Lesbians, but I read and re-read the passages that described "mannish" wimmin with short, cropped hair; who wore men's clothes; wimmin who were "tough" and "swaggered." Wimmin defined by their love of other wimmin. And I thought to myself, "That's me!" I was excited. I knew what I was! I loved other wimmin! Now I had a "name" for it! I was a "homosexual." The knowledge was priceless to me, and I carried it secretly and proudly inside me.

In high school, Penelope ventured into Miami's gay subculture, sharing community and a lexicon with gay men who understood her to be one of them: a gay butch.

In 1959, Penelope enrolled in Florida State University. At the time, the Florida Legislative Investigation Committee, led by state senator Charley Johns, was surveilling the state's public schools, firing and expelling suspected homosexual teachers and students. Founded in 1956, the McCarthyite committee had failed to identify Communist sympathizers in the state's NAACP chapter, the primary target of Johns's hate, and shifted its investigation to homosexuals instead. Penelope was one of the 110 casualties of Johns's campaign, only a handful of whom were lesbian women. In her freshman year, she was called into the dean's office. Known on campus for her "indiscretion," as she described it, Penelope was asked to leave FSU and was promised a "clean transcript" if she transferred to the University of Miami. The women in Penelope's dormitory wrote a petition to the university administration, claiming that she had "never bothered" any of them and that they didn't think her "personal problem was just cause for expulsion." Their protest went unheard.

Despite the dean's promise of a clean record, Penelope was received at the University of Miami with suspicion and animus. After eight weeks, she was expelled on the pretextual grounds that she had "men sleeping in her apartment." The gender swap here was presumably meant to preserve Penelope's dignity. Before she left Miami for the City College of New York, where she graduated with a degree in English and linguistics, the dean of students urged her to seek therapy because "society needed [her] mind." As Penelope recounted it, she replied, "How can you ask me to change, to not be myself, so that the very society that wants me to change can then have use of my brain?" The dean, she reported, "didn't have an answer for that; no one will."

While Penelope was in New York, the Johns Committee ignited a scandal that precipitated its undoing. In 1964, it published a pamphlet, *Homosexuality and Citizenship in Florida*, which subsequently circulated as "the Purple Pamphlet" because of the dark lavender abstraction on its cover. The pamphlet's purpose was to alert Florida's citizens to the so-called menace of homosexuality. "It behooves us all," the committee members wrote, "to know the nature of the homosexual . . . to define for him, and for ourselves, the conditions which govern his presence." This last line reads something like a premonition: the pamphlet's contents were meant as much for a gay reader as a straight one ("to define *for him* . . . the conditions which govern his presence"). But if gay readers were meant to be intimidated and indicted by the pamphlet, they could just as easily read it as an instruction manual.

The pamphlet included reproduced images of gay male sex (kissing,

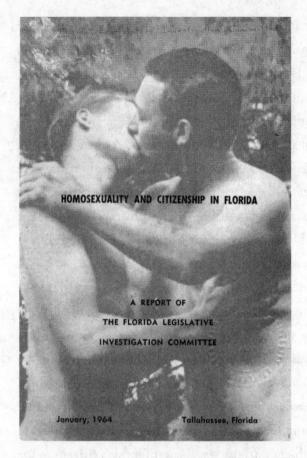

HOMOSEXUALITY AND CITIZENSHIP IN FLORIDA

A REPORT OF
THE FLORIDA LEGISLATIVE
INVESTIGATION COMMITTEE

January, 1964   Tallahassee, Florida

Title Page,
Homosexuality and
Citizenship in Florida,
1964.
CREDIT: University of
Florida Digital Collections.

bondage, a blow job through a glory hole) and reprints of child pornography reputedly found in the "catalogue of a supplier of homosexual erotica." Most of it, however, was devoted to a "Glossary of Homosexual Terms and Deviant Acts," with entries including:

ANILINGUS: Sexual pleasure obtained through the use of the mouth on the anus.

CHI-CHI: (Pronounced she-she). Usually a room or apartment very effeminately decorated. Lace works, drapes, etc.

DOG'S LUNCH: Either a normal or a gay person whose looks and actions are unattractive to the point of non-association.

RED LIGHT: A raid which is starting without enough time to leave safely. Only time enough to change places with the other homosexuals to make couples of the opposite sex and to destroy all incriminating material. This warning is given by rapid repetition through the club or bar.

TYPES OF QUEENS:

69 queen

Browning queen

Reaming queen

Belly-wh queen

Hand queen

Golden-shower queen

(All of the above are fairly well self-explanatory.)

It is little wonder that the Purple Pamphlet made its way up the East Coast, where it landed in New York City's smut shops, circulating as pornography. In the hands of New York City's gay readers, the pamphlet operated as Penelope's crosswords did: a way of signaling that "we" (queers) don't use language like "you" (straights) do. Difference, registered in language, is not just a way to be "outed"; it's also a way to be included—to be legible as "in."

In Miami and New York, Penelope's social identity was rigidly self-enforced, her behavior and identity adhering tightly to the prescriptions of slang definitions: she was a *butch* (a masculine-presenting lesbian), sometimes a *stone butch* (a butch who doesn't allow other lesbians to touch her, although she fucks other lesbians), and sometimes a *kept butch* (a butch who is supported by another woman, often a sex worker or mistress of a wealthy man). The social power that germinated in these names was made painfully evident to Penelope when she was only sixteen, after a night with a self-proclaimed *femme* named Stefanie. She wrote:

Stefanie wanted to know if I minded if she made love to me. Surprised, I said, "Of course not." But it was near dawn; I was exhausted and drunk. The last thing I remember is her beginning to make love to me. Then I must've passed out. It was afternoon by the time I made it down to the gay beach. One friend after another came up to me and asked me if I'd gone "femme." At first, I was puzzled, but after I'd been asked the same question a few times, I finally asked someone why they wanted to know. The reply is still accurate in my mind: "Stefanie is going up and down the beach telling everyone that you flipped for her. . . . She's saying you've turned femme for her." . . . I knew, as surely as I felt humiliated, that Stefanie was, by her claims, asserting that she had taken a large measure of power from me, and it was a "loss" I vowed never to repeat. . . .

For fifteen years, no matter how badly I might have wanted to let another woman touch me, no matter how badly I craved sexual release, I remained untouched and untouchable. By refusing to allow another Lesbian to give me any measure of pleasure, I felt in my guts that I thereby retained my power and my autonomy.

When, in 1972, Penelope began participating in the consciousness-raising groups of the feminist movement, she renounced the terms *butch* and *femme* altogether. Like *homosexual* a decade earlier, these terms had provided stability for her young identity, but their social props became psychosexual albatrosses. Feminism, she claimed, had released her from a self-punishing "stone butch" masquerade.

Penelope's thinking was highly informed by binaries: mind/body, in group/out group, but the antinomy that ultimately shaped her academic work was +MAN/-MAN, a semantic theory she defined to understand the Patriarchal Universe of Discourse. She wrote, "If one accepts the idea that biological sex is a significant feature [of language], one might suppose that this distinction would result in semantic features like +MALE and +FEMALE. But this isn't the case. Instead, sexual dimorphism is coded as +MALE and -MALE. . . . Females are -MALE in the semantic structure of English." There were no words, according to Penelope, that positively defined a woman. Woman was only ever defined by her lack of male attributes. Using her 1967 Random House dictionary as her evidence, Penelope demonstrated that while *masculine* means "having the qualities or characteristics of a man; manly; virile; strong; bold," *feminine* is merely the inverse of these qualities.

Penelope revealed the pervasiveness of this +MAN/-MAN structure by searching out its limit case in the words *womanish* and *mannish*. A womanish man (one who "cries . . . crosses his legs at the knee, bends from the waist down to pick something up") is behaving as a "not man," a -MAN. A mannish woman (one who "is aggressive, stoic, or withdrawn," who is "too tall" or "weighs too much") is behaving as a +MAN. This logic informed Penelope's principled repudiation of butch/femme relationships in the lesbian community, a position that allied her with a growing camp of pro-androgyny feminists but also antagonized many others. She wrote:

Lesbians shouldn't need to defend "femininity" or feel as though being gentle, kind, tender, interested in fabric and texture, or a host of other

personality traits has anything to do with being a female or a "femme." ...
Similarly, Lesbians can enjoy bicycling, playing softball, repairing cars, rid-
ing motorcycles, working in construction, and being hostile to men without
calling themselves "masculine" or "butch." Accepting those labels to describe
our predilections is a trap, and it perpetuates heteropatriarchal ideology as
though it belonged in a Lesbian context.

Penelope held fast to this position, using it as a cudgel against
lesbians who still identified as femme or butch, especially those who
practiced versions of homosexual sex that, Penelope felt, reproduced
heteropatriarchal ideology. Lesbian sex that involved penetration and
sex toys, sadomasochistic sex, and the production of lesbian erotica
became targets of her political suspicion and ultimately her ire. Identifying increasingly with the radical feminist and lesbian separatist
movements, Penelope felt that heterosexual feminists and lesbians who
enjoyed these performances of domination and submission—who celebrated a range of sexual practices traditionally associated with male
pleasure—were betraying the tenets of feminism.

Although the targets of Penelope's critique—sometimes called "sex-
positive" feminists or "pro-sex" lesbians—found her views to be repressive or reactionary, Penelope understood her politics to be consistent with
her long-standing rejection of the Patriarchal Universe of Discourse. In a
1992 essay called "The Lesbian New-Rotics: Bogus or Breakthrough?" she
attacked Audre Lorde and Sabrina Sojourner for their efforts to "reclaim"
the terms *erotic* (Lorde) and *femininity, cunt, slit,* and *gash* (Sojourner).
Lorde's famous 1974 essay "The Uses of the Erotic" enjoined lesbians to
see erotic satisfaction as a source of power and self-knowledge—and to
find in the experience of touching another woman's skin or feeling the
sun against their back a catalyst for physical, spiritual, and political ac-

tivation. Lorde was advocating an embodied Black feminist politics, but Penelope's unusually persistent investment in language had her parsing Lorde's words instead of engaging her political propositions.

For Penelope, efforts to reclaim words from their past circulation in the "male pornographic tradition" were indeed "bogus." She understood the project of "reclaiming" very narrowly: words that had "negative" connotations in the Patriarchal Universe of Discourse (*dyke, queer*) could be redefined positively for feminist and lesbian usage, but words that already had "positive" implications in PUD (*femininity, erotic, slit*) could not. She explained, "I can't think of a word we've reclaimed that is positively valued in PUD. Can we try to 'reclaim' a word so laden with positive associations in male discourse? Is it possible to eradicate all of its meanings and replace them with our own? I don't think so."

During the 1980s, Penelope's efforts at lesbian liberation intensified her own isolation from mainstream culture and from intersectional feminist community. She spent much of her time organizing and participating in women-only and lesbian-only festivals and retreats and penning angry essays in feminist and lesbian publications about the trans women and mothers who brought their male children to these events. Her language was defensive, indignant, and ultimately grossly transphobic: "They made a choice: they decided to have a baby. Fine. That's their choice. But what about OUR choices? What about my choice NOT to have a baby? What about my right to have a Lesbian-only space? What about the rights of Lesbians who say we don't want pricks in our space? Why are OUR rights ignored, trashed, ridiculed?" Her neat linguistic binary +MALE/-MALE may have contributed to her biological essentialism—her conviction that sex was strictly binary and that binary sex roles were always and only an expression of patriarchal dominance.

Gay men, transgender people, and bisexual and heterosexual allies became Penelope's explicit foes. As a visiting professor at Amherst College in 1988, she began organizing Northampton's Lesbian Liberation March. When, in 1991, the organizing committee was joined by gay men and bisexuals who wanted to rename the event the Lesbian, Gay, and Bisexual Pride March, Penelope was incensed again. "The rhetoric of inclusion," she wrote, "was a smoke screen for lesbian-hating." When she spoke at a committee meeting, defending the march's history and original name, "bis, hets, and gay men booed and hissed and tried to, literally, drown our voice," she wrote. Those with social privilege—male privilege, heterosexual privilege—were reproducing in queer spaces the discrimination that she had experienced her whole life as a lesbian woman. The "bis, hets, and gay men" saw it differently and launched a brutal campaign against Penelope and her peers. She recalled:

Outline, a local newsletter, published articles in which the lesbians organizing the march were called "lesbian fascists from hell" and accusing them of "oppressing bisexuals." Graffiti beg[a]n to appear regularly on the walls of the bathrooms at Bart's (an ice cream store in downtown Northampton) saying that "Lesbians are sexual Nazis, and Bisexuals are their Jews."

This was not the first time that she had been called a fascist; nor was it her last. Penelope's scrutiny and criticism of other women's sex lives— and her public dissent from Lorde and Sojourner, lesbians of color—had led women in the movement to call her a racist, a neo-Nazi, and a fascist and to compare her to J. Edgar Hoover, Jerry Falwell, Hitler, Stalin, and the Khmer Rouge.

In 1977, Penelope had organized a historic panel at the Modern Language Association on "Lesbian Language and Literature," featuring

Mary Daly, Audre Lorde, Adrienne Rich, and Judith McDaniel. More than seven hundred people attended. In her opening remarks, Penelope said, "Through language, I define myself to myself; I can see myself. My language goes before me, illuminating my actions; through my language, I create myself, for myself, and for other women." By the early 1990s, the only woman on the panel with whom Penelope still spoke was Mary Daly, a committed separatist who famously refused to teach male students in her Advanced Feminist Theory classes at Boston College. To the other women on the panel and many more, Penelope had created a rigid feminist lexicon and worldview that denied them their rights to be women and lesbians as they wanted to be. In response, they gave Penelope ugly names—names "recovered" from history that were meant to wound her as she had wounded them.

Though Penelope's inflexibility led her to exclusionary and even hateful positions, her commitment to lesbian separatism was, in her view, utopian. Imagining a world for women that, as historians told it, had never existed, she was building upon the recovery efforts of the feminist dictionaries that filled her puzzles and the work of the Lesbian Herstory Archives that she helped to found. Such recovery projects needn't be transphobic, and they weren't for Penelope's cofounders at the archive, who recognized trans women as women with herstories that had been expunged from existing collections. The traces of lesbian life before Stonewall—love letters hidden in attics, remains of Amazonian tribes—fueled their collective dreams of a world that valued lesbian experience. These recovered traces inspired their fantasies of a lesbian past that became a guide for the future they hoped to build. In these terms, recovery was not only an act of discovery but also an act of invention.

IN RECOVERING FROM ANOREXIA, I HAD TO DEFINE MYSELF ANEW: I couldn't simply return to who I was before my eating disorder. I could barely piece together the experience of my life before it. I used to dance and play basketball, activities I stopped because they fueled the appetite I wanted to suppress. I loved movies, but my obsessive fixation on food distorted my relationship to the screen. I would have been hard-pressed to tell you the plot of *Casablanca*, but I could tell you everything that was eaten at Rick's Café Américain. I had worked to deny my life before anorexia and to supplant it with a new identity shaped in "her" image. And though I had once been a nonanorexic child, I had never been a nonanorexic woman. In order to recover, then, I had to look as much to the past as to a speculative future, inventing the woman I wanted to be.

For some women in treatment, recovery extended the project of denying their past selves. A few moved permanently to Utah or to California, deeming the East Coast, the site of their disorder, a trigger. My fantasy of recovery was relational, not geographical. I was lonely, and I was looking for a new way of relating to women, as well as my own womanhood. This was why I came to value group therapy—not necessarily our biweekly meetings, guided by a therapist, of which I actually remember very little—but the practice of living with women and of learning to support each other in our shared recovery project.

When I told "my story" to the group, one woman was particularly cutting in her response. In her late thirties, she was the oldest of the patients. Having been to many inpatient treatment centers, she wielded her experience as strength, not weakness. She commanded respect, and although I wasn't prepared to admit it, I was scared of her. As I finished reading "my story" aloud, she was the first to break the silence that followed. In a turn of words that she knew would pierce me, she said I had "failed the assignment." I burst into tears, taking refuge in my therapist's office, begging him to reassure me that I was, of all irrelevant things, a good writer. I had clearly missed the point of the exercise on many levels. The next evening, after our last meal and snack of the day, she pulled me aside. She didn't apologize for calling me a failure—that would have been insincere, and she was implacably honest. She didn't bring up my story at all. Instead, she told me that she had noticed a disturbing pattern in my behavior.

At the start of treatment, we were given little choice in our meals: menus and portions were set, and plates were to be cleaned. During the three snacks of the day, we had more choice: bins in the snack closet were labeled 1, 2, and 3. It didn't take much deduction to figure out that these numbers stood for calories: snacks of 100, 200, and 300 calories, respectively. Depending on our meal plans, we knew how much we had to eat, but we could choose what we would. There was one caveat: each of us was only allowed one fruit a day. Our choices were recorded in a ledger that was inspected to ensure that we were not falling into "food ruts" or flouting any of our prescribed meal plans.

The aberrant behavior that she had noticed had gone undetected by the supervising staff: I was saving my one-fruit-a-day for my evening snack. I would have nuts, yogurt, crackers, and cheese as my first or second daily snack, but I waited before bed to have my apple or orange. I had created this ritual because fruits were, by comparison to the rest of the day's intake, "safe" in my mind. It was an inverted display of delayed gratification: I rewarded myself with fruit for making it through two "unsafe" snacks, breakfast, lunch, and dinner. This food rule of my own invention was a vital, if totally arbitrary and calorically insignificant, connection to my eating disorder, and I was terrified to break it. When she called me on this "behavior"—a treatment euphemism for "symptom"—I was horrified. More pathetic than attaching my self-worth to the time at which I ate an apple was someone else knowing the perverted mechanism I'd developed to maintain a relationship with anorexia.

Did she need to call me a failure again? Was she pleased with herself for finding the flaw in my otherwise spotless performance of recovery? I began to cry again, not sure if I should defend myself against her accusation or even accuse her of her own rehab crime: focusing on other women's food choices. Wasn't that a "behavior"?

Before I could embarrass myself more, she embraced me tightly, reminding me that holding on to food rituals would only delay my recovery. To get better—to regain control over my life—I would first have to relinquish control. I might even want to concede that a "spotless performance of recovery" was a fiction worth relinquishing too. She was firm but not punitive. Hers was the first hug I'd received from a woman other than my mother in almost six years. Holding another woman, another anorexic committed to recovery, was an unexpected form of therapy. We made knowing eye contact the next morning when, after breakfast, I picked a pear for my first snack.

It's a feminist truism that patriarchy pits women against each other, turning us into competitors for male attention and token professional achievements. I had heard horror stories about psych units and treatment centers in which anorexics fueled each other's disorders, becoming rehab rivals or, worse, teaching each other new ways to restrict food, burn calories, and manipulate the staff. I don't know why the women in Paradise were all so committed to recovery—or why I got so lucky—but ours was a collective liberationist project. We all wanted to be free from the disorder's grip on our lives. But freedom from anorexia is no feminist guarantee. Paradise didn't exist outside of patriarchy.

Twelve weeks into treatment I was convinced that I was approaching my "healthy weight range." The nutritionists and doctors on staff didn't tell us when we were getting close to the goal they had set for us; they only let us know when we had met it. After weeks of a steadily increasing meal plan, I anticipated each meeting with the nutritionist, desperate for her to tell me that I could begin "weight maintenance." The objective of this second stage of treatment was not "refeeding" but "intuitive eating." Over time, women in this second phase were given more control over their food intake: we could stop measuring portions; we no longer had to clean our plates. We were instead tasked with rediscovering hunger and fullness cues that had been effaced by years of self-imposed starvation. We were meant to confront our own "Cartesian dilemmas"—to begin heeding our body's requests for food over the prescriptions of our merciless minds.

My desire to stop refeeding and start weight maintenance was a wish held at once in good and bad faith. At that point in treatment, I was stuffed. I was uncomfortably full all of the time, even when I woke up. But, of course, my eating disorder was uncomfortable too. I was panicked by the weight I was gaining and increasingly anxious for my treatment team to tell me that I could stop. After one particularly disappointing meeting with the nutritionist, the youngest woman in the group approached me.

Just before I'd arrived in treatment, she had turned eighteen and was moved from the adolescent to the adult unit. We had lived together for more than two months but had spoken few words. She was beautiful. I broke the facility's rule of not talking about other patients' appearances to tell her that I thought she looked like Marilyn Monroe. She had no idea who I was talking about. I insisted that we couldn't have been more different. Her sexual confidence was not a French Feminist masquerade but something that seemed far more organic. Once when we returned from a meal in town—two of us crying over our entrees—she announced that she'd gotten the waiter's number. I exoticized her, I ridiculed her, and I admired her.

Sitting next to me after my meeting with the nutritionist, she leaned in to console me. She told me that, based on her stints in hospitals and her time at the adolescent unit, she thought that I was close to my "healthy weight range." It was as presumptuous as it was reassuring. "You're hot," she told me, still equating hotness with thinness, if not emaciation. "They don't want you to be *not* hot. What good would that do them?" We hugged. Hers was an anti-feminist pep talk—encouraging me to think that I could "reclaim" my femininity from my eating disorder, if not from heteropatriarchy. As much as her confidence encouraged me, it also scared me. I had to confess to myself, in terms more honest than I'd ever admitted—in terms that my anorexia had, in fact, been masking from me for years—how much I wanted to hear what she'd said.

The perverse dictates of my eating disorder—mandating when and how I ate fruit, for example—had allowed me to think that my relationship to hotness and thinness was more complicated than the directives of heteropatriarchy, which would simply equate them. I maintained that my eating disorder wasn't a symptom of vanity or an effort to conform to repressive beauty standards. I had to be more interesting than that. But maybe I wasn't. Maybe I had created yet another puzzle for myself when the answer to my distorted body image was devastatingly clear: I wanted to look good in the terms that I knew. I wanted to be beautiful, and I wanted to be thin.

———

The Riddles of the Sphinx

THOSE WHO SEE EATING DISORDERS AS AN ADDICTION RECOM-
mend that anorexics in recovery continue to call themselves anorexic.
Just as the sober alcoholic is never not an alcoholic, so the anorexic in
recovery is never not an anorexic. This strategy is meant to produce vigi-
lance against the forces that would have us relapse. When I left Paradise,
I held to this practice, firmly believing that even though my weight was
"restored" and my eating was "intuitive," I was still an anorexic. It was
hubris to claim a new identity for myself. I'm now ambivalent about the
value of claiming anorexia as a life-long condition. I identify inconsis-
tently: sometimes it's liberating to see anorexia as a "past self"; sometimes
it's liberating to say, "I'm an anorexic," knowing that the disorder was not
a parasite for which I was a passive host, but a part of me and "my story."

When gaining weight in treatment, I imagined the day that I would
wake up in a new, nonanorexic body. I would arise from bed both me
and not-me. This was the fantasy of my eating disorder in the first place:
at the age of fifteen, I woke up one morning and identified as anorexic.
I could be a new person—a sick person, sure—but at least my identity
would be stable. Defining my body as sick forestalled the discomfort of
having to claim it as my own. But instead of precipitous and surreal, my
physical metamorphosis in Paradise was slow and deliberate. I was surprised, if not somewhat confused, by the anticlimactic ease with which
I could claim, after months of weight gain, "My body is still my body." I
am still me.

In 1993, Julia Penelope wrote, "I've called myself a lot of things in
my life. . . . I'm not equally proud of all the labels I've chosen, but I won't
deny them." It is my belief that Penelope's affinity for labels and her "war
with her body" were psychic comorbidities. Self-identifying so strongly
with words allowed her to deny a basic identification with her body.

Ultimately, Penelope repudiated all of the labels that had defined her adult life: homosexual, butch, radical feminist, and lesbian separatist.

In 1994, she wrote a mass letter addressed to "lesbians who know me well, not so well, and some not at all," a Dear John to the lesbian movement. Penelope had just finished editing *Lesbian Culture: An Anthology*, when she learned that Caryatis Cardea, the editor of *Sinister Wisdom*, the lesbian quarterly that had published Penelope's work since 1976, was writing a public rebuke of the book and of Penelope herself. The authors included in Penelope's collection were too white (75 percent white by the journal editors' calculation); some of the included work contained "oppressive content" (a photo of a white woman wearing a parody T-shirt with the words "Camp Nonwannaweenie" on it; a poem that describes tofu as "slimy" and "weirdo"; a rap lyric by two white women; and a "lesbian fantasy about constructing a nipple atop a mesa in Australia called Ayer's Rock [sic]," a sacred Indigenous site). In short, Penelope's collection was far from representative of "lesbian culture."

In her sixteen-page letter to all the lesbians she knew and some she didn't, Penelope defended herself and her book against the charge. Most tragically, she confessed that she had reached out to several lesbians of color—Gloria Anzaldúa, LindaJean Brown, Paula Gunn Allen, Cherríe Moraga, and Barbara Ruth—none of whom wanted to be associated with her edited collection. Despite her resolute identification with the lesbian community, she could no longer realistically call herself part of it. She wrote:

I made a tragic mistake in 1972 when I wholeheartedly embraced feminism and then separatism. Now, in order to try to salvage something of the rest of my life, I am leaving. . . . In the more than twenty years I have considered myself a lesbian activist, a radical-lesbian, a lesbian-feminist, a lesbian separatist, I have been trashed and vilified by other lesbians. . . . All my life,

I have been hounded out of places, thrown out of schools, fired from jobs, not given jobs, been excluded from groups, dismissed, and . . . trivialized. Silly me. I believed, when I finally began to identify myself as a feminist and as a gay liberationist . . . that I had found a "home" finally. . . . I understand now that I do not belong among lesbians, and it hurts me more than any of you can imagine to have to say this. It means that I belong nowhere, and that is a painful realization for me.

Like Andrea Dworkin's 1983 essay "Goodbye to All This," in which Dworkin bid farewell to "Pat, cow, cunt, silly bitch, whatever obscenity you are organizing for the right to call other women this week" and "all you proud, pro-sex, liberated *Cosmo* intellectuals," Penelope was writing her goodbye to the fractious lesbian movement and its obsession with using the "right words" not the "wrong" ones. Unlike Dworkin, whose essay teems with self-righteous antagonism and the cackle of triumph over her former movement foes, Penelope's letter is a testament to her defeat. After all, she never really repudiated the rigid nominalism of the feminist and lesbian movements. Perhaps, in identifying so strongly with an idea—with radical feminism, with lesbianism separatism—Penelope failed to identify with the people who would be her community. In repudiating her "past selves" and old labels, she repudiated individuals too.

The editors at *Sinister Wisdom* actively discouraged lesbians from buying the *Lesbian Culture* anthology, which did not sell well among the readers Penelope most hoped it would reach. No longer attending lesbian-only and women-only festivals, no longer organizing lesbian liberation marches or lesbian language panels at conferences, Penelope focused the intensity of her political will on her handwritten crossword puzzles. They became the exclusive site of her feminist and lesbian activism and her unyielding desire for political change through linguistic change:

Eight letters for "One who is Self-identified"
    Answer: SPINSTER
Five letters for "Self-reliant, independent"
    Answer: CATTY
Nine letters for "She's not a governor's peer"
    Answer: GOVERNESS
Ten letters for "They were never peers of courtiers"
    Answer: COURTESANS

In her debates with other linguists, Penelope spent little time worrying about the field's "chicken-egg disputes": Does language change culture, or does culture change language? For Penelope, the debate itself was a way for academics to cede their responsibility to care for others through language—to cultivate a lexicon and grammar that doesn't exclude or insult. "Every time we step into our classrooms," she wrote, "we must ask ourselves: 'which changes in whose language by what methods for what reasons?'"

Moving from classroom to classroom, from departments that wouldn't promote her because she was an out lesbian or who dismissed her work as unserious, Penelope stopped trying to find teaching positions in 1988. She assumed freelance copy editing and lexicography jobs and began treating the crossword puzzle as her new classroom, the new arena for her pastoral care of the English language. Penelope was an expert at dismantling the arguments against her activist approach to language. "We need to examine the strategies utilized by opponents of linguistic change in order to understand why reason and justice have failed to convince a majority of our colleagues," she wrote. To that end, she outlined the "six arguments against eradicating sexist usage," summarized here:

1. Denial: Language is neutral. Speakers use language in sexist ways only if they are sexist.

2. Negativity: Sexism is a structural problem. We have to readdress the systems that perpetuate it (compulsive heterosexuality, employment discrimination) before language will change as a consequence.

3. Creativity: Asking speakers to change the way they use language stifles their creativity.

4. Trivialization: The problem of sexism in language is trivial by comparison to "real" issues like equal pay.

5. Aesthetic: There is sexism in language, but changing it sounds "awkward" or "clumsy."

6. Censorship: Feminist censors are curtailing free speech.

Although Penelope's political trajectory might lead us to want to simply renounce her and give her new labels in the meantime—a TERF (trans-exclusionary radical feminist), a narrow-minded white feminist— her analysis here remains illuminating, in spite of itself. The arguments she outlined against the political evolution of language are, after all, familiar; they're the same ones mobilized today against the use of nonbinary pronouns and the elimination of texts with racial epithets from college syllabi.

Penelope reduced these arguments to two basic positions: either language is relatively meaningless and not worthy of political scrutiny (the foundation of arguments 1 to 3), or language is aesthetically and politically significant (the foundation of arguments 4 to 6). But despite assuming different orientations to language, arguments 1 to 6 are often mouthed by the same person, someone eager to maintain the status quo. "On the one hand," Penelope wrote, "feminists are told to abandon our attempts to change language because the way people talk isn't important, or, on the other because altering their terminology somehow threatens their ability to express themselves adequately and clearly. . . . Removing sexist usage either affects meaning or it doesn't."

———

IN THE LAST TEN YEARS, CROSSWORD PUZZLES IN MAINSTREAM outlets (the *New York Times*, the *Washington Post*, the *LA Times*, and the *New Yorker*) have become hot zones for cultural anxiety about common usage. Should the crossword puzzle be a classroom, as Penelope envisioned it, a place to inform solvers about the political evolution of language? Are there words that simply shouldn't be included in a puzzle—not because they flout the "Sunday morning breakfast test" but because they're politically retrograde?

I have been told, mostly on Twitter or in the comment sections of crossword puzzle blogs, that my crosswords include too much "trivia." It's a strange plaint, considering that crossword puzzles are, by definition, full of trivia: obscure facts, dates, and names that are hopefully interesting, if nonessential to quotidian life. Even clues whose solutions hinge on wordplay, using a synonym or pun to mislead the solver, can be called trivia: a way of using language that is intentionally of little consequence and unreasonably indirect. I understand this complaint about my puzzles to be a lightly veiled way of calling my entries not trivia but *trivial*. Feminist authors, gay slang, neologisms that stem from movement politics or academic fads—if solvers find these entries obscure, not worth knowing or learning, they will seem trivial. And my puzzles will be trivialized.

All three words—*trivia, trivial, trivialize*—stem from the Latin *trivium*, the lower division of the seven liberal arts in the medieval university. These lower fields included grammar, rhetoric, and logic—the disciplines that Penelope's scholarship understood to be the foundation of political and ethical relationships. They're also the tools required to solve a crossword puzzle. They're trivia, perhaps, but far from trivial.

The question of which words are "puzzle-worthy"—worth knowing or learning via crosswords—is no less fraught than the question of which words should be excluded from a grid. In 2019, the *Times* issued a formal apology for including a racial epithet in a Tuesday puzzle. BEANER, a slur against Mexicans, was clued otherwise: *six letters for* "Pitch to the head, informally." Alarm from solvers, again mostly signaled on Twitter or in the puzzle blogs, took two forms: regardless of the clue, the word's associations included a derogatory term; solvers, especially Mexican solvers, shouldn't have had to confront it in their puzzles. Constructors, meanwhile, pointed out how easy it would have been to change the offending corner of the grid. Switch around a few letters, and the word would disappear. An obscure, "informal" use of language could have been replaced with a more familiar word—one more "puzzle-worthy" in both aesthetic and political terms.

Policing the language of a crossword puzzle may be seen variously as a misunderstanding of language's basic neutrality; a distraction from more important, structural inequities; a limit on the constructors' creativity; a red herring; clunky; or a limit on free speech. These are arguments 1 to 6. Where, the concerned solver might ask, is the line? Which words are valid, and which are politically suspect? Isn't this self-serious commitment to cleaning up the crossword an invitation to parody in the style of *chairperone* and *feperone*?

I've been asked by puzzle editors to remove the following words from my puzzles: NRA, ESKIMO, and the admittedly awkward ATE A TON (which could, I was told, offend solvers with eating disorders). Some constructors refuse to put BIDEN in a puzzle, as he was accused of sexual assault; one won't clue TRUMP as a verb because she doesn't want to look at the word due to its likeness to a certain proper noun. A solver once told me that my needless inclusion of Ivanka Trump in a clue and (Samuel) ALITO as an answer disrupted her otherwise pleasant experience of the puzzle. She did crosswords to distract herself from the Trump administration and the Supreme Court's conservative majority. I have since taken these words out of my crossword lexicon and have tried to avoid falling into the defensive posture that would have me call these solvers overly sensitive or hysterical. Language is meaningful, and removing sexist, racist, and other hateful language from the crossword puzzle isn't particularly stifling or a curtailment of the constructor's free speech. It's a problem of rhetoric, an exercise of the trivium.

Julia Penelope was always "telling her story," and it is, ultimately, a cautionary tale. "Words wound" was her mantra, and although she committed her professional life to softening their blows, her rigid use of language caused significant harm. As a professor, crossword constructor, feminist, anorexic—and any number of labels I might reasonably claim—I'd like to think that language's potency is its most brilliant resource. We can use its constraints to harden our self-conceptions, to resist the painful ineffability of embodied experience, and to crystallize our difference from others. We can wound, and we probably always will, but we can try not to.

POLITICIZING
A PASTIME

VI

When Computers Replaced Women

IN JULY 2013, AFTER I HAD RETURNED HOME FROM PARADISE AND had graduated from college, Will Shortz asked me to be his assistant. To my mind, his invitation had little rationale. It arrived on the heels of minimal correspondence: two emails in which he had accepted two of my puzzles with minor revisions. He had wanted me to remove TMAC from a grid, the sobriquet of NBA all-star Tracy McGrady (or, as Shortz put it, an "oddly spelled nickname that not everyone may know"), and he asked me to avoid the crossing of ALMIRA (Handel's first opera) with DAPS (fist bumps, slangily), which he feared would create a Natick for some solvers. These are all debatable entries—debatably mainstream, debatably "puzzle-worthy"—as so many are. McGrady was nearing retirement when I submitted these grids, so his relevance (and his nickname) was waning in common usage. It was a high point for DAPS discourse, as Michelle and Barack Obama's affectionate fist bumps had become fodder for political punditry, a pretext for lightly veiled outrage over the First Couple's irrefutable blackness. ALMIRA is more obscure and easier to deem "crosswordese," or words found more frequently in crosswords than in everyday speech, words useful to constructors for their high vowel-to-consonant ratio or the unusual adjacency of two consonants. Like all crossword editing, Shortz's request that I remove these entries involved judgment calls about language and its use that could hardly be called politically neutral. What is mainstream language? Does its ambit overlap neatly with the common knowledge of *New York Times* crossword solvers, as Shortz imagined them? What, after all, are "puzzle-worthy" words?

These became perennial themes of my conversations with Shortz when I worked for him four days a week, for eighteen dollars an hour, in 2013 and 2014. I didn't accept his invitation without hesitation. I doubted Shortz's motives for hiring me as much as my qualifications for the job. Surely there were many more prolific and talented young constructors to assist him. The only thing that distinguished me, I thought, was my gender. Before hiring me, Shortz was clear that I would work with him only between August and the following May, when his longtime summer assistant Joel Fagliano would graduate from college and could assume the job full-time. I assumed, in other words, that I was not only a pinch hitter but a diversity hire.

This account has since been humbled by the memory of my inbox, which provides a much more extensive correspondence between me and Shortz before the summer of 2013. I had selectively remembered the two acceptances but not the three rejections. I had also repressed a long chain of emails about the possibility of a Bloomsday puzzle, commemorating the publication of Joyce's *Ulysses*, which he nixed ("For solvers who aren't familiar with *Ulysses*—which would be a large number of people—I don't think this puzzle would be very satisfying"). Apparently, I had been courting Shortz's attention and approval for three years before he offered to hire me. And once I got it, I negated it. My revisionist history protected my ego (only two emails, two acceptances), just as it exposed me to more ego-withering insecurity: Shortz barely knew me; I had no track record; he only offered me the job because I was a young woman in a field rife with men.

I'm not sure how I knew that crossword constructors at the time were mostly men. I had never met a constructor, nor had I scrutinized puzzle bylines. I knew nothing about the many women who shaped the early life of the crossword—before highly educated women entered the American workforce en masse, before the advent of digital constructing technologies, before the rise of the male-coded nerd stereotype in the 1950s, whose contours increasingly defined my understanding of the average crossword fan. If anything, the puzzles I enjoyed most were those in *New York* magazine by Maura Jacobson, who, for thirty-one years, wrote weekly puzzles that were spoiled with puns and consistently avoided the combined pitfalls of crossword construction: dull repetition and excruciating corniness. But despite Jacobson, and despite my own commitment, somehow I knew that to think of crossword constructors today—if one thinks of them at all—is to think of men. And not just any men, a particular kind of American man, the Nerd, the Word Nerd: white, STEM-educated, and charmingly (or brazenly) undersocialized.

Ultimately, despite my misgivings, I accepted Shortz's offer. If my understanding of his motives for hiring me was a paranoid misread, my premonition about the ethos of contemporary puzzle-making was confirmed.

———

THE BATHROOM IN WILL SHORTZ'S ARTS AND CRAFTS–STYLE home, unrenovated since he purchased the house, is tiled with black-and-white squares. He considers this a good omen. His kitchen cabinets are filled with canned soup, his daily lunch, often accompanied by a peanut butter and jelly sandwich. Immersion in the World of Will becomes a professional necessity—and often delight—for his assistants, at least one of whom has slept on his couch during summer internships or have joined him for games of table tennis at the club that he owns in Pleasantville (the second largest in the country). Shortz's life is highly routinized—hours of puzzle editing, followed by hours of table tennis, sleep, and repeat—and our work took on a similarly predictable cadence. Each week we went through seventy-five to one hundred puzzle submissions (still, at the time, an analog process, sent through the mail); I was responsible for sending rejection and acceptance emails; he and I edited clues together (rewriting up to 95 percent of them in every puzzle); and I typed up completed puzzles, preparing them for print.

The most illuminating and challenging part of our work was selecting puzzles and rewriting clues, where the question of "puzzle-worthy" entries became most glaring. So too did the difference in our frames of reference and the subjectivism of our collective work. When determining what words, phrases, and references were "fit to print," Shortz and I mostly agreed. In his thirty years at the *Times*, he has made it his explicit mission to introduce a more varied vocabulary—including brand names, popular culture, neologisms, and slang—into the daily puzzle. Though some version of Farrar's "Sunday morning breakfast test" still applies, its scope has narrowed. Some oblique references to sex have appeared during Shortz's tenure (PORN, CONDOM, KINK), as have certain diseases (ALS, BIRD FLU, MAD COW), "private parts," and their attending "public" displays (AREOLA, D-CUPS, G-STRING).

When possible, Shortz will clue these terms to avoid sexual or bodily reference. KINK, for example, has appeared in thirteen Shortz-edited puzzles but has only once been clued as "Unusual sexual preference." The twelve other entries have all referenced chains, hoses, necks, and other devices that might be "kinked" to the point of disuse. This tendency to err on the side of prudence can sometimes override Shortz's other values for "puzzle-worthy" entries like timeliness and broad-ranging relevance. Unlike his predecessor, Eugene Maleska, Shortz likes to avoid obscure or arcane definitions; he wants every entry to be something a *Times* solver could be expected to know, and he often uses the language of excitement to praise or reject a word or grid. It "just didn't excite him enough," he instructed me to write to constructors whose puzzles we were rejecting. Alternatively, he was "excited" to see the words VINE-RIPE and INCOME GAP debut in my puzzles. They'd never been in a *Times* crossword before, and he deemed them relevant to everyday life and therefore deserving of a place in its pantheon. Perhaps he saw these words and phrases at the grocery store or on his AOL News homepage. For whatever reason, they excited him, and he wanted them to excite *Times* solvers too.

But Shortz's "relevance" policy, to say nothing of his "excitement," no longer holds when the entry is AREOLA. Because of its high concentration of vowels, this often-used term has been clued twice in the *Times* as "Nipple ring?," but it is much more frequently clued as some version of "Interstice on an insect's wing" or "Part of the iris surrounding the pupil." Neither an entomologist nor an ophthalmologist, I wouldn't know these latter definitions if it weren't for crossword puzzles. I have no use for them. But when these kinds of entries emerged—which is to say, those that make references to the body and might have emphasized the differences in our gendered bodies—Will and I mostly kept silent, rarely discussing, but mutually understanding, that discretion tops relevance when it comes to AREOLA or KINK. I understood that our lack of discussion around these terms existed in deference to Farrar's legacy, while also protecting us from engaging the awkward fact of our difference.

Because our job required us to draw on our life experiences—how we use language, what words occur in our daily lives—it was necessarily intimate work. If Shortz and I implicitly agreed that we best avoid brainstorming cute or explicit clues for body parts, we more often disagreed about a word or phrase's "relevance." Relevant to whom? Shortz was prone to reject words or phrases because they were "too niche," hoping, as he explained it to me, to satisfy the largest possible audience of solvers. The paradox of Shortz's goal for inclusion was that his image of a mass audience for crossword puzzles often instituted a tacit policy of exclusion. Like the imagined viewers of American television before the diversifying output of cable channels, Shortz's vision of the *Times* solving community was fairly homogeneous: college-educated and gender and racially "neutral," which is to say, not apparently catering to women or non-white solvers. In brief, Shortz pictured an audience that looked like him. There's evidence for this implicit bias in the words and phrases that he has deemed *not* "puzzleworthy" (because "too niche"), a sample of which I have gathered from fellow constructors, as well as my own time in Pleasantville:

BELL HOOKS
MARIE KONDO
LATINX
LORELAI (clued to the protagonist of *Gilmore Girls*)
SULA
RADIOLAB
RICK ROSS

MATCHA

LAVERNE COX

GARTER STITCH

BTS

SNCC

MALE GAZE

A pattern develops when looking at these words: they have their origins in non-white and/or woman-produced culture, even if I and others have protested that they have broken through to a (white male) mainstream. Shortz and I used the shorthand "But is it a thing?" to determine an entry's suitability for the *Times* puzzle. Often, I would turn to Google hits or references in the pages of the *Times* to justify a word or phrase's "thingliness": LATINX (72.4 million Google hits), BELL HOOKS (29 million Google hits); MALE GAZE (referenced 218 times in the *Times* before 2014).

This strategy only worked to a point. In 2022, for example, the constructor Rachel Fabi had an extended correspondence with Shortz and Joel Fagliano about the inclusion of the makeup tutorial vlogger Nikkie de Jager in an accepted puzzle. In the southeast corner of her grid, Fabi included DE JAGER because, as she wrote, "She's definitely famous to people of a certain age, and has been for some time, but I was most excited to highlight a trans woman in the puzzle." Fagliano replied that YouTube influencers are generally not seen as "puzzle-worthy" because of their questionable staying power (the timeliness problem) and because DE JAGER was unknown to Shortz, Fagliano, and the puzzle's test solvers—one of whom protested that she shouldn't have to know any YouTube influencer by name (the relevance problem).

To her credit, Fabi replied that "trying to diversify the names and references in puzzles to include identities that have historically been underrepresented is more important and satisfying than trying to ensure that imaginary 'typical' solvers are kept comfortable." Fagliano conceded the point, and Fabi assumed that DE JAGER would be included in her grid. She was understandably surprised to learn, when she was sent the proofs for her puzzle, that DE JAGER had been changed to DOWAGER, and that a clue for MSNBC no longer included a reference to Rachel Maddow. Fabi's response, gracious but forthright, is worth reprinting at length:

I have a concern, which is that you have edited out two LGBTQ+ women (Rachel Maddow from a clue and Nikkie DE JAGER from the grid(!)), at a time when LGBTQ+ rights are once again under attack. It's particularly upsetting that I received these proofs on the day that MARGARET COURT, famed homophobe and anti-LGBTQ+ activist, got a full-length theme entry in the puzzle. . . .

I don't think it's particularly compelling to say that because a single test solver feels that they don't want to encounter names from YouTube, no one should have to encounter names of YouTubers. I don't particularly care about golf, but I have learned who ISAO AOKI is over time! . . .

All that to say, I am willing to accept the ire of a few disgruntled solvers in exchange for the message that it sends when we include a prominent trans woman in the puzzle.

Shortz reverted the grid to Fabi's initial construction. He had wanted to change her Maddow clue to one referencing Al Sharpton, but Fabi protested that "as a queer woman myself, I don't love that we replaced a reference to a queer woman (Rachel Maddow) with a reference to a man who has made public homophobic statements in the past." They compromised, and Shortz changed the clue to "Network with Joy Reid's 'The

ReidOut.'" In response to the puzzle, crossword blogger Amy Reynaldo wrote, "I appreciate the effort Rachel made to be inclusive of women in this puzzle: MADAM C.J. Walker, JOANNE and Lady Gaga, Tina FEY, DE JAGER, BETTE Midler, DELLA Reese, RITA ORA, Joy Reid."

Ultimately, the question of "puzzle-worthiness" is a negotiation between the constructor's voice and that of a publication's house style. Fabi's case is extraordinary because usually, at major publications, individual voices are dimmed by the standards of the house. In the case of crosswords, where editorial oversight has been fairly limited to puzzle editors, house style is set to the voice of Shortz or Mike Shenk (at the *Wall Street Journal*) or Rich Norris (who edited the *LA Times* puzzle from 1999 to 2022).

I've never published in the *Wall Street Journal* or the *LA Times*, but another constructor informed me that Shenk and Norris also deemed the following entries "un-puzzle-worthy":

GUCCI MANE
RAJON RONDO crossing (Nicki) MINAJ
COME CORRECT
SI SE PUEDE
HBCU
DEETS
ANGSTY
(Howard) ZINN crossing NIHAO and BANH MI
RIOT GRRRL
An entire puzzle whose theme centered on WNBA teams

I was both shocked and not surprised to learn of these rejected submissions. Mine was a lazy indignation. But the problem of an entry's "relevance"—intimately tied to editors' unthinking proclivity for exclusion—has high stakes for the fate of this lively art. It requires editors and constructors to ask not just "*who* is a crossword puzzle for" but also "*what* is a crossword puzzle for." Is it meant to satisfy loyal solvers who have come to expect the gratification of perfectly filled grids and increasingly faster solving times? Or is it meant to shape and expand the boundaries of common knowledge—pushing solvers to see an unknown word or phrase not as a stumbling block but as an opportunity to learn. I am strongly of the opinion that looking up an unknown word or phrase is not cheating but learning. But I am also not a speed solver and will disable the timer function on any crossword solving web application I'm using. I rush enough; enough of my life has been gamified against my will; and I still think that the primary purpose of solving a crossword puzzle is to waste time, not beat it. If I encounter a phrase or person I don't know—and sink even more time into researching their YouTube makeup tutorials and impeccably draped 2021 Met Gala gown—all the better.

Not a speed solver and not a man, when I started working for Shortz, I also wrote crossword puzzles by hand, "the old-fashioned way." In 2013, these traits made me three times an outlier among *New York Times* constructors. Like crossword solving, crossword constructing has become a digital process. When writing Shortz's rejection and acceptance emails, I was often disturbed to see how quickly constructors could turn around puzzle revisions using software. "Your southwest corner is a little inelegant," I would write, aping Shortz's voice in an email from his account, and within the hour, I would receive, in reply, a new corner—or sometimes two or three new grids to choose from. The same task would have taken me an afternoon by hand. At the time, I couldn't disentangle the use of technology from intelligence: Was I just not as smart as these guys?

Every move to digital has its naysayers and analog fetishists who can be ungenerously labeled reactionary or twee. It's not a type with which I'm quick to identify, but I didn't use constructing software until 2016, after ten years of constructing by hand. My anachronistic impulse might have been a little reactionary and a little twee. I might have also worried that using software was "cheating." But if I didn't believe that solvers could cheat—that instead they could only learn—why was I unwilling to learn the constructing software?

Reactionary, twee, hypocritical—my motives were also quite simple: I enjoyed creating puzzles by hand. The process was frustrating and slow, requiring an intensity of concentration that was as punishing to pursue as it was exhilarating to complete. It required me to think about language as a material clump of letters, allowing me to feel almost weightless as I navigated the grid's matrix of words, focusing on their material constitution, not mine.

Constructing by hand and constructing by software couldn't be more technically or phenomenologically distinct. Programs like Crossword Compiler and CrossFire allow puzzle-makers to build or import wordlists that include rankings of individual entries, depending on how "puzzle-worthy" a constructor deems them. The work of revising one's wordlist and shaping the algorithm's inputs could not, by any measure of my experience, be called transcendent. Database management doesn't require the constructor to abstract words into letter units; as a result, it doesn't allow her the conceit that her mind is abstracted from the body at her desk. The constructor using software rarely thinks about language as strings of letters, divorced from their meanings, because that is now the work of the computer. Instead, she thinks almost exclusively about meanings—and whether a word in her database is "puzzle-worthy"—constantly reminding her of her most embodied interactions: how a word or phrase makes her feel, where she was when she first encountered it, the contexts in which she uses it. In short, constructing by software doesn't allow her to think of the puzzle as a virtual "place" she goes to escape quotidian life, but a constant engagement with life's routines.

Filling in the words in a puzzle by hand can feel interminable, but it does have a discrete *beginning* (insert black squares), *middle* (fill letters in white squares), and *end* (clue the entries in the puzzle). Bounded in time, analog constructing creates a quasi-therapeutic space that feels, paradoxically, out-of-time or beyond it. By contrast, the process of cultivating one's wordlist, like tending to one's garden or managing one's inbox, is never-ending. A constructor invested in creating timely and "exciting" puzzles is always adding, reranking, or deleting words from their lists. The puzzle is no longer a "space" but an ongoing activity.

Although today's constructors have offloaded a tremendous amount of make-work onto the computer, this is not to say that the software itself merits authorship. The constructor is still responsible for the puzzle's theme (if it has one), its design, and its clues. Often the software will alert the constructor to a quadrant of a grid that is simply "unfillable" by its own algorithm. In this scenario, a constructor can try to outsmart the machine, or she can change her grid, adjusting the placement of black squares or the position of certain words, and "autofill" again.

There are still many basic tasks that analog and digital constructors share. Whether constructing by hand or with software, a puzzle-maker's first step is to determine whether she is creating a "themed" or "themeless" puzzle. The distinction is as simple as it sounds: themed puzzles feature three or four entries that share some gimmick (like Harold T. Bers's "Catalogue" theme from 1958), whereas the entries in themeless puzzles share no relation—they are determined only by the limits of a grid's design and the constructor's whim. Typically, themeless puzzles have fewer black squares, more white space (and therefore longer entries), and are harder to solve, with more difficult clues and fewer short words that would otherwise provide solvers footholds in the grid's pattern. Some outlets publish only one kind of puzzle or another; the *Times* runs themed puzzles Sundays through Thursdays (on a sliding difficulty scale) and themeless puzzles on Friday and Saturday, the "hardest" days of the week. Using software infinitely expedites and improves the quality of themeless grids. Before I started using CrossFire, I mostly stuck to themed puzzles. The few themeless crosswords that I wrote by hand never saw print. Full of arcana and initialisms to make my crossings work, they just weren't very good.

Although themed puzzles can be easier to create, they are, in some ways, harder to conceive. Crossword themes can be simple (all of the theme entries in a grid are related to cats, for example) or complex (all of the theme entries are puns that hinge on the same kind of wordplay: tricks of grammar or syntax, spoonerisms, or anagrams). Ideally, a themed puzzle will also include a "revealer," an entry that explains its gimmick. To complicate things yet further, all theme entries must be placed symmetrically in the grid, adding another constraint for the constructor to manage. Two of my favorite themed puzzles from 2022 offer clarifying examples for those unfamiliar with the form (the number of letters are provided to demonstrate how the constructor has maintained the theme's symmetry in a fifteen-by-fifteen grid):

New Yorker themed puzzle by Sarah Kay and Ross Trudeau

Theme Entry 1:
Clue: "What catfishers might use as bait"

Answer: PROFILE PICS

(eleven letters)

Theme Entry 2:
Clue: "Accurate rink attempts"

Answer: SHOTS ON NET

(ten letters)

Theme Entry 3:
Clue: "Conclusion that ties everything up improbably neatly"

Answer: HOLLYWOOD ENDING

(fifteen letters)

Theme Entry 4:
Clue: "Fizzy mocktail made with citrus"

Answer: LIME RICKEY

(ten letters)

Revealer:
Clue: "Verse derived from an existing source text . . . or what the [bolded letters] might be described as"

Answer: FOUND POETRY

(eleven letters)

New York Times themed puzzle by Karen Lurie

Theme Entry 1:

Clue: "Drink from a spring" Answer: MINERAL WATER

(twelve letters)

Theme Entry 2:

Clue: "Steakhouse option" Answer: MEDIUM RARE

(ten letters)

Theme Entry 3:

Clue: "Queasy, perhaps" Answer: FEELING ILL

(ten letters)

Revealer:

Clue: "Nitpicker's lead-in . . . or a Answer: WELL ACTUALLY
response to [the theme entries], if
they were posed as questions" (twelve letters)

I used to think that inventive themes could only be created "by hand," which is to say, without the assistance of software—informed by the force of a constructor's imagination alone. But the poet Sarah Kay and the constructor Ross Trudeau relied heavily on digital tools to create their *New Yorker* crossword theme. They thought of their "Found Poetry" conceit without digital tools, but to develop their theme entries, they used RegEx, short for Regular Expression, a search operation that represents strings of letters, numbers, or symbols within a database of text. Constructors can use RegEx to search for "all words that begin and end with the same vowel," say, or "all words or phrases that include the consecutive string of letters 'ODE.'" A RegEx search for the latter would have offered Kay and Trudeau almost 3,000 results (IN TOO DEEP, WE ARE SO DEAD, for example) and more than 300 results for words and phrases that contain EPIC (APPLE PICKING, ICE PICKS, GET THE PICTURE). Their project, at this point, was to select answers of symmetrical lengths—and answers that might be fun to write clues for—building up their theme material *ex machina*, not *ex nihilo*.

By contrast, Karen Lurie's puzzle seems more likely to have been conceived and executed without the use of code. It would take far more sophisticated feats of natural language processing for a computer to know that WELL ACTUALLY has dramatically different meanings when its words are separated by a comma—and, to my mind, inconceivable feats for a program to recognize that WELL, ACTUALLY could be a response to MINERAL WATER, MEDIUM RARE, and FEELING ILL if those phrases were asked as questions. To me, the joy of this theme is that it feels so human—as though Karen's voice, and not a string of code or an editor's hand, emerges from the puzzle upon discovering its gimmick. Even, and perhaps especially, when the line between the human mind and that of the computer is increasingly imperceptible, Karen's puzzle generates an interpersonal feeling, despite the multiple forms of technological mediation (CrossFire, wordlists, track changes, solving web apps) that no doubt stood between her and her solvers. If I were feeling particularly sentimental, and maybe a little hyperbolic, I might call her ability to conjure that feeling through a crossword puzzle theme a bit of found poetry.

Despite the romantic ideal of the solitary constructor—themes and crossings emerging from her mind like Athena from Zeus's head—there is, ultimately, no construction *ex nihilo*. There never has been. Even if I liked to imagine that my early grids were the products of my unassisted, disembodied brain, I was always relying on dictionaries I referenced, books I read, TV shows I watched, and supermarket aisles I wandered to cull words and phrases for my puzzles. Even when constructed "by hand," my crosswords were always the product of my mind, assisted and informed by my social and technological world.

When I worked for Shortz, we didn't discuss why I constructed by hand. Around that time, Michael Sharp, better known by his crossword blogging alias Rex Parker, and Ben Tausig, editor of the indie crossword platform AVCX, both encouraged me to start using software. They were flattering me: *If you make these kinds of puzzles by hand, imagine what you could do with software.* But they were also explicitly hoping that if I created puzzles faster, I would create more of them, helping to introduce more women-made puzzles into an industry and community run by men.

By 2013, a wave of discourse about the puzzle world's gender imbalance was building among constructors and avid solvers. It crested in the spring of 2014 at the American Crossword Puzzle Tournament. My responsibilities at the event, which has been organized by Shortz since

1978, were threefold: I was there as a judge, as Shortz's assistant, and as a constructor with a puzzle in the tournament. The logistics of the weekend, which sound like the start of a bad joke ("How do you fit seven hundred crossword solvers into a conference room?"), had occupied me and Shortz for months. This was my first ACPT—my crossword cotillion—and I spent the first night's mixer matching faces to bylines.

Among the speed solvers at the ACPT, there was, and continues to be, an equal number of men and women participants. Those in the top ten, however, are consistently men (with the noteworthy exceptions of Ellen Ripstein, Miriam Raphael, Anne Erdmann, and Stella Zawistowski—all of whom have landed in the top ten, if not the top three, with Ripstein winning the tournament in 2001). There is no reason to believe that men are better solvers than women—just as they aren't better constructors. They do seem to be faster, though, a function of social factors that began to crystallize for me over the course of the weekend.

On the tournament's first morning, I was invited to a breakfast for women constructors. There were ten of us in attendance. The point of the breakfast was not to address the lack of women publishing puzzles in mainstream newspapers, but that was inevitably what we discussed. Some suggested that the pastime had become too competitive for them— that the popularity of puzzle blogging left constructors vulnerable to vicious comments, draining the once humble activity of its joy. Most of the women—all, except me, over forty—conceded that they barely had the time to make the few crosswords they did. They attributed the scarcity of women constructors to the imbalance of household labor: where men may have the leisure time to craft puzzles and train for speed-solving tournaments, women do not. In an email exchange following our breakfast, constructor Tracy Bennett wrote me, "Not only do I work full-time, but I parent full-time as well. So I have to make excellent puzzles (still working on that), because I can't make that many. And if I'm making fewer puzzles, I'm getting feedback from the editors at a slower rate, and my learning curve may take more time because of it. . . . I've accepted that I'm a tortoise in this race."

On the second night of the ACPT, the topic of the crossword puzzle's "gender problem" emerged from the mouth of its most unlikely messenger: David Steinberg, a seventeen-year-old puzzle wunderkind. Steinberg's first crossword was published in the *Times* when he was just fourteen; he has since had more than one thousand puzzles published there and is currently the Puzzles and Games Editor at the Andrews McMeel Universal media company, where he edits syndicated crosswords that run in the *Boston Globe*, the *Philadelphia Inquirer*, and the *Miami Herald*. At the ACPT, Steinberg was given the podium to present data on the history of women in crosswords that he had collected for his high school science research course.

To the disappointment, but not the surprise, of many in the audience, Steinberg revealed that the gender disparity among constructors had steadily worsened in the past two decades. Under the two editors before Shortz—Will Weng (1969–1977) and Eugene Maleska (1977–1993)— women constructed 35 percent of all puzzles, and in the reigning "Shortz era," Steinberg reported, women accounted for 19 percent of all puzzles. Moreover, most of the woman-made grids in Shortz's time appeared on Mondays or Tuesdays, the week's easiest puzzles, or the "M-T ghetto," as one puzzle blogger has called it. At this point in his speech, Steinberg suggested that the ever-widening gender gap in crossword constructing might be explained by the field's shift to software.

Steinberg offered cogent data to support the hypothesis that as puzzle-making became increasingly informed by programming, it began to replicate the gender imbalance of tech culture. He invoked the "numerous studies that suggest that females are far less likely than males to enter computer and other technology-related fields," suggesting that "as the practice of puzzle-making moved from graph paper and dictionaries to word databases and algorithms, it became 'less of a literary exercise and . . . more of a mathematical exercise.'" Women, he posited, may have been "left behind" as a result.

Steinberg's analysis stung, but not just because it had been "boysplained" to me. Still constructing puzzles by hand, a woman alienated by the digital turn in crossword constructing, I confirmed his findings—just as I found them troublingly reductive. One doesn't need to know how to code to use Crossword Compiler or CrossFire, but the sensibility of crossword culture had, by 2014, merged with that of Silicon Valley. Even Aimee Lucido and Zoe Wheeler, two young women constructors who published their first puzzles in the *Times* around the time I did, were then starting a job at Facebook and a PhD in computer science, respectively. The gender imbalance among constructors was, for them, par for the course. But for me, working with Shortz was a stop on the way to graduate school in literature and media studies, a year-long cultural immersion in a world of puzzle fanaticism that I knew to be not really my own.

Since Steinberg's speech, the website XWord Info has started tracking data on the gender of *New York Times* crossword constructors. Gender is one of many metrics that the site's developer Jim Horne monitors—including "Youngest Constructors," "Grids with the fewest black squares," and "Puzzles with the longest average word length"—

but it's undoubtedly the most controversial. Notably absent are any statistics on constructors' race or ethnicity, which, unlike gender, by way of gender prefixes, the *Times* doesn't ask constructors to provide. And Horne, I think understandably, doesn't want to resort to profiling to trace constructors' racial demographics.

Meanwhile, the data that he has collected on gender is as useful as it is divisive. Horne tracks the number of puzzles that are "women solos" (puzzles written only by women), "all-women collaborations," and "collaborations with men." He also tracks the days of the week that women publish puzzles. (In 2014, 35 percent of Monday puzzles were made by women, 2 percent of Saturday puzzles were made by women, and only 15 percent of *Times* puzzles had women's bylines overall.) Horne has amended these statistics with a caveat: "Collaboration puzzles are counted here as 'by Women' if there is at least one woman constructor. One could argue that this overstates their contributions and the more accurate percentages are even lower."

There is real value in having these statistics, however dispiriting, on hand. Data can start conversations, alert people to trends, and hold editors accountable; but it can't change a culture. I'm also not sure that it helps with how underrepresented constructors feel. Does it feel good to know exactly how much of a minority you are? Or to feel like a data point? Is it possible that these numbers actually reinforce the supremacy of gender as an arbiter of crossword culture? Horne's graphs don't account for nonbinary constructors, but he has changed the gender of constructors who have transitioned since their puzzles were published. One trans constructor asked Horne for access to XWord Info so they could change their gender whenever they wanted to. Their motive may have been to disrupt Horne's project just as much as it was to gain agency over their representation in its plot. I like to think that the request was an act of gender abolitionist protest, saying to Horne in so many words: *Your stats are doubling down on gender binaries; give me the access codes, and I'll blow them up.*

As Horne told me, "I realized from the beginning that [the gender statistics page was] fraught. I've thought about just removing it, and I've asked people who have complained about it whether they thought I should. Mostly I get 'No, no, no, no, don't remove it. But it's just awful!'" Horne knows that the explanatory power of data is limited, but perhaps because so much data on crosswords is available—and constructors are already engaged in so much data work themselves—analyzing it seems irresistible.

Antony Lewis, the developer of Crossword Compiler, sent me demographic data about his program's users: bar graph representations of the number and gender of those who have downloaded his constructing software since its advent in 1993. Per his calculations, in the United States, women accounted for roughly 45 percent of Crossword Compiler downloads in 2000, and about 35 percent of users in 2020. These numbers far outpace the number of women published in mainstream newspapers. One is tempted to use these statistics, and their difference from those that Horne has compiled, as a departure for speculation: Are women downloading constructing software but just not using it? Are they using it, but just not very well? Are they using it well, but just not being published? In other words, is the problem time, facility, or bias? In his email to me, Lewis implied yet another theory for the disparity, writing, "This [data] of course includes people like teachers making educational puzzles, who may have distinct demographics from the newspaper folk." His suggestion, as I understand it, is that women may be downloading his software for use in feminized professions like teaching, whereas men are using it in male-dominated professions like publishing.

Lewis wouldn't share with me how many people had downloaded Crossword Compiler, so I don't know his sample size, but he did explain how he determined the gender of his customer base—not by asking his users their gender identity (as Horne does at XWord Info), but by deriving it through yet another computerized operation. He wrote, "I don't track the gender—I used the first names stored in the database where I have them, and then [I] weighted [them] by the sex ratio of each name in the US population as given by a name table." In other words, he used a social construct (naming) to reverse engineer another social construct (gender) to project a claim about the way that crosswords are, well, constructed.

How has this happened? How did crossword constructing evolve from a feminized pastime—once conflated with first-wave feminists and bored housewives—to a male-dominated industry, its pervasive gender imbalance tracked, analyzed, and visualized by men prominent in the field? While the rise of constructing software in the 1990s doesn't fully explain the masculinization of crossword labor and culture, it does offer some clues. After all, computer programming itself is an industry that has, over the second half of the twentieth century, become masculinized. It began with women at the helm but has since become the domain of men (or, as they have been called since the early 1960s, "computer boys," so named because of their tendency to start young and their typically stunted maturity levels). To understand—and perhaps even to redress—the systematic exclusion of women from contemporary crossword constructing, one needs to understand the parallel history of the much larger, and more obviously consequential, field of computer programming. Both spheres have been shaped by economic, social, and technological forces that have created and reproduced a culture in which women feel unwelcome, underutilized, and underestimated.

IT IS BY NOW COMMON KNOWLEDGE THAT THE EARLIEST "COM-puters" were women—employees of corporations or wartime government agencies whose job was to crunch numbers by hand and to input data into the earliest electronic computer prototypes. These early "computers"— people who did computations, not machines—have resurfaced in popular culture with the success of the 2016 film *Hidden Figures*, which depicted the largely Black team of women whose work was essential to NASA's operations during the Space Race. It has also risen to mainstream promi-nence because of the 2011 and 2014 launch of Apple's Siri and Amazon's Alexa—women (or women-presenting) virtual assistants, who dutifully retrieve data on command. Big Tech's feminized bots, it seems, represent not a newly subservient role for women in the history of computing but a return to the industry's origins.

Historian Jennifer S. Light's 1999 article "When Computers Were Women" was one of the first and most significant projects to rediscover the women who pioneered early computing—and to explain why they, as opposed to household names like Bill Gates and Steve Jobs, have largely been forgotten. Light's essay is a social history of technology that can be traced through the evolution of naming. With the 1945 invention of the ENIAC, the country's earliest electronic computer, the women whose responsibility was to use the new machine and to aid in its calcu-lations became increasingly known as "programmers," not "computers," as the machine itself took on the title that once belonged to them. But, as Light has explained, "The job of the programmer, perceived in recent years as masculine work, originated as feminized clerical labor." Men involved with the ENIAC were engineers; the role of the programmer, meanwhile, assumed distinctively feminized connotations. (I have often wondered when crossword constructors became known as such. When did we become "constructors" and not "puzzle-makers," a near echo of the woman-coded "pattern-makers" and a term that lacks engineering connotations? Did our job's title change when its gender demographics did?)

To call a professional role "feminized" not only suggests that women are more prone to do it but also accounts for the position's lack of prestige, depressed salary, and limited professional advancement. Feminized labor, like that of early programming and early puzzle construction, presumes that women workers are financially dependent on men (and therefore don't need an equitable salary) and that they lack the leadership, administrative, or technical skills that have historically been attributed to and developed in men. The feminization and masculinization of industries and professional roles are rooted in social and economic forces that may no longer hold—women are increasingly financially independent and have, for two generations, been the beneficiary of leadership and technical training—but have nonetheless been naturalized over time.

The received wisdom about World War II is that, because of the draft, masculinized industries were newly open to women. Women entered the US labor force en masse, and working-class women took up jobs in American factories and shipyards, a phenomenon that has since crystallized in the popular imagination in the figure of Rosie the Riveter. Lesser known is what happened to women with college degrees—especially those with degrees in math and engineering—who, before the war, would have sought jobs after graduation as teachers, perhaps only until they were married. During the war, the US government explicitly solicited these women's technical expertise to perform the calculations underpinning ballistics operations and to decrypt Japanese and German codes. To do this work, women programmers became ENIAC experts: encoding information so it could be legible to the machine, threading the tape on which this information was inscribed through the ENIAC at the correct point of tautness, and discovering and remedying the bugs or glitches that emerged from these processes. As a result of their experience with the ENIAC, college-educated American women were some of the nation's earliest and most adept programmers, underrated as that label (and their work) was at the time.

Their names still go unremarked in many histories of computing: Agnes Driscoll, Adele Goldstine, Grace Hopper, Kay McNulty, and Betty Snyder among them. However crucial their work was to an Allied victory in the war, their computing and programming positions were understood to be less prestigious and demanding than combat. As Light explains, programming was considered clerical work—an extension of the secretarial pool, itself an extension of women's work in the home: neatening, organizing, and managing the operations of the family unit. Like Margaret Farrar, tidying up the ungainly crossword puzzle at the *New York Times*, the women programmers of World War II were solicited precisely because of skills that their employers understood to inhere in women: those that translated seamlessly from the home to the office.

Despite Rosie the Riveter's manual, male-coded labor, the World War II economy was still heavily structured by sex-typing, with professional roles based on a biologically reductive notion of gender. Women programmers were responsible for software because of their soft skills; men engineers were responsible for hardware (and the credit of invention). Although the work didn't divide so neatly—in order to use the ENIAC, women programmers developed a more robust understanding of the machine's hardware than many of its engineers—the realm of software programming was nonetheless considered meticulous and repetitive, ideal for the mid-century woman worker. This was not implicit bias, but highly explicit. As Evelyn Steele, editorial director of *Vocational Guidance Research*, wrote in 1943:

It is generally agreed that women do well at painstaking, tedious work requiring patience and dexterity of the hands. The actual fact that women's fingers are more slender than men's makes a difference. Also, women adapt themselves to repetitive jobs requiring constant alertness, nimble fingers and tireless wrists. They have the ability to work to precise tolerances, can detect variations of ten thousandths of an inch, [and] can make careful adjustments at high speed with great accuracy.

Although crossword constructors were never explicitly sex-typed in this way, the requirements for being a good programmer overlapped heavily with those of crossword enthusiasts. Or at least the US government thought so. As Liza Mundy discovered in *Code Girls*, her comprehensive history of the women code breakers during World War II, women graduating from elite private colleges were asked two questions before being recruited for computer programming jobs: (1) Do you like crossword puzzles? and (2) Are you engaged?

In the middle of the twentieth century, before the advent of the nerd stereotype or the "computer boy," crosswords and computing were not seen as markers of intelligence per se. But they were evidence of a woman's shrewdness, her tireless work ethic, and her fastidiousness—all highly compatible with the mid-century workforce, so long as she wasn't yet committed to building a home. By the war's end, the history of the

ENIAC was written to exclude women programmers. Instead, post-war press tours triumphed the intelligence of the men who developed its hardware and that of the machine itself. Newspapers and magazines touted the machine's "brain" while failing to account for the women who operated it. It's almost as if the woman programmer's intelligence had been subsumed by that of the machine—as if her work developing the computer was some of the first to be replaced by computing itself.

Computer programming is one of many professions that have become masculinized since the "grunt work" of the job (encoding data, reproducing usable code, fixing bugs) can now largely be done by the computer itself. Other once-feminized jobs whose "women's work" has been replaced by that of computers—and whose fields have subsequently been masculinized—include film editors and librarians. In the days of silent cinema, most film editors were women, using their "nimble fingers" to piece together bits of film stock on a Moviola. If the analog crossword constructor weaves with language, the work of the celluloid film editor can be similarly sex-typed: she sews film together; she makes work of celluloid decoupage. Just like computer programming, early film editing work was understood to be suited for women because it was precise and mechanical. It is only in recent years that women film editors like Jeanne Spencer, Winifred Dunn, and Margaret Booth have come to be recognized for the pre-digital artistry and intelligence of their work.

To call American library science a masculinized field is a less obvious claim. Women still make up the majority of librarians in the United States, but library leadership roles are increasingly given to men. In 2010, 83 percent of academic librarians were women, but 40 percent of their libraries' directors were men, and women's weekly earnings averaged just 81 percent of men librarians' pay. There is reason to think that the computerization of the field—its infrastructural transformations from card catalogs to databases—has contributed to the disproportionate role of men in library leadership positions. As early as 1985, the faculty in library science education was sex-typed in ways we have come to expect: women educators specialized in materials and services for children and young adults, while men taught classes in information science, library automation, and management theory.

That women have largely stopped being involved (or involved at high levels) in these various fields—programming, film editing, library science, and crossword constructing—isn't because they stopped being good at the job once it was digitized. Nor is it because the job now requires a higher or different kind of intelligence because it is computer-assisted. It is, rather, because the work of the computer overlaps neatly with the kind of work that women have historically been allowed to do. Since the computer can perform many of the operations of traditional "women's work"—or support work—women have been displaced from the many jobs available to them, having to fight instead for jobs with the prestige, titles, salaries, and social roles that have historically gone to men. Jobs, in other words, that they have been discriminated against holding from the start.

Light's essay "When Computers Were Women" could just as easily have been called "When Computers Replaced Women"—an examination of how machines edged college-educated women out of careers and into the home. This white-collar warfare between woman and machine is acutely dramatized in *Desk Set*, a 1957 Katharine Hepburn / Spencer Tracy romantic comedy. Hepburn plays Miss Watson, the head of the Research and Reference Department of the fictional Federal Broadcasting Company. (Staged in a near replica of Rockefeller Center, the film leaves the viewer with little doubt about who Miss Watson's employer—or what, for that matter, her IBM namesake—is meant to evoke.) Her job is to be on hand for radio broadcast announcers, answering questions as various as "Which poisons leave no trace?" and "Which baseball player has the highest lifetime batting average?" Unlike her colleagues who use reference books to assist their work, Watson apparently knows all of these facts from memory: she's a data repository personified.

Tracy, meanwhile, plays an efficiency expert and inventor of the EMERAC (nicknamed "Emmy"), an electronic computer that is meant to replace the women of the Research and Reference Department. Emmy can answer any and all questions just as fast as Miss Watson can, and far faster than her office mates. With the entrance of the machine, Miss Watson is slated to lose her job, and, by the end of the film, she is no longer a "miss" at all. Hepburn and Tracy get engaged and embrace, as the mainframe computer spells out the words: *THE END*. But is that really the end? What is Hepburn to do with all that free-floating knowledge—the origin of every Bible quotation, the words to every Longfellow poem—that she's flaunted throughout the film? Maybe she'll start writing crossword puzzles.

MY IMPRESSION THAT THE COMMUNITY CONGREGATED AT THE 2014 American Crossword Puzzle Tournament wasn't really *my own* was a function of crossword culture's masculinization. Although you don't need to know how to code to create or solve crossword puzzles digitally, the set of factors that masculinize an industry (computerization, increased prestige, lack of accommodations for parents) has transformed the culture of the puzzle. Like every masculinized field, crossword constructing has had exceptional women working at every level of production: not only champion speed solvers like Ellen Ripstein and Stella Zawistowski but also women who developed grid-filling software of their own, years before concerns that constructing software had "left women behind."

In the early 1980s, for example, Mary Virginia Orna, a chemistry professor at the College of New Rochelle, was using her lab equipment to help her construct crosswords, twenty-eight of which she published in the *New York Times*. Orna wrote her puzzles with graph paper and pencil, but when it came time to submit her puzzle to Maleska at the *Times*, she used an x-y plotter to create professional-looking grids. As she described it, "By entering the required code, one could have the plotter do simple graphics, and crossword puzzle grids are simple graphics. I taught myself how to write the code, and it was so much easier to print out the grids, numbers and all, and when prompted, also the solutions."

Most developers of crossword-constructing software are also puzzle constructors, but not all of them. Some are just natural tinkerers or AI enthusiasts who want to see if a computer can replicate human behavior. And of all human behavior, crossword constructing is remarkably well-suited to automation because there are so many constraints governing its operation. (It is, you might say, debatably human in this regard. I liked doing it precisely because it made me feel nonhuman.) All words must be at least three letters long, and all letters must be "checked" by two words—which is to say, all letters must exist within two crossing words, giving the solver two opportunities to fill them it. In 1974, two computer science majors at Wesleyan University took these constraints as an opportunity for software design. David P. Anderson and Matt Ginsberg, both of whom are now computer scientists, made grid-filling programs using early computing languages. Both insist that their programs were rudimentary and basically unsuccessful. At that point, computers didn't have the processing speed to match the human mind in feats of natural language.

The first major breakthrough in crossword-constructing software arrived in 1989, when Eric Albert, a computer scientist who had worked at Bell Laboratories and BBN (which, he told me, "*really* invented the internet"), began trying his hand at constructing software. Albert wanted to create a program that not only could fill a grid with words but also could make the kinds of aesthetic decisions that make for "good grids" with "good words." To that end, he invented the process of ranking words in a database, developing a thirteen-category system that would allow his algorithm to distinguish between "fabulous" words and "very yucky" words, as he described them. In an essay he wrote for *Games* magazine outlining his innovation, Albert provided his aesthetic categories with telling examples:

0–Fabulous (KUMQUAT, QUICK FIX)
1–Great (NEW YORK, AL HIRT)
2–Very Good (AMAZON, JAWBONE)
3–Colorful (TULIP, BABOON)
4–Above Average (ASPARAGUS, MACAO)
5–Average (INN, ECONOMY)
6–Below Average (TIPS, KNOCKED)
7–Boring (LATERALLY, ELLS)
8–Flawed (YOU'LL, OCT)
9–Stretching (COWY, BITERS)
10–Yucky (COWIER, ANOA)
11–Specialized (UCALEGON, <obscene>)
12–Very Yucky (BERT L, SHILFA)

Explaining these rankings, Albert wrote, "Categorizing entries is subjective and somewhat arbitrary. . . . In my scheme, multiple-word phrases and full names rank very high. Hipness, vividness, and interesting quirkiness raise an entry's value. So do rare letters like J, K, Q, X, and Z." What's both so fascinating—and so goofy—about Albert's rankings is that, like an eighteenth-century aesthetician, he was formalizing, for the first time, solving experiences that had previously been tacit. In trying to get a computer to judge language the way a crossword constructor does, this retired software engineer became the crossword community's Edmund Burke.

In his *Games* magazine essay, Albert described the combination of life events that led him to pursue constructing software. He and his wife had a newborn child, and they decided that he would stay at home while his wife returned to her job at BBN. In looking for a job that he could do freelance and from home, Albert began work on his program. As he described it, "I began considering puzzling as a profession . . . [but] after finding out the pittance paid for most puzzles . . . I [learned] that few people could grind them out quickly enough to afford both food and shelter. But could a computer fill crossword grids, I wondered, and do so at a professional level?" Paradoxically, then, Albert developed constructing software—the alleged death knell for women constructors—when he began his life as a homemaker. Puzzles became his profession, like so many housewives before him.

Crossword Compiler and CrossFire, both produced by men, launched in 1993 and 2008, respectively. Although they have cornered this niche market, they are not the only programs available. When Karen M. Tracey began creating crosswords, for example, she wanted more agency over the software than Crossword Compiler allowed. Specifically, she wanted software that even more effectively replicated the kinds of control that analog constructors have over discrete segments of the grid. A computer programmer between jobs, Tracey started using Crossword Compiler in 2003. At the time, the application didn't allow constructors to see all of the possible entries that could be entered into a certain place in the grid, depending on the entry's length and how many other letters were already filled. All of that information was stored in the algorithm's Black Box. Nor did Crossword Compiler allow constructors to isolate certain quadrants of the grid to "autofill." It simply filled the entire grid or got stuck. Tracey made her own program, named Crossword Builder, that she never licensed or sold. Using Crossword Builder, she could stop and start her program's "autofill" function, digitally filling some parts of the grid and fine-tuning other parts by hand.

In 2010, Tracey stopped making crosswords. She started a new job, had less time for puzzling, and began work at a cat rescue that took up most of her leisure time. She also grew tired of submitting work to Shortz at the *Times*. Now that the process of constructing puzzles was infinitely expedited with software, why was he still receiving printout submissions through the mail? Why was a puzzle that was submitted in 2010 accepted in 2011 and then published in 2012? Might words and phrases that are "fabulous" in 2010 be merely "very good" two years later? Couldn't Shortz's editorial work be automated and expedited too? For Tracey, the digitization of the CrossWorld had not gone far enough. As a result, she lost interest.

IN 2020, THE PUZZLES AND GAMES SECTION OF THE *NEW YORK TIMES* made significant changes that were meant to redress complaints lodged by constructors and former Shortz employees about everything from the process of submitting crosswords to concerns about implicit bias in puzzle editing. The submissions and editorial processes are now digitized with edits track-changed for constructors to see, pay has increased, and the newspaper's Games section has hired three women editors, Everdeen

Mason, Tracey Bennett, and Wyna Liu. In 2022, the paper also introduced a "Diverse Crossword Constructor Fellowship," a mentorship program aimed at "increasing the number of puzzles created by underrepresented groups, including women, people of color, and those in the LGBTQ community." With this effort, the *Times* was following the lead of crossword constructor, champion speed solver, and now *USA Today* puzzle editor, Erik Agard. In 2018, Agard launched a Facebook group dedicated to connecting aspiring constructors from underrepresented groups with experienced constructors. Alongside these changes at the *New York Times*, in 2022 the *LA Times* replaced editor Rich Norris with longtime constructor and fierce advocate of gender parity Patti Varol. None of these changes were made in a vacuum.

Since 2014, when I stopped working for Shortz, the crossword landscape has changed dramatically. New outlets have proliferated, including prestige print publications that have introduced crosswords on their websites (the *New Yorker*, the *Atlantic*, *New York* magazine's Vulture) and a spate of indie puzzle sites, some of which explicitly publish puzzles by women for women (the Inkubator) or puzzles by queer constructors for queer solvers (Queer Qrosswords). For the glossy magazines, online puzzles were simply good business: digital advertisers calculate pay based on how long users stay on a certain webpage. On average, a solver will struggle over a crossword far longer than a reader keeps an article as an open tab. The indie puzzles, however, emerged as a direct result of constructors' experiences of marginalization at the *New York Times*, the *Wall Street Journal*, and the *LA Times*.

All of these new puzzle platforms have put implicit pressure on Shortz to raise constructors' pay (now $500 for a constructor's first and second *Times* puzzles and $750 for any succeeding publications). They have also put explicit pressure on Shortz to diversify the constructors he publishes and ideally, as a result, the entries included in *Times* puzzles. When the *New Yorker* launched its online puzzle in 2018, gender parity was baked into its organization. Instead of a submissions-based process, web editors David Haglund and Liz Maynes-Aminzade chose six constructors, three men and three women, to comprise a roster of constructors who alternated puzzles week-by-week. As the magazine's Puzzle and Games section has grown, with Maynes-Aminzade at the helm, the *New Yorker* has expanded its roster but maintained an unwavering policy of gender parity.

Also in 2018, Laura Braunstein and Tracy Bennett founded the Inkubator. For five years, they solicited and published puzzles from women to remedy what Shortz has seen as a pipeline problem: he simply gets far more crossword submissions from men than women. Their ambition, as they described it, was threefold: to deliver subscribing solvers entertaining and challenging puzzles, to "help women new to the field develop their constructing skills," and to "provide a venue for women to exhibit and get paid for high-quality puzzles, especially (but not exclusively) puzzles that may not have a chance at mainstream publications due to feminist, political, or provocative content."

Braunstein and Bennett knew that puzzles with feminist themes will often be deemed niche at the *Times*. That, at least, was my experience when, in 2016, I sent Shortz a puzzle featuring boxes containing circles in the pattern of three "waves" and one "intersection." Once the solver finished the puzzle, the words FIRST WAVE, SECOND WAVE, and THIRD WAVE appeared in the waves, and INTERSECTIONAL appeared in its center circles.

Shortz rejected the grid, claiming that many solvers "won't know the significance of first, second, third wave, and intersectional—especially

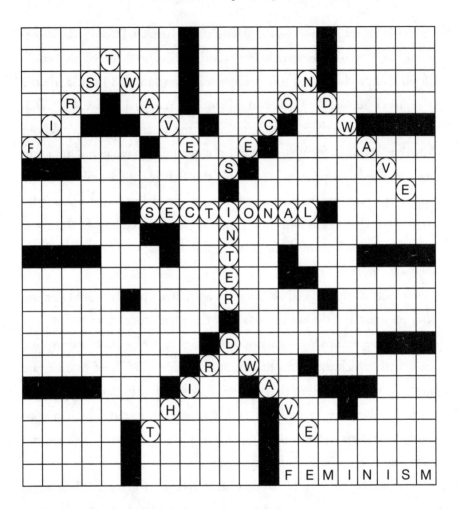

the last one," and that he found the whole thing "not playful enough." I heard this as: *Your feminist puzzle is the product of a special interest, and what's more, it's humorless.* This is when I stopped submitting puzzles to him; in fact, I assumed I was done constructing.

I was in graduate school, where my interests in literature and media studies had developed into a dissertation and where few people knew about my crosswords or my eating disorder. I didn't hide these parts of my personal history, but nor did I lead with them. Instead, I would sometimes invoke either subject as a party trick: I had stories and theories that I could unveil if either happened to emerge in conversation, and I could use the disconnect between my past and present as a narrative device. I'd watch people recalibrate their understanding of me when I'd tell them about "the time I worked for Will Shortz" or "when I was in rehab in Utah." I'm not sure how therapeutically advisable this lightly exhibitionist relationship to my past was, but I found it socially gratifying—as if holding up anorexia or crosswords as a curio from my past evinced how far I'd come from the time when they'd been integral to my self-understanding. Now they were more like trivia.

In fact, if my father had once thought that my life would get too busy for anorexia, the inverse was now true: with food rules and weight no longer preoccupying my daily thoughts, I had new time and psychic space with which to build a life. In practical terms, it's hard to overstate how important food is to that project, how significant slices of pizza and glasses of wine are to building and maintaining friendships. I had to learn these social rituals like a second language. Starvation had left me both cognitively and socially impaired.

And yet, before I went to treatment, I remember fearing that I wouldn't be smart—or that I couldn't get good grades—if I didn't also restrict my food. I worried, I think, that if I released myself from anorexia's "discipline," as it were, it might make for a domino effect: I might slack off in other ways too. It's a stupid thought—a quintessentially anorexic thought—yoking the disorder's value to my other values in order to justify its own perpetuation. But in recovery, I was smarter—less distracted by hunger, sure, but also more able to understand human beings (by way of philosophy, literature, and the other objects of my study) now that I actually understood myself to be one. My life in recovery, inflated with new possibility, was getting too busy for crossword puzzles. They were no longer my coping mechanism; they had never been my professional aspiration; and I knew that my sensibility wasn't compatible with that of the *Times*. Constructing, and certainly constructing by hand, wasn't worth the trouble.

At the time, the Inkubator didn't exist, and I went without writing or solving puzzles for about a year, until Haglund and Maynes-Aminzade asked me to help launch the *New Yorker*'s crossword puzzle. It was then that I learned how to construct using software, as they wanted one themeless puzzle a month (impossible for me, by hand) and then two, as the magazine's puzzle section expanded. Also in 2018, Ben Tausig, editor of the AVCX crossword platform, solicited a puzzle from me. Instead of drafting him the conciliatory email that I had planned—*So sorry, but fuck crosswords*—I told him about my feminist puzzle. He swooped up the grid and helped me retool its theme. The resulting puzzle, much better than my submission to Shortz, featured SUSAN B. ANTHONY, GLORIA STEINEM, and REBECCA WALKER (icons of the first, second, and third feminist waves) hidden in the circled letters, and it was equipped with the title "Feminist Movements," which was also the clue to its revealer in the southeast corner of the grid.

In other words, Tausig mentored me. This form of mentorship has not, historically, been how Shortz defines his job; it is, however, how Braunstein and Bennett have defined theirs. Of course, a feminist puzzle need not be so literal as mine was. In the wake of Donald Trump's presidential election, I was—channeling Julia Penelope—trying to consciousness-raise in puzzle form. I look back on the exercise with some embarrassment: this puzzle was my pink knit pussy hat. But with Tausig's help, it managed to be a little more than that: timely, well executed, and maybe even "exciting."

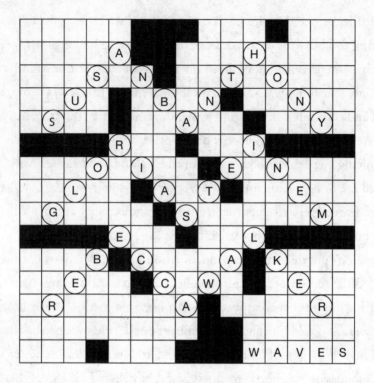

When I asked Braunstein and Bennett if, in soliciting women construc-tors, they were also looking for women-focused themes and entries—and if they saw those projects as necessarily related—they answered quickly and unambiguously, "Yes." Their assumption is that women will make puzzles that represent women's interests and experiences. But this can involve some cajoling on their part. As Braunstein put it, "we are often 'womaning up' the clues"—tying words and references back to women (even women or artifacts that the constructor may not know or identify with) in the edit-ing process. If, as a result of their editing, a twenty-something constructor learns about Bella Abzug, all the better.

It is intuitively but not necessarily true that a woman constructor will include "women's references" in her grid. What, after all, are "women's references"? Are they like pornography, per Justice Potter Stewart—do you just know them when you see them? When adding words to my wordlist, I am sometimes thinking about cultural representation—about adding words and phrases that I know to be marked, however implicitly, as "female." More often, though, I am simply adding words that I like, new coinages or familiar phrases from the mediascapes that I inhabit (academic publishing, film Twitter, book reviews, and celebrity gossip accounts, among them).

Constructor Portia Lundie describes her process similarly, culling her wordlist from her interests. "My crossword dictionary is heavy on comedy, sci-fi/fantasy, and pop culture," she wrote on the X Word Info blog when her puzzle was published in the *Times* in February 2021. Her puzzle's theme was "Let Your Hair Down," with that phrase running vertically down the grid as its revealer. Her theme answers—DISCOMBOBULATED, TOMB RAIDER, and PERMAFROST—also ran vertically and included hairstyles (BOB, BRAID, AFRO) hidden in their forms. When I spoke to Lundie, she mentioned how important it was to her that the answer to 1-Across in her puzzle—JADA, clued to actress Jada Pinkett Smith—was something that her mother could get. "People in my community, in my family," Lundie told me, "will just put [the puzzle] down because they're like 'Oh, I don't know the first three words, I must be stupid. I must just not be good enough for this.'"

Lundie is the second Black woman to publish a crossword in the *Times*, although she has been making batches of themed "midi" crosswords (nine-by-nine puzzles) for the *Times*'s puzzle app since 2019. The first Black woman to publish a *Times* crossword was Soleil Saint-Cyr, whose puzzle was published just days before Lundie's during "Black Constructors' Week" in 2021, in which, as Shortz described it, "every daily crossword this week, Monday to Saturday, is made by an African-American contributor."

Lundie's puzzle included references to sci-fi ("Star Trek director") and pop culture ("Music genre for Billie Eilish") as well as Greek mythology (Lundie was a classics major at Wesleyan) and Black American history ("Deliverer of a noted speech upon the death of Martin Luther King Jr., in brief"). She began creating puzzles after college with the help of her friend Milo Beckman, who had been publishing *Times* crosswords since he was fifteen. "He was gracious enough to teach me," she told me, adding, "So much of crossword-making is gatekept. Something you notice about people who value intellect is that there is this pride in being the 'only person' who can do something. [It cultivates] the idea of genius, which I understand to be related to access and privilege."

Lundie's parents didn't solve crossword puzzles when she was growing up, and it wasn't until she published hers in the *Times* that she learned that her father, a lawyer, was the editor and judge of a crossword competition in Guyana before immigrating to the United States. He stopped solving crosswords when he arrived, embarrassed by the limits of his knowledge of American culture, as it was reflected in the grid. "Turns out," she wrote in an op-ed in the *Washington Post*, "I was robbed of a chance to learn about crosswords at a young age in part because crossword culture does not encourage learning—rather, it rewards already knowing."

Black Constructors' Week was variously received: Was it a sign of good faith or a virtue signal from the *Times*? A tokenizing effort or an inclusive one? One commenter on a crossword blog went further, writing, in response to a puzzle that week, which featured the word REPARATIONS in the center of its grid, "I prefer puzzles to be fun, not dry activist treatises that promote political ideology."

As of my writing, neither Saint-Cyr nor Lundie has published another puzzle in the paper, and constructor Enrique Henestroza Anguiano has even suggested that the percentage of non-white puzzle-makers has declined since the paper introduced Black Constructors' Week and its diversity fellowship. Anguiano's data is roughly composed, based on the photos that constructors upload to XWord Info when their puzzles are published. He's taking the risk of assessing constructors' race based on their appearance to prove a point: a week devoted to Black constructors and a mentorship fellowship are paltry efforts to wrest the puzzle from its hundred-year history of racial exclusion. Systemic changes are needed, and many puzzle-makers are turning to the word database—the source material for all digital crossword construction—as the engine for that change.

———————

DURING BLACK CONSTRUCTORS' WEEK, THIRTY NEW WORDS AND phrases were introduced into the *New York Times* crossword word database, including NERDCORE, DISH IT OUT, HERSTORIES, FLOW STATE, BODAK YELLOW, BLACK OR WHITE, GOOD TROUBLE, FREEDOM RIDERS, POP TRIO, and ESSENTIAL WORKER. Those words are now available to all constructors who use the *Times*'s downloadable wordlist as the data to feed their own constructing software's algorithm.

By trade, crossword constructors learn a truism about tech culture: the algorithm is never neutral. The standard wordlists that most constructors begin with—and that the "autofill" algorithm sources—are all made by men or are heavily informed by them. XWord Info offers a free list for constructors to download that includes all of the words ever featured in a *New York Times* crossword. Constructor Peter Broda also offers a free list on his website, peterbroda.me. For more than ten years, Broda has collected (or "scraped," in programmer parlance) words from mainstream and indie crossword outlets and supplemented them by scraping other online resources: "important movies, Billboard hit songs and artists, world capitals, etc," as he describes his corpus.

For constructors willing to pay $200, XWord Info offers a list developed by *New York Times* constructor and XWord Info site manager Jeff Chen. Chen's list is astoundingly rich, and he does no scraping. Instead of importing words and phrases from other online dictionaries in a single data dump, his process is analog and subjective. He always carries a notebook with him, taking note of new words when he goes to dinner or rock-climbing or to the movies, adding them to his wordlist every day. Like Margaret Farrar's little black book—or the Notes app I use—Jeff's list is an inventory of words he likes. He averages fifty to one hundred new entries a day.

If a constructor using these lists doesn't manually update them to reflect her own values, her software's algorithm invariably reproduces the priorities of the lists' compilers (and the limited, and sometimes ugly, list of words sanctioned for use by the *Times*). Some constructors have worked together to remedy the algorithm's bias. Anguiano and constructor Brooke Husic have organized an ongoing project called "Spread the Wordlist." They've collected and are periodically updating a wordlist, culled from words used as crossword entries in the *Times* since 2019, as well as those used in puzzles from the *New Yorker*, the *LA Times*, and other indie outlets. (They decided to only take words that have appeared in the *Times* since 2019, based on a basic distrust of the paper's editorial standards for "puzzle-worthy" words before then.) Husic and Anguiano rank their words with minimal aesthetic bias: all words that are passable (that aren't arcane variants or underused initialisms) are a 60. Constructors can then determine "fabulous" or "exciting" words on their own, ranking them higher for themselves.

Because constructing software allows puzzle-makers to use multiple dictionaries, Husic and Anguiano also rank many words a zero, so that their wordlist will overwrite (and effectively delete) words in other dictionaries that they have deemed "un-puzzle-worthy" for political reasons. Words ranked zero on their list include all racial epithets and any person ever accused of sexual assault. The point, as Husic described it to me, isn't to police other constructors' language—or to "cancel" anyone by scrubbing them from the wordlist. Constructors are free to find a person whose name is given a zero in their list (ANSARI, BILL CLINTON, or KANYE for example) and change its ranking if they so choose. "If you decide you're okay with [a word that we've ranked zero] then opt into it," she told me. "Don't assume that everything in the wordlist you're using is kosher just because it's been used in the *Times* before."

Other efforts to remedy the exclusions and biases of the most commonly circulated wordlists have relied on crowdsourcing. These open-source operations are meant to allow constructors to reprogram their algorithms collectively. In the text that introduces her "Expanded Crossword Name Database," for example, constructor Erica Hsiung Wojcik asks, "Frustrated by the overrepresentation of the same white men's names, organizations, works of art etc. in your crosswords? Me too! This database was started to give constructors a list of new proper nouns to include in their puzzles." Wojcik solicits "names of famous contemporary or historical women, nonbinary, trans &/or POC that you'd like to see in a grid" as well as "famous contemporary or historical places or things that represent groups/identities /people that are often excluded from crossword grids." The resulting lists are accompanied by descriptions, presumably meant for constructors who may want to diversify their wordlists but lack fluency or familiarity with the "expanded" cultural touchstones represented in the compilation. The first ten entries on the names and places/things lists are as follows:

FULL NAME	FN_ Length	FIRST	F_ Length	LAST	L_ Length	Description
AALIYAH	7	AALIYAH	7		0	Aaliyah Dana Haughton: "Princess of R&B" and "Queen of Urban Pop"
AARON SANCHEZ	12	AARON	5	SANCHEZ	7	Mexican celebrity chef and star of *Chopped* on Food Network
ABBY PHILLIP	11	ABBY	4	PHILLIP	7	CNN senior political correspondent
ABIGAIL THORN	12	ABIGAIL	7	THORN	5	Trans woman, creator of left-wing YouTube channel Philosophy Tube
ADA LOVELACE	11	ADA	3	LOVELACE	8	Credited with first computer programme
ADANIA SHIBLI	12	ADANIA	6	SHIBLI	6	Palestinian novelist
ADORE DELANO	11	ADORE	5	DELANO	6	(he/him) or (she/her) nonbinary drag queen and singer
AGNES MARTIN	11	AGNES	5	MARTIN	6	Painter
AGNES VARDA	10	AGNES	5	VARDA	5	Filmmaker
AIDY BRYANT	10	AIDY	4	BRYANT	6	Actress (*SNL*, *Shrill*)

NAME	Name_ Length	Alt Name	Alt Name_ Length	Description
AACM	4		0	Jazz non-profit, Association for the Advancement of Creative Musicians
ABENAKI	7		0	Algonquin group indigenous to contemporary northern US and Quebec
AFROFUTURISM	12		0	
ATLANTA DREAM	12	DREAM	5	Atlanta WBNA team, originators of the "Vote Warnock" campaign; co-owned by WNBA champ Renee Montgomery
AUTOSTRADDLE	12		0	LGBTQIA+ digital publication: http://www.autostraddle.com/
BROWNSVILLE	11		0	Former African-American community where Frostburg State University now stands. It was founded by two formerly enslaved women, and residents were displaced in the 1920s and 1930s as land was acquired by unfairly low prices by the state
CHARLOTTE STING	14	STING	5	Charlotte, NC, WNBA team
CHEWING GUM	10		0	Michaela Coel show (Netflix)
CHICAGO RED STARS	15	RED STARS	8	Chicago NWSL (women's soccer) team
CHICAGO SKY	10	SKY	3	Chicago WNBA team

The lack of a description for AFROFUTURISM and the extensive description for BROWNSVILLE is telling. I have often entered phrases into my wordlist that, months or years later, make their way into my puzzles, at which point I'm staggered by the project I've tasked myself with. Thinking about the database, and not the puzzle it will produce, I'm left with ridiculous questions like, *How do I write a ten-word clue that's at once descriptive and maybe even playful for QUEERBAITING or RACE SCIENCE?* Privileging political representation over the puzzle form itself, I marvel at how far I've strayed from the project of crosswords as I once understood it.

When faced with these words "autofilled" in my grid, I can become nostalgic for the days when I constructed by hand, when the puzzle in my notebook was an index of that very day's preoccupations and obsessions—not the projection of my past self's intervention in a database. This is not to say that I think the focus on diversifying wordlists has made the crossword puzzle "too political." Far from it. Crosswords have always been an artifact of power, defining the horizons of common knowledge and the canon of language's use. To me, what makes for a "good" crossword word doesn't lie in its concentration of Js, Xs, or Qs or its vowel-to-consonant ratio. It resides in recognition, the pleasure of finding something you know fit neatly into the cramped corners of a newspaper or digital grid. To see increasingly more of the world reflected in this admittedly specialized leisure-class activity is not just satisfying; it's political.

What troubles me about the focus on wordlists is, perhaps perversely, their open-source distribution and use. Is it a political victory if people who don't know AALIYAH or AUTOSTRADDLE are putting those entries in their puzzles because an algorithm told them they would fit? If a constructor publishes a "new" word in the *Times* puzzle—one that has yet to enter the XWord Info list, Jeff Chen's list, or Peter Broda's list—it will automatically be inserted into all of those downloadable text files. This could be a leveling device for women and other minoritized puzzle-makers, a way to diversify the language and trivia deemed common knowledge by the paper of record. But like all diversity efforts, this system is double-edged. Constructor Elizabeth Gorski, for example, has debuted a staggering 1,514 words in the *Times* crossword lexicon. More than 600 of them have been reused by other constructors in her debt. But were ANNE SEXTON, CHICK FLICK, TUBE TOPS, and STATESWOMEN already colloquial to the men constructors who used these terms after Gorski debuted them? Did they put those words into their puzzles actively, or were they automatically introduced into their wordlists and then autofilled? Is the result of Gorski's labor a diversified crossword dictionary or algorithm-assisted appropriation? Is it a triumph or a violation—a flight or a theft, to use Hélène Cixous's turn of phrase—to see a woman's contributions to a subculture published under a man's byline?

To ask these questions is to concede to such a thing as women's language, a separatist lexicon that maybe shouldn't be used by or for men. It is to sit between unsavory cultural stereotypes, on the one hand, and gender essentialism, on the other. Such is the familiar defensive posture assumed by feminist writers for generations. How can women fight for cultural equity without conceding their difference in the very terms that would objectify them? Can women ever create in a culture that is not properly their own? These were the very questions that plagued the French Feminists, the American sociolinguists, and their critics fifty years ago. They puzzle me now.

Such questions would feel less hopelessly thorny if gender parity were a reality among writers of all stripes. Incubated, crowdsourced, and algorithm-reproduced, crossword culture is changing, and there's momentum in the direction of parity. The result of these various efforts may be to rediscover the woman in the crossword puzzle—the housewife, the feminist, the computer. She was, after all, always there.

VII

The Paradoxes
of Ruth von Phul

IN MARCH 2020, THE COVID-19 PANDEMIC TRANSFORMED AMERI-
can lives and lexicons: definitions of safety and precarity had to be revised
daily, according to new data and CDC recommendations; neologisms
marked our speech (*doomscrolling, elbow bump, unmute*) and old words,
like old wounds, sloughed off their scabs of disuse (*quarantine, herd im-
munity, clinical trial*). The global crisis registered in our language, and
language games distracted from the global crisis: "You can't think of
your troubles while solving a crossword," Margaret Farrar said at the
start of the country's intervention in World War II. And as I understand
it, at the start of the pandemic, many Americans found comfort in the re-
liable grid, engaging their minds to disengage from anxious thought. By
way of mini or midi crosswords, Words with Friends or Wordle, puzzle
solving increased as most other forms of recreation ceased.

When my classes moved to Zoom and word of the hiring freeze in
academia reached my campus, I was also thinking of crosswords. Days
before lockdown, I had received a call from Claire Muscat, a constructor
and test solver for the *New York Times* who was quitting her job at the

paper. Claire reached out to me to vent—she was leaving her position because it had become untenable and unfun—and by the end of the call we were organizing an open letter to the director of the paper's Puzzle and Games section. As Claire described her situation in our letter, which we coauthored with constructor Natan Last, "She was made to feel like a lesser solver and constructor than her male colleagues; she was told that her 'primary role' was to be a female censor. . . . Yet even when her feedback [on clues or answers] was gender-related, it was often met with such skepticism that she began to feel as if her role was essentially nominal; that the most important part of her position was the 'diversity' requirement she fulfilled."

Natan thought our timing propitious—subscriptions to the *Times*'s paywalled puzzle were on the rise because of the pandemic—but I think we all worried, as I so often did, that we were taking crosswords and ourselves too seriously. If puzzles were trivial before COVID-19, what were they in its wake? *Trivial* too was a word whose definition was changing, inflating to accommodate so many once-serious concerns that had been eclipsed by the magnitude of the virus's path. But we carried on with our letter, honoring Claire's experience and our own, making three concrete requests of the *Times* puzzle team: "we ask that constructors receive access to proofs before their puzzles go to print" (this, to prevent an insensitive clue, or one that doesn't accord with the constructor's worldview, from running under her byline without her knowledge); "we ask that women and/or non-binary people comprise at least half of Will's test solving team" (to ensure that no one is asked to serve as spokesperson for their gender); and finally, "we want the *Times* to make a public commitment to adding diversity to its editorial staff." Our letter concluded: "We love the *New York Times* crossword puzzle.

It continually makes our day and, for some of us, it has made our careers. But in order to feel confident supporting the institution with our work, we want our voices heard and our authorial rights recognized." Within a day, we had more than six hundred cosigners, including at least eighty of the *Times*'s most frequent puzzle contributors and one great-granddaughter of Margaret Farrar. Our requests were met swiftly and, as far I know, without contest.

Three days after we circulated the open letter on Twitter, I received a galley for a new book about crossword puzzles, a history and journalistic account of the people who create them, by Adrienne Raphel. I found myself in the book's first chapter—"A new, brilliant figure making waves in the crossword world—and not only is she a woman, she's attractive, young, and fashionable to boot!" Slipping into the fawning register of the puff-pieces written about me while I was working for Shortz, Raphel was drawing attention to their almost explicit misogyny. She was also comparing my publicity—and the public persona I had developed—to that of Ruth von Phul, the winner of the first two crossword puzzle tournaments, hosted by the *Herald Tribune* in 1924 and 1926, whose victories made her a press sensation. Von Phul was profiled in national papers and in the *New Yorker*, where she was praised for her "distinct charm, both of appearance and of manner." A twenty-year-old "with light brown hair and blue eyes," she was "the sort of vivacious young lady one would not look to see going through life with Noah Webster . . . and Roget." According to Raphel, von Phul and I were "crossword ingénues" separated by a century. Neither "geek" nor "granny," as she wrote, we were subverting the "anticipated types" associated with the puzzle, making the crossword "the vehicle for the woman to whip off her glasses and flip from bedraggled bookworm to sexy librarian." In other words, we had disrupted two retrograde stereotypes (geek and granny) only to fall into another. Between von Phul and me, Raphel wrote, "the story still hasn't moved beyond the novelty that a crossword expert might be a smart young woman—and, by implication, that a young woman might be an expert at anything at all."

While I can't disagree with Raphel's conclusion, the description of me I encountered in her pages made me recoil. Of course, I could corroborate this "me." Sometimes self-consciously, sometimes implicitly, I had worked since age fifteen to develop this contrivance of Good Girl and Bad, routed through the crossword puzzle. But I was just as alienated by the twenty-first-century "crossword ingénue" as I was complicit in her invention. As a teenager, the image of the crossword constructor had been the working material of my psychic misrecognition. I self-fashioned in her terms (perfectionistic, nerdy, disciplined) in search of self-knowledge. But my alienation from that very same identity, fifteen years later, was only a function of another misrecognition: I needed to disavow this past self to fit the contours of a new one—one who now finds "crossword ingénue" incompatible with who I'd like to be and how I'd like to be perceived.

While reading about myself in Raphel's book, I chose not to contend with my self-alienation—with my disdain for this persona I'd worked so hard to develop. Instead, I defended myself against it, directing my criticism toward the book in which I featured: the comparison between me and von Phul was half-baked and under-historicized. My story couldn't be "*exactly* the same . . . as [hers] a century earlier" because the worlds in which we moved, the social and professional expectations for women that both enabled and curtailed us, had changed. So too had the culture of the crossword puzzle. Von Phul, for example, couldn't subvert the geek stereotype in the 1920s because it hadn't yet developed. (It, and its Alfred E.

Neuman / *Mad* magazine trappings, was a product of the 1950s.) And while von Phul conformed to the image of the crossword-crazed flapper that splashed across covers of *Judge* magazine in the 1920s, I didn't conform to the new image of the crossword-programmer in the 2010s. I was unwilling to identify with the crossword ingénue and therefore with von Phul—unwilling to make connections with the puzzling women who came before me, connections that I now court and cherish. At the time, I imagined that von Phul and I were alike only in the sexist coverage we had both received, coverage that I felt Raphel was, however ironically, reproducing.

I had been captured as I no longer wanted to be seen, but instead of wrestling with my past, I parried it. I was mobilizing a defense that my therapist has called, in a simple construction that belies its emotional anguish, "Going 'one-up' because you feel 'one-down.'" (The crossword-like implications of this turn of phrase no doubt eluded her at the time.) This defense against insecurity takes on many more vernacular forms—call it *snark, cattiness,* or *snobbery.* But Raphel was, of course, right to compare me and von Phul, and not just because we'd exposed ourselves to press coverage that recognized our expertise, only as it reflected off our appearance.

Like so many of the women I have written about here, von Phul and I used the crossword puzzle, of all things, to negotiate the stereotypes, or expectations, of how a woman ought to look, act, and think—in the 1920s or 2020s—sometimes conforming to them, and sometimes subverting them.

RUTH VON PHUL WAS BORN RUTH LOIS FRANC IN MANHATTAN IN 1904. She was the child of wealthy German Jewish parents, whose belief in education was held more religiously than their commitment to any

Jewish theology. "My parents were very advanced and gay," she reported in a 1979 profile in the *New Yorker*. "My mother even smoked." It was her second profile in the magazine. The first had appeared fifty-four years earlier, when von Phul won her first crossword tournament. "We thought it was time we looked her up again," the uncredited magazine copy read. With the hindsight of those fifty-four years, von Phul explained her path to becoming a crossword champion; her life as a wife, mother, and grandmother; and her late-in-life discovery of James Joyce, an encounter that activated her hyperkinetic mind more than any crossword could.

At seventeen, von Phul had enrolled in Wellesley College, dropping out two years later because, as she put it, "I discovered Harvard and Harvard discovered me." It's a telling euphemism for someone who shared her parents' devotion to the life of the mind, especially when polished by higher education: von Phul, after all, didn't discover "Harvard" in 1922, so much as she discovered her husband, William von Phul Jr., a Harvard student and future civil engineer from New Orleans. (In an interview after her tournament win in 1924, von Phul reported, "He is both a civil engineer and a civil husband, [who] . . . thinks the puzzles are silly, but I have three sisters-in-law, a mother-in-law, a mother and a sister just as keen about them as I am.")

A self-proclaimed "slave to the puzzles," von Phul entered the *Herald Tribune*'s crossword tournament on a lark. The contest was held over two days, with the first devoted to separate rounds for women and men. She handily won the women's trophy, completing the puzzle, created by *Tribune* crossword editor Mrs. Helen Haven, in four minutes and twenty seconds. It was three full minutes before the second-place contender finished hers. In a strange publicity stunt, one of the tournament's judges, Ruth Hale, brought a "bevy of Ziegfeld chorus girls" into the auditorium, as one paper reported, and "the judges proclaimed the cross word puzzler [von Phul] superior in charm to the chorus girls." The stunt seems more likely a product of the Algonquin Round Table's freewheeling imagination than Hale's own, as three Ziegfeld performers were also tasked with solving von Phul's winning puzzle, but "none . . . was able to get through the three-letter words."

In the second round, von Phul defeated the men's champion, William Stern II, although Stern and his wife, who as *Time* magazine reported, "advocate vocabulary jousts as an antidote to divorce," became national mixed doubles puzzle champions. After two wins in 1924 and 1926, von Phul couldn't participate in the paper's third tournament because her husband's work took her to Colorado—and then Baton Rouge, Dallas, and Los Angeles—forcing her to relinquish her title. Over the course of the next five years, however, she continued to create and solve puzzles, with one paper suggesting that it had become her career.

In the 1924 introduction to Simon & Schuster's first crossword book, edited by Margaret Farrar and "officially endorsed" by Hale, von Phul wrote advice to novice solvers and a "Ballade of Cross Words," confessing her devotion to the pastime in rhyme:

> Once from the world I sought surcease
> > Between a novel's covers pressed;
> No longer there I look for peace;
> > Of anodynes I've found the best.
> > So, when the sun sinks in the west
> Sunk, too, are husbands, friends and cook—
> > Where do I find my treasure chest?
> All in the leaves of the Cross Word Book.

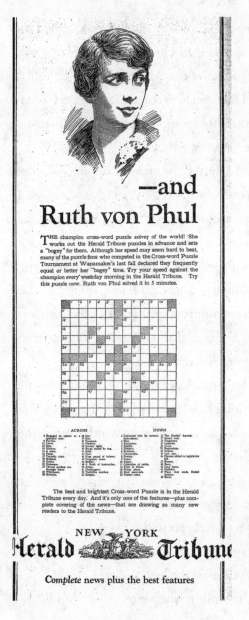

Ruth von Phul sets the official "bogey" time for the daily crossword puzzle, New York Herald Tribune, *April 24, 1927.*

Between 1926 and 1928, von Phul also served as the "bogey" for the *Herald Tribune*'s crossword, setting the benchmark time against which other solvers could test their wits. Having solved each puzzle a day in advance, von Phul sent her solving time to Haven, who published it above the grid (with cryptograms or clever blurbs that Haven wrote herself).

But crossword puzzles were never von Phul's career, as a career was never her aspiration. She was a wife and mother of two daughters, and she also wanted recognition for her tremendous intelligence. Crosswords were only one outlet for its display. At the start of the Second World War, von Phul took a course in cryptanalysis at Hunter College, where she was recruited to be an assistant censor in a special security division of the New York Office of Postal Censorship. Her job was to search, as she put it, "for secret messages in correspondence, with a hundred or more people working under me." After the war, von Phul was twice offered cryptanalytical jobs, both of which she declined. "I had had my fill of that kind of work," she said. Perhaps she also refused the job offers because she was moving again for her husband's work—this time to San Antonio, where, as her granddaughter described it, "she always felt like a transplant" and where she became an active member in the League of Women Voters.

In 1957, von Phul brandished her intelligence once again before a mass audience. She appeared on the hit TV quiz show *$64,000 Challenge*. After four stints, she won $8,000, bumbling a question about the definition of the word *rescissible* (capable of being rescinded or repealed). When asked why she had made a star turn on television, she replied, "I didn't mind much. I earned four free round trips between Texas and New York."

The TV appearance was a detour—or relapse—through middlebrow forms of entertainment that she had, at that point in her life, disclaimed. "When Nixon railed against the snobs of the East-Coast elite," one of her granddaughters told me, "I think she took it as high praise." Her grandchildren describe a woman devoted to theater, ballet, and modern art, who dismissed or even ridiculed their tastes for fashion or commercial fiction. She stringently corrected their grammar—"Don't use a pronoun without an antecedent!"—and strictly enforced genteel standards of dress: "A lady always wears gloves," she said, and slacks were only appropriate for housework. These weren't the dictates of a tyrant but relentless demonstrations of von Phul's class pride.

In the 1960s, von Phul found the ultimate outlet for her advanced logophilia: the works of James Joyce. Between 1963 and 1982, she was a frequent contributor to *James Joyce Quarterly* and *A Wake Newslitter*, writing on topics as varied as the "architectonic" structure of *Finnegans Wake*; the influence of Kierkegaard on *A Portrait of the Artist as a Young Man*; and the name of Leopold Bloom's would-be mistress in *Ulysses*, long suspected to be a cryptogram of the name of one of the novel's other characters. "There is obviously a connection between my interest in crosswords and cryptography and my fascination with Joyce," she told the *New Yorker* in 1979. "When you're solving puzzles, you let your mind float with respect to words. It's very Freudian, dealing with puns and tricky word associations, and you almost have to know several languages. In that respect, Joyce was incomparable."

In the years that she was refining her self-taught Joycean scholarship in print, von Phul was also composing a five-thousand-page Freudian analysis of *Finnegans Wake*. In this work—a magnum opus that one Joyce specialist deemed "scatologically oriented"—von Phul exercised her encyclopedic knowledge and graphomania no less ecstatically than Joyce did himself. As the project's one published excerpt suggests, von Phul was working to connect Joyce's own psychosexual development to those of his characters and the structure of his tetralogy—*Portrait, Ulysses, Exiles*, and *Finnegans Wake*—as a whole. The author's life cycle—from infancy to manhood to old age (as the Sphinx would have it)—became the trope that von Phul used to decrypt Joyce's work.

The author bio that accompanied her 1962 excerpt called von Phul "a housewife and grandmother," which must have been jarring to the volume's degreed contributors, many of whom shied from the more imprudent and impudent aspects of Joyce's canon that von Phul fearlessly broached. In an article about *A Portrait of the Artist* in the academic journal *Modern British Literature* in 1976, von Phul's bio read "retired undefeated crossword puzzle champion of the world." (It was "a surprise to me, but sounded nice," von Phul later confessed.) She was, of course, all of these things: decorous housewife and grandmother, undefeated crossword champion, and intrepid Joycean scholar. Perhaps these epithets constitute a paradox, although not in von Phul's terms.

In a 1974 issue of *Harper's* magazine, von Phul was a runner-up in the publication's "Hip Haiku" contest. She wrote:

> What a paradox
> Is an unbending person
> Who cannot unbend

The syntax is cryptic: the singular *is* can be read as standing in for two (what a paradox *is* / *is* an unbending person); or the first line might be clipped—an expressive, punctuation-less lament (what a paradox!). The message is no clearer: an unbending person cannot bend; an unbending person is uppity, straight-edged, rigid. And yet, the wisdom of von Phul's haiku is its acknowledgment that an unbending person's stubbornness can leave her locked in a wrongheaded (or wrong-bodied) arrangement. Unbendingness can leave you unable to unbend.

Perhaps it's a bit of self-critique: von Phul's granddaughters wouldn't exactly describe her as flexible. But if this oblique haiku about paradox is a confession or mode of self-reflection, it's a highly intellectualized one, a way of routing feeling through the mechanics of her electric mind.

The haiku also offers a neat figuration for all of the women in this book, many of whom were unbending to the point of self-sabotage: the militant suffragist who wouldn't break the rules; the editor with an illustrious career who would not be a career woman; the second-wave feminist accused of sexual harassment; the lesbian-separatist linguist who used language to alienate her allies; the anorexic with an outsize appetite—for recognition and a sense of self.

———

I HAVE OFTEN BEEN TOLD THAT INTELLECTUALIZATION IS A COPING mechanism of mine, but I know that when I heard this term, like *perfectionism* before it, I misunderstood it, repressing its final syllables. When I was told by various clinicians that I "intellectualize" (I hold feelings at bay by processing them as thought), I heard that I was an "intellectual" (someone smart). Even if the term was presented to me as an accusation or reproach—*Don't intellectualize*—I took it as a compliment. I wasn't just making a cognitive error. My thought about what the words meant—and what they meant about me—had been distorted by the static noise of feeling: by the feeling that I wanted to be recognized as smart; by the feeling that I wanted to know myself better than any therapist or doctor could. I was confident that I could think myself out of the mental illness that I so stubbornly thought myself into. I wanted to use my words to make sense of myself, while avoiding the soft sensations of vulnerability.

It's a cliché of recovery narratives that they're not linear: the addict or anorexic should try to see backsliding or even relapse as experiences of recovery, not its undoing. I understand the message in the abstract. To consider relapse a "failure" of one's recovery is to fuel the paradigmatic thinking that the disorder feeds on (relapse = bad; recovery = good). To expect a perfect recovery is, in other words, an anorexic expectation of the self. It's a psychological trap—a paradox. How do I protect my recovery, cherish it even, without using its maintenance as a new disciplinary metric for my self-worth?

I still see the therapist who wouldn't treat me unless I went to Paradise. Sometimes I think of my commitment to her as a token of my commitment to my recovery. There are others—symbolic gestures that remind me of my past, even as I try to project myself out into a future unencumbered by anorexia. I don't weigh myself, and I still ask doctors and nurses to "blind weigh" me at annual appointments. (I turn around on the scale, and they record its number without disclosing it to me. It's a mildly humiliating performance.) I know, at this point, that I could handle the information of my weight—that I wouldn't misuse it—but I don't want to have to. It also feels hard and perhaps therefore significant to ask medical providers to accommodate my recovery in this small way.

While in grad school, I once confessed to my therapist that I didn't think I could relapse—that I didn't have the capacity to starve anymore. I wasn't bragging about my recovery; I was feeling defeated, nostalgic even, for the smug sensation of being *too thin* as an anchor for my self-esteem. She chastened me. In fact, her tone was almost intolerant: *Of course you could starve.* I imagine that she didn't want me to romanticize the disorder or some past self who had more willpower than my present-tense experience of me. It wasn't only her tone that was aberrant; our subject matter was: we rarely talk about anorexia anymore. Instead, we discuss all that has filled its vacuum in the aftermath of treatment. This isn't to say that anorexia never emerges in my life, interfering with my relationships, corrupting my mood or self-image. But when it has emerged—when I have felt anorexic in the years since Paradise—it hasn't manifested as a set of restrictive food habits, so much as a power play, a battle of wills between *it* and *me*, and between *me* and *men*.

Years after I stopped fasting, I held on to the vocabulary of anorexia to help me express anxiety, insecurity, or self-loathing. I would describe these feelings to myself and also to the men I was dating as "body dysmorphia." It was a shorthand, but in retrospect, an imprecise one: I wasn't seeing or feeling fat on my body that wasn't there, but I was having a physical reaction to more commonplace forms of emotional pain and self-doubt, and so I used the language of psychosomatic illness that had been familiar to me. There were benefits to this form of misrecognition. When I communicated to men that I was feeling dysmorphic, I was able to use my clinical history to secure their care. In fact, I was using diagnostic language to suggest that I needed *extra care*, that I needed to be taken *extra seriously*, that I wasn't like other people or other women. Even though it didn't determine my eating—or how I was feeling with regard to my weight—the thinking underneath this behavior is, in my mind, classically "anorexic." It's self-pitying, manipulative, and competitive—a reflexive performance of woundedness that inevitably left my partner feeling inadequate and me feeling monstrously unbent.

I have worked hard to protect myself—and my relationships with women and queer friends, in particular—from anorexia's triple-threatening performance of emotional anguish: self-pity, manipulation, and competitiveness. I haven't, however, always cared to protect straight men from these treacheries. With them, I can fall into a ritualized dance of brazen autonomy and frenzied dependence. I can be a fiercely independent woman until I'm not. At that point, I'm tempted to claim, *I'm anorexic! Help!* It has taken me many years since Paradise to understand that, as a person, I am entitled to care—and can, in fact, provide it to others. I need no mark of clinical distinction to license or request it. I understand this, but I don't always feel it. How many women do?

In some way, then, when my therapist and I are talking about my romantic attachments to men—and how I do or don't express my needs—we are still talking about my eating disorder. Sociolinguistics and psychoanalysis can be instructive here. Perhaps the pervasive linguistic relation +MAN/-MAN that Julia Penelope identified in her scholarship has always made me feel *less than* the straight men I've dated. Maybe anorexia or body dysmorphia, in giving me a name for my negativity (my minus, my lack), allows me to feel that I can do or say anything to even my odds against them. Maybe, in other words, I'm just resentful. Or perhaps, in learning to see myself as other women's equal, I have finally submitted to the grammar of sexual difference. In isolating me from other women—from identifying *as* a woman, no better or worse—anorexia had insulated me from its injury. Maybe my recovery has, in fact, "unmasked" my disorder's comorbidity—a comorbidity I want to call gender.

I take some pleasure in these theories but try to hold their seductive power at bay. They're so heady, and even if they stem from felt experiences, they don't long remain there. They're symptomatic; they're intellectualized. This is to confess that my dumb malapropism—mixing up *intellectual* and *intellectualize*—still motivates much of my thinking. It may have even motivated this book project at the outset, leading me to believe that I could describe my past (my eating disorder, my crossword puzzles) as a memoir deflected away from feeling, a memoir wrapped in a cultural history.

If that's how this project began, it is not, at least to me, how it has ended. In writing about women who have wrestled with the norms of gender by rigidly attaching themselves to the norms of language (Ruth Hale, Margaret Farrar, Jean Stafford) or militantly attacking them (Jane Gallop, Julia Penelope), I have discovered connections that can't be intellectualized. I feel for these women—melancholically and admiringly—and in feeling for them, I feel for myself. They are not role models—new material for misrecognition, objectified figures though which to route my subjectivity—but I have recognized versions of myself in their efforts to fashion a self through language, a project that so often alienated them from their bodies and from other women.

Despite our many differences, historical and social, we have all negotiated the Riddles of the Sphinx. We share a desire to work and create in a culture that is not properly our own. We have tried to retreat from the hard fact of our embodiment into a world of words, into its order and disorder—caring for it as we try to care for ourselves.

RESEARCH NOTE

I've never loved books. In fact, I treat them poorly. But, as I hope is obvious from this book, I love words and ideas, and despite the technological advances of my lifetime, I know of no better medium for their communication. There are hundreds of books to which this one is indebted—books that have altered the trajectory of my recovery and the course of my life. Those that have schooled me in the inexorable mystery of the unconscious—and whose authors have made it their explicit goal to retain Freud's discoveries for the feminist movement—deserve special recognition, including Juliet Mitchell's *Psychoanalysis and Feminism* (1974), Jane Gallop's *Feminism and Psychoanalysis: The Daughter's Seduction* (1982), Jacqueline Rose's *Sexuality in the Field of Vision* (1986), and Diana Fuss's *Essentially Speaking* (1989).

Janet Malcolm's *Psychoanalysis: The Impossible Profession* (1977) and *In the Freud Archives* (1984), as well as Jamieson Webster's *The Life and Death of Psychoanalysis* (2011) and *Conversion Disorder* (2018), have guided me in the art of writing about the unspeakable and making personal claims about people we cannot really know, including, of course, ourselves. Already mentioned in the text of this book are Lauren Berlant's

Cruel Optimism (2011) and Sabrina Strings's *Fearing the Black Body* (2019), both of which have helped me come to terms with my inner life by directing me beyond it—to the social and historical forces that have made it so.

The research for this book was inspired by a gut feeling: I knew about Ruth von Phul's crossword tournament wins and Margaret Farrar's influence at the *Times*, and so I guessed—and hoped—that there were more women like them, and more to learn about the conditions that would have led them to this peculiar outlet for their intelligence. The large share of my research was culled from magazine and newspaper clippings, but I couldn't have begun to undertake it without the assistance of Cynthia Farrar, Andrew Farrar, and Michael Thaddeus—Margaret Farrar's grandchildren. Some of Margaret's letters are housed in John C. Farrar's papers at the Beinecke Library at Yale University, but most of her correspondence, publications, and clippings remain in Andrew's attic. With his generosity, I was able to encounter Margaret in her own words and the words of her late-in-life assistant, May Dikeman. I was also directed to Ruth Hale and Jean Stafford's devotion to the crossword, as they were registered in books and magazines that Margaret saved.

Not much has been written on Ruth Hale, Margaret Farrar, Julia Penelope, or Ruth von Phul, although I couldn't have written about Hale without Susan Henry's *Anonymous in Their Own Names* (2012) or Heywood Hale Broun's *Whose Little Boy Are You?* (1983). Nor could I have broached Jean Stafford's steely relationship to language without the help of Ann Hulbert's *The Interior Castle: The Art and Life of Jean Stafford* (1992).

Kelly Wooten, librarian at Duke University's Sallie Bingham Center for Women's History and Culture, turned me on to Julia Penelope's

Crossword Puzzles for Women, and Joan Nestle, cofounder of the Lesbian Herstory Archives, provided invaluable context about Julia's fractious development within the feminist and lesbian separatist movements. *Speaking Freely: Unlearning the Lies of the Fathers' Tongues* (1990) lays out Penelope's most comprehensive theory of the Patriarchal Universe of Discourse, and many of her most polemical autobiographical essays are collected in *Call Me Lesbian: Lesbian Lives, Lesbian Theory* (1992). *Sinister Wisdom*, the journal that first published Penelope and also first repudiated her in print, celebrated the forty-fifth anniversary of the Lesbian Herstory Archives with a phenomenal 118th issue in 2020.

Janet Abbate's *Recoding Gender* (2012) and Nathan L. Ensmenger's *The Computer Boys Take Over* (2012) provided useful framing on the masculinization of the tech industry, developing the historical and theoretical insights of Jennifer S. Light's "When Computers Were Women" (1999), an essay that has indelibly shaped my own thinking about the intersections of labor, gender, and technical expertise in the United States.

Katherine Hinds and Emily O'Dell, Ruth von Phul's grandchildren, were tremendously generous with their time and helped me understand their brilliant, relentlessly paradoxical grandmother, while dozens of members of the contemporary CrossWorld took the time to speak with me about their experiences in it. I relied heavily on the data visualizations and constructor interviews performed by Jim Horne and Jeff Chen at XWord Info, as well as David Steinberg's Pre-Shortzian Puzzle Project, which has digitized thousands of *New York Times* crossword puzzles between 1942 and 1993, when Will Shortz became editor. The limitless curiosity and collective goodwill of the CrossWorld has made researching this book a delight.

ACKNOWLEDGMENTS

This is a strange text: panoramic and particular, historical and, at times, theoretical. I lost faith in it many times, but my editor, Rakesh Satyal, and my agent, Alia Hanna Habib, didn't. I couldn't have written it without their encouragement and guidance. I am also indebted to the Klarman Fellowship at Cornell University, which has given me three years to write, sponsoring my work in various academic and nonacademic idioms, including the language of crossword puzzles.

Several writers informed every sentence—not only because I have learned so much about writing from them, but because I knew that they would be my first readers. Elizabeth Anker, Anne Anlin Cheng, Merve Emre, and Patricia White all read portions of this book as a manuscript in progress. Tobi Haslett, Sam Huber, and Ava Kofman remind me every day how rich a "life of the mind" can be—and how far it is from what I imagined as a sad teenager. There's much more laughter. D. A. Miller was my confidant throughout the drafting of this manuscript. He has taught me how to approach the familiar, the *tired*, with all the wary and excitement of a first encounter. I am tempted to call this a lesson in defamiliarization, but if it is that, it is also a lesson in joy.

Acknowledgments

Cynthia Farrar, Andrew Farrar, and Michael Thaddeus, and Katherine Hinds and Emily O'Dell were phenomenally generous resources, helping me to understand their grandmothers, Margaret Farrar and Ruth von Phul, respectively. Joan Nestle endowed me with the courage and compassion to tell Julia Penelope's story and inspired me to see the value in telling a version of mine. I conducted some of this book's research when COVID-19 restrictions made going to libraries impossible. Thank you to the staff at Duke University's Sallie Bingham Center for Women's History and Culture, as well as Jessica Modi and Hailey Andrews at Yale University, who helped me access archives remotely, and to Madelyne Xiao for thoughtful, careful fact-checking.

I interviewed and corresponded with many people to help me grasp the current state of crossword constructing beyond my experience in it. I'm tremendously grateful for their time and candor: Erik Agard, Eric Albert, David P. Anderson, Enrique Henestroza Anguiano, Tracey Bennett, Laura Braunstein, Jeff Chen, Kameron Austin Collins, Rachel Fabi, Matt Ginsberg, Elizabeth Gorski, Mary Lou Guizzo, Anna Gundlach, Malaika Handa, Helene Hovanec, Brooke Husic, Natan Last, Wyna Liu, Aimee Lucido, Portia Lundie, Claire Muscat, Soleil Saint-Cyr, Ben Tausig, Finn Vigeland, and Robyn Weintraub. I am especially indebted to Liz Maynes-Aminzade and David Haglund for pulling me out of crossword retirement and allowing me to reencounter the form with unusual creative freedom. The entire *New Yorker* crossword editing team—Andy Kravis, Nick Hernandez, Sara Nies, Kate Chin Park, and Sonali Durham—has continually pushed me to think more critically about the politics and play of our coauthored grids. David Remnick and Tyler Foggatt encouraged this book when it was just a skein of ideas about bodies and language that I thought might be worth trying to knit together. Will Shortz deserves all the credit he gets (and more) for investing in young constructors and for bringing together the crossword community at the ACPT and in the *New York Times*, reminding us how social the crossword puzzle is, even when it's created or solved in solitude.

I could not have gone to treatment without the trust and support of my father, Paul Shechtman. He and the staff and patients at Avalon Hills as well as and Danielle Shelov, merit more than thanks. I owe them everything, knowing that they want nothing from me but to live well. Many friends offered me patience and wisdom during the writing of this book. I am forever grateful to Elias Altman, Sammy Chamino, Pierre Foillet, Erica Getto, Lidija Haas, Dana Hammer, Menachem Kaiser, Anna Levine, Chris McGowan, Max Nelson, Maru Pabón, Timmy Pham, Emily Remensperger, Zelda Roland, Arthur Wang, and Alex Weintraub.

My mother and sister, Bonnie Yochelson and Emily Shechtman, to whom this book is dedicated, have not only watched me transform our family history into prose, they have also had the courage to help me understand it. I love them more than words can express, although I know we'll keep trying to find the right ones.

ABOUT THE AUTHOR

Anna Shechtman is a Klarman Fellow at Cornell University and will begin as an assistant professor in the Department of Literatures in English in 2024. She writes biweekly crosswords for the *New Yorker*. Her free-lance essays and reviews have appeared in *Artforum,* the *New Inquiry,* the *New Yorker*, the *New York Review of Books*, *Slate*, and the *Los Angeles Review of Books*, where she is an editor-at-large. She lives in Brooklyn.

CROSSWORD SOLUTION

K	O	S	SHE/HER	D	E	L	I	■	■	H	O	R	E	B
O	B	S	E	S	S	E	D	■	C	A	N	A	P	E
A	I	R	P	L	A	N	E	■	I	S	O	B	A	R
N	E	I	L	■	T	A	B	S	■	B	U	■	THEY/THEM	
■	E	W	W	■	O	C	T	■	I	L	O			
S	A	W	E	N	S	■	M	O	I	S	T	E	R	
P	R	O	B	Y	C	A	B	■	P	O	E	T	I	
A	R	R	S	C	I	P	SHE/HER	S	■	S	A	T	S	
C	O	D	E	S	■	A	T	L	A	S	■	R	E	O
E	G	O	T	I	S	M	L	I	E	■	S	S	T	
C	A	F	■	A	T	M	■	D	A	D	■			
A	N	THEY/THEM	■	R	A	S	A	■	R	U	T	H		
M	T	E	T	N	A	■	O	L	D	M	O	N	E	Y
P	L	A	C	I	D	■	U	P	R	O	O	T	E	D
S	Y	R	I	A	■	THEY/THEM	O	T	SHE/HER	L	O	D	E	